Analytics the Right Way

Analytics the Right Way

A Business Leader's Guide to Putting Data to Productive Use

TIM WILSON
JOE SUTHERLAND

WILEY

Published by John Wiley & Sons, Inc., Hoboken, New Jersey.

Published simultaneously in Canada.

For general information on our other products and services or for technical support, please contact our Customer Care Department within the United States at (800) 762-2974, outside the United States at (317) 572-3993 or fax (317) 572-4002.

Wiley also publishes its books in a variety of electronic formats. Some content that appears in print may not be available in electronic formats. For more information about Wiley products, visit our web site at www.wiley.com.

Library of Congress Cataloging-in-Publication Data:

ISBN: 978-1-394-26449-0 (paperback)
ISBN: 978-1-394-26451-3 (ePDF)
ISBN: 978-1-394-26450-6 (epub)
LCCN: 2024946991

Manufactured in the United States of America

SKY10093096_120524

Cover Image: © Paul M. Lyren
Cover Design: Wiley

To Julie and Sarah

Contents

Acknowledgments

Together, we'd like to thank our publishing and editorial team at Wiley—Jim Minatel, Cathleen Small, Pete Gaughan, and Sara Deichman—without whom this book wouldn't have been possible. Paul Lyren provided both comical wit and a talented hand in illustrating our book, taking our goofy ideas of what passed for "comedy" and making them actually funny; the herculean task of illustrating no fewer than 11 chapters worth of content about analytics—yuck!—is a feat, and we deeply appreciate him doing so. Mike Gustafson and our many colleagues at Search Discovery deserve credit for bringing the two of us together, and for supporting our harebrained ideas, for whatever reason—it was Mike's light touch that led us to build a friendship and point of view for how the analytics business is and should be.

Tim: I would like to thank everyone from whom I learned something that worked its way into the ideas and examples in this book. But then the editors said that would be several orders of magnitude beyond the appropriate word count, so this list is tragically abbreviated. Matt Gershoff is quoted in the book, and I've learned that "minimization of regret" means jumping at every opportunity to have a drink, a meal, or a walk with him—be the topic reinforcement learning, decision-making at the margin, the cost of reducing uncertainty, or the relative merits of European versus American restaurant payment systems, it's always a delight. Another Matt—Matt Coen—is responsible for giving me the language of "the two magic questions." I was loosely applying the idea, but it was during our relatively brief work together when he articulated them (it was purely my cheekiness that then branded them as "magic"). John Lovett—a coworker twice over—provided an on-the-job master class in how to listen to business partners and clients effectively, and he provided encouragement and advice ever since this book was the faintest of glimmers in my eye back in 2017. Val Kroll and I have been collaborating for more than a decade, although we didn't realize we were codeveloping a shared point of view until we became coworkers several years ago, and she's now my cofounder (and podcast cohost), so that collaboration continues. Alison Ferguson, Jim Sterne, Eric Peterson, and Matty Wishnow all took leaps of faith (twice in Matty's case!) that moved my career and my professional growth forward—giving me the opportunity to develop and practice many of the ideas included in this book. The on-stage practice of those ideas—at industry conferences and in meetings with clients—went much better than they could have thanks to concepts and techniques I learned from Lea Pica, and her friendship and encouragement to tackle the authorship of this book at all was a valuable boost.

The Analytics Power Hour is a podcast that has given me more opportunities to have deep discussions with smart people—the cohosts and the guests—for a decade (and counting) as of the publication of the book, and I don't think the book would have been possible without those discussions. I'm indebted to Jim "Analysts Don't Do Anything" Cain for being the spark that got that rolling. Michael Helbing—the smoothest voice in explicit analytics podcasts—has been my cohost, my mentor, my manager, and my sounding board and has calmly talked me down from countless temper tantrums in all of those roles, so most importantly, he is my dear friend. Moe Kiss joined the show near the start, and her brilliant perspective, friendship, and willingness to hash out just about any topic on or off the mic has made me a better analyst and a better consultant. Julie Hoyer was a coworker long before she became a cohost, but her ability to nail the weaknesses in any idea, as well as to build on any idea that has some underlying merit, and to do so instantaneously terrifies me just a little bit, but she contributed directly to expanding and solidifying several of the techniques described in the book.

Joe: I'd like to thank my family and friends for providing ample leeway and grace during the work on this manuscript. The late nights, rain checks, and vacation days spent working on this book can add up, and I appreciate their kindness and support during the process. My wife, Sarah, deserves special appreciation for giving me the space to peck away at the manuscript while we gleefully anticipated the arrival of our son.

Some of the themes in this book, which fed into the mind meld Tim and I achieved in producing this book and wouldn't have been developed if not for our partnership, were the culmination of practical ideas from my two-decade journey through software engineering, scientific inference, and executive service. It was a public library in my youth (and its staff and patrons) that I must thank for setting me on a path to fully learn and appreciate the power of engineering, machine learning, and artificial intelligence in an applied business context (it all started with a book on *How to Learn BASIC* when I was a kid). My Washington University in St. Louis, Columbia, Princeton, Johns Hopkins, and Emory colleagues helped me develop entirely new perspectives through which to view data, analytics, and business. The ideas of counterfactual reasoning and evidentiary weight owe homage to my work with, and learning from, Don Green, Andy Gelman, Greg Wawro, Bob Shapiro, and Suresh

Naidu. I credit Jon Rogowski, Andrew Reeves, and Dan Butler for launching me on my academic odyssey, which has proven enjoyable and rewarding.

It is impossible to recount all who in the course of my business inspired and guided the ideas that are reflected in this work; we stand on the shoulders of giants. Evan Schnidman and Bill Macmillan encouraged me to use data and analysis in what was an entirely new way at the time: to forecast Federal Reserve policymaking from unstructured texts. My colleagues and clients at Peachtree AI, Search Discovery, Cisco, and Amazon, lent me the experiences needed to operationally enable these ideas in the business context.

Finally, thank you to Emory University, the Department of Quantitative Theory and Methods, the Center for AI Learning, the Weidenbaum Center, and the Woodruff Library, for enabling me to work on this book.

About the Authors

TIM WILSON

Tim started his career in architecture, pivoted quickly to technical writing, and then found himself working in marketing communications just as the internet was starting to become a thing that businesses took seriously in the early 2000s as a means of finding, acquiring, and keeping customers. In retrospect, he realizes he was in the right place at the right time to have this weird and wonderful thing called "web analytics" land in his lap—a primitive but useful set of technologies for collecting and analyzing the behavior of visitors to the website of the high tech B2B company where he was working at the time. He went on to head up the business intelligence department at that same company before stepping into the agency and consulting world: creating and growing the analytics practices at three different agencies that worked with a range of large consumer brands; consulting with the analytics teams at various Fortune 500 companies on the their strategies, processes, and tactics for effectively putting analytics to actionable use; and then cofounding a consultancy, facts & feelings (factsandfeelings.io), dedicated to helping organizations productively employ research, analytics, and experimentation to drive growth. Tim is a long-time creator of pragmatic content for analysts and marketers, including, in 2008, cofounding the still-running Data and Analytics Wednesday monthly meetup in Columbus, Ohio, and cohosting the biweekly Analytics Power Hour podcast (analyticshour.io) since 2015. He has been a regular conference speaker across multiple continents on a wide range of topics: data visualization, data storytelling, the R programming language, marketing and digital analytics, and, of course, many of the concepts and techniques addressed in this book. While Tim is physically based in Columbus, his heart and soul maintain joint custody with Austin, Texas. He holds a bachelor of science from the Massachusetts Institute of Technology, an MBA from the University of Texas at Austin, and a Certificate of Amazement from Joe that a hillbilly raised in Sour Lake, Texas, can, indeed, learn the fundamentals of causal inference.

DR. JOE SUTHERLAND

With a career spanning the White House, the Dow Jones 30, and America's top universities, Dr. Joe Sutherland has served as executive, public service leader, and educator. Sutherland is the founding director of the Emory Center for AI Learning, where he serves as lead principal investigator of the Emory branch of the US AI Safety Institute Consortium, associate faculty of the Empathetic AI for Health Institute at Emory Healthcare, and fellow of the Weidenbaum Center on the Economy, Public Policy, and Government at Washington University in St. Louis. He is a professor in Emory's Department of Quantitative Theory & Methods. Sutherland's professional experience spans public service in the White House, technology entrepreneurship, executive roles including as chief executive officer of an AI company and at Amazon and Cisco, and academic positions at Columbia, Johns Hopkins, and Princeton. Sutherland founded two startups that were later acquired: Peachtree AI, a professional services firm specializing in artificial intelligence integrations, and Prattle, a fintech company that uses natural language processing to forecast both the Federal Reserve's monetary policy decisions and the performance of publicly traded companies. From 2011 to 2013, he served in the White House Office of Scheduling and Advance for President Barack Obama, traveling with the president in support of various policy initiatives.

His research exploring the utilization of machine learning and AI in a wide variety of topics is published in top peer-reviewed journals, and his work has been featured on *FOX 5 Good Day Atlanta, Atlanta Journal Constitution, Forbes, Georgia Trend, Government Technology, MIT Sloan Management Review*, and many other venues. In 2017, the National Science Foundation recognized his work in state politics and policy with Honorable Mention, considered a national honor. Sutherland earned his PhD, MPhil, and master's degrees in political science from Columbia University and his bachelor's degree in political science from Washington University in St. Louis. He lives in Historic Brookhaven, Atlanta, Georgia with his family, where he enjoys playing golf and tennis.

CHAPTER 1

Is This Book Right for You?

You picked up this book, which means you're thinking that something about the way you and your organization use data and analytics is not "right." Time and again, the executives, managers, and new hires who make up our clients, colleagues, and friends have expressed to us their anxieties related to how they and their teams are using data and analytics:

> "We have plenty of data, but the actionable insights we get from it are few and far between."

> "Our team consistently invests in the latest data tools and platforms to ensure we're collecting and storing all the data we might need, but the recommendations we generate from those data never really increase in quality or volume."

> "We work with agencies and consultancies that do a lot of reporting on the results they're delivering for us. Those tend to be lengthy presentations with a ton of charts, but I often feel like I'm just having data thrown at me that may or may not be representing real business value being delivered."

> "I never feel comfortable investing the millions we invest in paid media; it's unclear if we're actually getting the returns our agencies report, or if they just tortured the data until it confessed a positive answer."

> "We have talented analytics and data science teams, but it feels like we're talking past each other when I interact with them. I really need them to generate insights and recommendations, and they seem frustrated when I tell them that that's not what they're providing."

> "My data engineers over-promise what their machine learning and AI techniques can do for our stakeholders; it tanks our credibility when we promise magic but don't understand the nuts and bolts well enough to do it right."

> "My product teams build these exotic proofs-of-concept using the latest and greatest AI tools. But to scale them up is way too expensive, and the production engineers tasked with doing so can't understand the opaque mathematical techniques being used."

> "Our technology platform partners sell us licenses to their latest technology and their latest AI or machine learning, and they share

eye-popping stories for how effective they are. But when we dig into the pilots, the platforms don't offer anything more than what we're already doing. I wish I could see through these sales pitches earlier."

"We have a ton of automated dashboards, and I understand most of the data that they include, but I still struggle to figure out how I should be using that data to make decisions. Where do I start?"

If any of these quotes feel familiar, then this book is for you. We've heard these frustrations in every data-related function in nearly every industry, ranging from pharmaceuticals to health care, retail, financial services, and consumer packaged goods. And we've worked with clients in all of these industries to shift their approaches. Putting your data to use can be productive, profitable, and even fun! That's why we wrote this book: to guide business leaders who want to *use their data effectively*.

THE DIGITAL AGE = THE DATA AGE

A common theme across all of the frustrations we hear from organizations about their struggles to effectively and consistently extract meaningful business value from their investments in data and analytics is that, well, *there's just so much data*. Our instincts have long been that more data is better, but the shifting of all aspects of our lives from analog to digital over the past three decades has wrought such an extreme version of "more" that it has left many managers questioning those instincts. The origins of the internet are often traced back to the mid-1960s and the creation of ARPANET as a distributed control computer network funded by the US Department of Defense. It was not until 1989, though, that Tim Berners-Lee at CERN conceived of an easier-to-use evolution of what had become "the internet" that would become the "World Wide Web." Within four years, Marc Andreesen, a student at the University of Illinois Urbana-Champaign created the Mosaic web browser while working with the National Center for Supercomputing Applications (NCSA), and the internet was on its way to catching mainstream fire. From the several hundred websites that existed by the end of 1993, to the more than 20,000 in 1995, to 17 million in 2000,[1] the growth of digital content was exponential.

---

[1] Internet Live Stats. (2009). *Total number of websites—internet live stats* [online]. Internetlivestats.com. Available at: https://www.internetlivestats.com/total-number-of-websites/.

Organizations began transitioning every aspect of their businesses to digital formats. Digital bits and bytes trumped paper on countless fronts: storability (a room full of file cabinets was replaced with a thumb drive), searchability (leafing through those file cabinets pulling out folder after folder and scanning the pages within those folders was replaced by a rectangle on a computer screen into which keywords could be typed), portability (traipsing to the library or the records room or a coworker's office was replaced by launching a browser from any device connected to the internet, and seemingly *every* device is connected to the internet). At a macro scale, global life began going through an analog-to-digital conversion:

- Rather than sending a letter, we could send an email.
- Rather than going to a brick-and-mortar establishment to buy a book, or leafing through a publisher's quarterly catalog, we could search for one online and order it immediately.
- Rather than receiving a book in the mail, we could read it instantaneously in a digital format.
- Rather than advertising on billboards, in magazines and newspapers, or with direct mail, we could advertise on the personalized screens that consumers were spending more and more time looking at, by running ads on websites and search engines.
- Rather than staffing a customer service representative to help prospects find what they need, we could use data science to offer our customers personalized recommendations in real time.

As early as 1994, *BusinessWeek* reported, "Companies are collecting mountains of information about you, crunching it to predict how likely you are to buy a product, and using that knowledge to craft a marketing message precisely calibrated to get you to do so [...] Many companies were too overwhelmed by the sheer quantity of data to do anything useful with the information [...] Still, many companies believe they have no choice but to brave the database-marketing frontier."[2] The digital data revolution was in full swing.

For companies, perhaps the most exciting aspect of this pervasive transformation to a digital-first world was the increased scale and fidelity of the data that could be collected along the way. Ask a retailer how their customers walk through one of their physical stores, and they would have to hire a set of observers to position themselves in the store and take

---

[2] Berry, J. (1994, Sept. 4). Database marketing. *BusinessWeek*.

copious notes. And they would only have data for the periods when those observers were on site. *And* they would run the risk of affecting their customers' behavior in the process, the so-called "observer effect." Ask a retailer how their customers navigate their *website*, though, and they are just a few clicks away from being able to pull up a report in a digital analytics platform like Google Analytics.

Expectations were high. With *all of this data*, it seemed obvious that *amazing things were possible*! And amazing things *can* be done with data. But over the last 25 years, businesses have slid into what Matt Gershoff, the chief executive officer of Conductrics, refers to as a "big table mentality." They have begun the never-ending and ever-increasing pursuit of gathering "all" the data—striving to clean, store, integrate, and maintain all of the data has become a goal in and of itself. "We can predict, discover, and engineer *anything*, if only we can observe *everything*," the philosophy suggests. "We're going to be truly scientific with all of this data" is the *idea*, but a misunderstanding of scientific principles and their application leads to ineffective and frustrating results rather than the "actionable truths" that we expected.

We (the authors) absolutely believe in the value of data. But we also have personally observed the negative results of flawed approaches and misguided expectations of how to realize that value. These negative results force leaders to seek external correction (many times, that's where we would be hired), or in the worst cases, lose the trust of their customers. We hope more leaders will proactively seek the knowledge this book offers to start reversing this trend. If you've ever felt frustrated, fascinated, forestalled, or fired up with the industry of data and analytics, this book is for you.

WHAT YOU WILL LEARN IN THIS BOOK

We are data enthusiasts, and we believe that data and analytics have near limitless extraordinary potential. But we have seen that the best intentions to put data to productive use can still lead to ineffective and even destructive activities. In this book, we will give you the tools to use data to enable effective decision-making and automation with clarity and purpose.

In Chapter 2, we explore the root causes that have led many organizations to invest extraordinary amounts in their data infrastructure, in reporting and analysis technology, and in substantial data and analytics teams without realizing the business value they expected. Myriad forces—economic, institutional, and psychological—inadvertently reinforce misconceptions of data and analytics and the misguided allocation of resources and efforts. Once these forces are called out, you will have a hard time not seeing them everywhere you look. (Yikes!) But you will be armed with the ability to push back when these forces try to drag you and your organization into an unproductive analytics abyss.

In Chapter 3, we develop the roles of decision-making and actionability in the analytics process, which we believe contribute to the "right" approach to getting value out of data. We discuss the *potential outcomes* framework, a mental model through which to view decision-making and the possible versions of the world that may emerge as a result of the decisions you make (or that *could have* emerged as a result of a decisions you made in the past).

In Chapter 4, we outline a framework for data usage. This structure highlights three fundamentally different ways that data can be used within an organization to drive value: measuring performance, validating hypotheses, and enabling operational processes. While activities in each of these areas may rely on some of the same underlying data, they are fundamentally different business activities, and they need to be approached in fundamentally different ways as a result. Methodologies from machine learning and artificial intelligence also play different roles, depending on the type of business activity. Chapters 5 through 9 dive into these three uses of data.

Chapter 10 explores how these different uses are, in practice, often interconnected. For example, if performance measurement shows that an operational process is not delivering the expected business results, then hypotheses get developed and validated to determine the root cause and recommended corrective action. Digitally enabled, profitable, AI-first enterprises are distinguished by the leader's ability to elegantly weave the three uses of data together.

Throughout the book, we share real-world vignettes based on our experiences working with clients. These vignettes will demonstrate the application of the framework and tools described within the book in a way that we expect you will be able to link to the situations you may encounter, or have encountered, in your career.

WILL THIS BOOK DELIVER VALUE?

As we just described, one of the core ways that data can be used to deliver value is through effective *performance measurement*, which we detail in Chapter 5.

We want this book to deliver meaningful value to *you*, so we're going to practice what we preach: you will have the opportunity throughout this book to report its performance for you online. We will state our intentions for the book using the "two magic questions" of performance measurement, which we will describe in much more detail in Chapter 5:

> **Magic Question 1: What are we trying to achieve with this book?**
> We want to arm you with a clear and actionable framework and set of techniques for efficiently and effectively getting more value from your data and analytics.
> **Magic Question 2: How will we know if we've done that?**
> While this could be measured in numerous ways, we're going to keep it concise by asking you to respond to two statements as you complete each chapter in the book:

1. The information and ideas presented gave me a new and better way to approach using data.

Strongly Disagree	*Somewhat Disagree*	*Neutral*	*Somewhat Agree*	*Strongly Agree*

2. I expect to apply the information presented to the way I work with data in the next 90 days.

Strongly Disagree	*Somewhat Disagree*	*Neutral*	*Somewhat Agree*	*Strongly Agree*

If you respond with "Somewhat Agree" or "Strongly Agree," then we will consider that we've achieved what we hoped to with you. Our target is to have more than 85% of respondents answer "Somewhat Agree" or "Strongly Agree" to these questions.

At the end of each chapter, we will remind you to visit https://analyticstrw .com and respond to these two questions. We will not be capturing anything other than what chapter you have just completed and the answer to these two questions. In other words, this will be entirely anonymous data that you are providing. But each pause for that assessment is an opportunity for you to reflect on whether you are getting value from the book.

If this feels a little gimmicky, well, maybe it is. But it's a way for you to see performance measurement in action in a situation that, at first blush, may seem difficult to measure. And, as we noted, we'll dig into this approach in much more detail in Chapter 5.

So now you've stuck with us through the introduction, which means you are at least a little intrigued. This is a good chance to pause and ask yourself if this book is worth continuing to read. Or, in data terms, will this book deliver *meaningful value* to you as a business leader?

MEASURE THIS CHAPTER

If you haven't already done so, it's time to contribute to the performance measurement of this book by visiting https://analyticstrw.com and answering the two-question survey for this chapter.

CHAPTER 2

How We Got Here

Scientists say that gathering data used to be like a walk in the desert. To get any water, you would have to hang out a giant tarp and wait for a small drop of rain to fall on it, only to hope it would travel down into a thermos to quench your thirst. Today, gathering data is easy. You walk out the door and are deluged by a torrential stream of bits.

Gathering reams of data, storing it, and accessing it has become easier and easier, but organizations are regularly frustrated that they're not seeing a steady and voluminous flow of actionable information as a result. At the root of these frustrations are a series of ideas about "data"—how it works and what it can do—that are, frankly, incorrect.

Getting *data* does not mean you get *insight*.

To begin to understand why, consider the journey we've been on for the past few decades. Many of us were stranded in that metaphorical desert. A drop of water in the desert is precious, and so its uses are meticulous. With such limited water, you're careful to use it in exactly the way you need to achieve your goals. When you're flooded with cheap and easy water in the suburbs, you water your lawn until it's practically submerged. If you had lived through the desert and found your way to suburban utopia, you would take pride in your reckless abandon.

Generic data are cheap and omnipresent today, and those of us who lived through the data revolution can tend to, undeservedly, feel like royalty.[1] But even those who didn't go from the desert to the suburbs, the trappings of this royal feeling have captured the majority of professionals. And it is, in part, this feeling that our data today are an unexpected bounty of pure "gold" in and of themselves that lead to misconceptions that hurt our ability to use data productively.

Metaphorical comparisons like "data is the new oil" are trite, and perhaps not fully informative. Oil is a high-priced *commodity*, and finding it on your property can feel like you have found gold in your backyard. But oil requires refinement before it can generate profits. Without refinement, oil is simply a sticky dark substance found on your property. Data work the same way. You

---

[1] Note that we say *generic data*, not all data. We mean this intentionally; most data that are readily available are not necessarily as useful as the data you would develop to answer the specific questions you care about answering the most.

have to refine the data in order for it to produce profitable value. The difference is that, without refinement, data aren't worth the bits and bytes they're stored on.

Another difference is that it is predictable what oil's outputs are, and therefore, any oil from anywhere can produce a profitable output. Although machine learning is often treated as though it can magically convert commodified data into useful insights and outputs, the missing ingredient is usually the appropriate theory for how the data were generated and how they should be used. Whereas with oil, the outputs are fairly constrained and replicable without additional knowledge (notwithstanding the plastics industry), with data, the outputs are nearly infinite. When something is infinite in nature, you have to know where to look. That is what necessitates this missing ingredient of theory, and you can inject it through hypothesis validation, a topic into which we will drill deeply starting in Chapter 6.

In this chapter, we argue that the mental models and techniques analytics required to process data into good decisions have been ignored in favor of a much larger lucrative enterprise: the collection of data. We have become hooked on the *promise* that the data bring. We mine for data in our backyards just as we once rooted around for oil, but we've forgotten that oil too, before refinement, is a boring, not-very-useful goo.

MISCONCEPTIONS ABOUT DATA HURT OUR ABILITY TO DRAW INSIGHTS

Data are not valuable in and of themselves. You have to interact with the data in a particular way to get any insight from it. You have to know what you'd like to learn, and then you have to know the analysis technique to apply to it in order to learn it.

In an age of artificial intelligence (AI) and machine learning, it's commonplace to assume that simply offering our data for consumption by the analytics techniques and AI tools we now have available will simply "generate insights." This idea has even made its way into our popular culture: anyone who's seen the android AI character named "Data" on *Star Trek* knows that the crew rely on him to autonomously perform insightful analysis quickly and at the drop of a hat. But in truth, even these tools are useless without a good idea to test.

Our society—including "the industry," broadly—has misidentified "the data" as an end in itself. We are not sure exactly why, and this book certainly does not suffice as a comprehensive research report on the topic, but we have identified four misconceptions underpinning the data and analytics zeitgeist that have put us in this situation. In fact, this idea that data are the be-all, end-all, is driven by forces that are sneakily powerful (hard to combat) and well-intended (the people behind these forces are misguided rather than malevolent) but are, arguably, quite destructive.

Consider the following four statements about data:

- With enough data, uncertainty can be eliminated.
- Data must be comprehensive to be useful.
- Data are inherently objective and unbiased.
- Democratizing access to data makes an organization data-driven.

How many of these four statements do you agree with—completely or in part? In the remainder of this chapter, we will explore why each of them is a dangerous misconception.

Misconception 1: With Enough Data, Uncertainty Can Be Eliminated

Most of the world's processes are inherently *random*. When a process is random, it means that the outcome cannot be determined with *exact certainty*, and there's absolutely nothing anyone or anything can do about it. In life, we want to be certain we're going to win—or at the very least, be certain that we won't lose. Randomness is the root cause of most intense discomfort in life because it makes almost everything, to some degree, *uncertain*. After all, we would never rationally choose to put ourselves in a losing situation.

We deal with uncertainty by gathering information. For example, one of the authors was uncertain if his wife would like the purse he bought for her as a holiday gift. If she didn't, it would cause him discomfort because she would feel obligated to like it and not return it, but she would never use it. He knew he would have to gaze upon his failure daily—a lonely and unused accessory permanently hanging from a hook in the closet. So, he asked his mother-in-law for an indication as to whether his wife would like it or not. When she replied, "She's been telling me for a year she wants that one," it reduced his uncertainty about his wife's reception of the gift. The author gathered information to reduce his uncertainty.

To executives, having lots of data available is even better than having your mother-in-law on speed-dial.[2] With data, they can reduce their uncertainty without even having to pick up the phone! In fact, search advertising, which is today one of the most lucrative advertising strategies, works exactly like a

---

[2] Did we just say that?

robot mother-in-law. You don't need to wonder if a user wants a Dior handbag if that user types, "buy black Dior handbag" into the search bar.

As the volume of data available to businesses has exponentially increased over the past few decades, technology vendors in the business of helping other companies collect or manage data are incentivized to promote the idea that, given sufficient data, advanced analytics and predictive models can deliver "the truth" without ever having to phone anyone. While business leaders may have some intuition that the data will never turn them into truly omniscient beings, they also generally accept as a fact that "more data is better."

The reality is that, while data play a key role in reducing uncertainty:

- having a large amount of data doesn't mean you have *any* information that reduces uncertainty regarding the decision at hand;
- even with the best information, the natural law of uncertainty still governs;
- data can cost more than the benefit you get from collecting it; and
- it is impossible to actually collect and use "all" of the data.

Having More Data Doesn't Mean You Have the Right Data

With even a relatively small volume of raw data, the outputs are infinite—data can be combined, added, multiplied, and extrapolated in countless ways.[3] That means, in effect, that without an idea of where you are trying to go with the data, any amount of data, even tremendous amounts of data, cannot help you to get there.

The Library of Babel

Consider the Library of Babel, which Jose Luis Borges introduced in 1941. This fictional library contains a seemingly infinite number of books. Each book was written by a computer that was trained to scramble all of the letters of the alphabet into every one of its possible permutations. So, for the first book, the computer would take all of the letters of the alphabet, shuffle their order—including the As, the Bs, the spaces, the punctuation, etc.—and it would write 300 pages of that, bind the pages together, and then put the book on the shelf of the library. The computer continues to do this until every possible string of letters, spaces, and punctuation have been represented in the library.

---

[3] In fact, even the number of permutations of characters possible in a single 280-character social media post exceeds the total number of atoms in the observable universe.

In this library exists every possible idea any person ever has or will have. That means that the library contains the patent for Windows 95. The library contains the greatest literary work ever to be written, from a future century, that has not yet come to pass. The library contains, if it is possible, the technology required to travel through outer space at a speed faster than light. The library would even contain a history of your life's past, present, and future— enabling you to live just as Biff Tannen did in *Back to the Future*, winning horse bets and conducting stock trades to amass the largest fortune ever known. By scrambling these letters, we have generated every solution to any problem that humanity has ever or will ever face. There is the ultimate level of certainty in this library of all possible iterations of knowledge.

The problem is, how do you find anything in this library? There are simply too many books available to know where to look. Most of the books in the library are complete gibberish, and many of the books, while coherent sets of words, are fiction rather than fact (the tale of a small online bookseller called Amazon that went bankrupt and ceased to exist after a mere 2 years in business). And the process that you would use to search through the books, or order them, would require you to have read all of them in the first place. Ironically, having access to the ultimate level of information means that now you have absolutely no certainty about where to look for it.

Perhaps one solution is to have an artificial intelligence tool based on a large language model (LLM) framework review all of the materials and find the books that seem most promising. However, in order to know what is most promising, the tool has to know what ideas it should be looking for. The problem is that LLMs are only familiar with the ideas that we have available today and how influential they have been up until now. They do not know what the influential ideas of the future will be. Well, dang!

Let's say we go one step further. We give the LLM tool the ability to implement the hypothesis validation techniques we discuss in this book (see Chapter 6), and we give it the authority to start testing the ideas it finds to see if they have any value or merit. The amount of time it would take to test every possible idea it finds, in the order in which it finds them, is still in excess of the amount of time we would have available in a million lifetimes.

Therein lies the problem with data. Because data can be refined into an infinite number of applications, we have to have an idea of where to look for those applications before we can successfully see value from them. We have to bring ideas about where we should be looking in order to advance our ability to apply data. It is not the fact that we have data available in and of itself that creates insight; rather, it is the application of the data to the right idea at the right time that generates our ability to create history through the actions we take. We are, in this sense, charting our own path forward by deciding what to test and act upon, even if the future history of the world is entirely predetermined, as some people believe.

The Streetlight Problem

Let's make this point more specific. Imagine that we come across a gentleman looking for his keys in the street. We say, "Can I help you? Where do you think you've lost them?"

He replies, "I think I lost them over there near the grass, not here."

We ask, "Why are you looking over here if you lost them over there?"

And he replies, "Well, this is where the streetlight is, so I can see what I'm looking for."

Because the streetlight is setting the agenda for where he should look for the thing he wants to find, he will, by definition, never find it. Uh...sound familiar?

We see this a lot in business. New questions that are valuable to the actions the business needs to take are often unable to be answered by the data at hand. And if we try to answer them with the data that we "found in our backyard," then we will always get the wrong answer. Just because data are available doesn't mean they are the right data for the job.

For instance, consider one of our clients: an insurance provider to frontline professionals that provides coverage for medical problems and catastrophic occurrences that some frontline professionals endure in the line of duty, like exposure to COVID-19. The insurance provider wanted to release a new insurance product that would change the price of the insurance premium based on the lifestyle characteristics of the frontline professional seeking insurance. They gave us a data set, including factors such as whether the professional smoked, whether the professional had a pre-existing heart condition, etc., and asked us to predict whether these factors changed the risk the company would assume by writing a policy for the professional. So, in theory, a professional who does not smoke—a factor known to be correlated with cancer diagnosis—could be given a cheaper premium than a person who does, because it creates less risk for the company.

And so the first question we asked was, "What do you mean by risk? Is risk the probability that you have to pay out a claim? Is it the amount of the claims paid? Is it the probability that the person is catastrophically harmed? Is it the probability that the person will be readmitted to the hospital several times after a single admission?" There are several outcome factors used to quantify risk in the insurance industry.

The client responded that, in an ideal world, the risk we compute would be related to the total amount of claims that would need to be paid out over the lifetime of the insured professional. But then the client pointed out that they did not have this data available. They only had, on short notice, data related to the satisfaction of the insured professionals with the services that the company provided. Couldn't we just use that?[4]

Well, no. You can't look for an answer in the place where you already have the data, just because that's where the data already are. And any analysis using that as the outcome variable would not ultimately produce something that would help the client actually reduce their uncertainty with respect to the insurance policies.

Even with an Immense Amount of Data, You Cannot Eliminate Uncertainty

Okay, so we've talked about instances in which we did not have the right data, or at the very least, the ability to find where the right data are. But what if we do have the right data? Is it possible to eliminate uncertainty when we do? The answer is, unfortunately, also no. The natural laws of randomness that govern uncertainty, as we discussed earlier, have a pernicious way of preventing our ability to make perfect predictions.[5]

Consider a situation in which an investor comes to your business and offers to invest $10 million in your company. But she'll only give it to you if

---

[4] Relatedly, there were only factors that correlated with worse outcomes in the data; there were no factors that correlated with better outcomes. Because there were no data that could potentially decrease the absolute premium, all an analysis of this data could actually do is show us where premiums would be relatively higher or lower. This would produce a potentially flawed number of insights, as we discuss further in Chapter 8 on descriptive evidence.

[5] Wow, that was a nice alliteration. T-shirts, anyone? Visit: https://analyticstrw.com/store.

you take a gamble based on a coin flip: "If it's heads, you give me 10% of your company. If it's tails, you give me 90%."

Is that a good bet?

With no information (data) at all, it's impossible to know what side the coin will land on; you would predict that it has a 50% chance of landing on heads and a 50% chance of landing on tails. It's perfectly random what would happen.

What data could you collect to improve that prediction? You could gather data on 10,000 flips to build a "model" and gather a bunch of additional data about the conditions around each flip: the starting position of the coin pre-flip (is heads or tails facing up?), the flipping technique (a flick from the top of a thumb vs. simply throwing the coin from being pinched between the thumb and index finger vs. throwing it up from the palm), the landing material (concrete, dirt, carpet, wood, the surface of the moon?), the speed with which the coin is thrown, the amount of rotational force applied to the coin, and the temperature and humidity in the space.

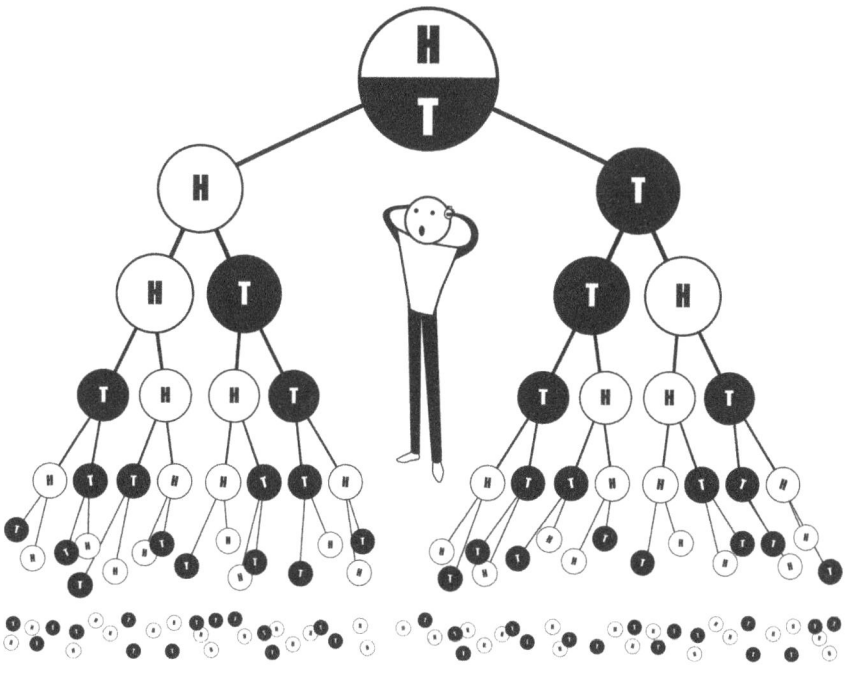

With all of this collected data (and, presumably, a pretty tired thumb), how much do you think you would be able to improve your prediction?

Well, not that much at all: ultimately, it's still a random coin flip.

This is a simplified and silly example, but the underlying idea applies just as much in the real world of business. Even when we're talking about something as simple as a coin flip, we can expend an enormous amount of effort in collecting and crunching the data and still not get to anything close to a perfectly accurate prediction.

In business, most situations have an unfathomable number of variables at play, and it is always a better framing of the challenge as "reducing uncertainty an appropriate amount given the cost of that reduction" rather than "eliminating uncertainty (no matter the cost)."

Frame the challenge as "reducing uncertainty" rather than "eliminating uncertainty."

Data Can Cost More Than the Benefit You Get from It

On top of these issues, we will add that collecting immense amounts of data in an effort to reduce uncertainty comes at significant cost. Once they are collected, they have to be stored. Storing data is quite expensive, especially in the cloud. Paying to store data that are never used makes the executive who decided we needed to store it look foolish. So the data need to be used. Scanning data artifacts to use them is expensive, especially when the scans are done indiscriminately. And so data usage must be governed to optimize costs. And having catastrophic data breaches can expose the company to lawsuits, and they can cause the company to cross the ethical Rubicon, and so on, etc.

The simple choice to collect data leads to a sequence of further, increasingly expensive choices that must be made, all ultimately incentivized to be made such that they justify the further existence of the data.

It Is Impossible to Collect and Use "All" of the Data

If you work in business and data today, you've likely come across this concept formally called *causal determinism*, or *scientific determinism*. It makes the rounds every century or so. The nineteenth-century scientist Pierre-Simon Laplace called it the "clockwork universe" theory, which Stephen Hawking mentions in his published 1999 lecture, "Does God Play Dice?":

> *In effect what [Laplace] said was, that if at one time, we knew the positions and speeds of all the particles in the universe, then we could calculate their behavior at any other time, in the past or future. There is a*

probably apocryphal story, that when Laplace was asked by Napoleon, how God fitted into this system, he replied, 'Sire, I have not needed that hypothesis.' I don't think that Laplace was claiming that God didn't exist. It is just that He doesn't intervene, to break the laws of Science.

The idea is this: every event we've ever witnessed was caused by a sequence of preceding events. If we could observe perfectly every event happening today, and then apply clever predictive thinking, then we could perfectly predict the events that will happen tomorrow. In fact, if we could encapsulate as data the state of the world at every moment, down to the position of every atom, and then train a model that predicts every moment as a function of the moments that came before it, then we could perfectly predict what's about to happen. We can know the future perfectly because the future state of the world is entirely determined by the current state of the world and the processes that map the current state to the future.

Seems great, right? Well, not when you realize that collecting, storing, and analyzing all of that data would actually exceed the matter capacity available in the universe itself. Yes, trying to use the universe to predict the universe (or the universe plus one millisecond) would require a universe exponentially larger in size just to make the calculation—which by the laws of physics is infeasible. And even if we could find that universe, an intimidating sounding idea called *chaos theory* kicks in: once we start making predictions based on predictions, our predictions get inaccurate really quickly. Let's not even mention the cost of the cloud bill.

It's not useful to collect all of the data. And it's impossible to even use it.

Scientific determinism still rears its head periodically. These days, it's when the press or some Silicon Valley know-it-all decides that omnipotent AI can solve all of our problems. But don't be persuaded. In fact, it is infeasible that any such AI could ever exist, as it would break the laws of physics. The best way to advance is to ensure you collect the right data to answer the right question, and then apply the right technique to answer it. We discuss methodologies to do this in the coming chapters (see Chapters 6 through 9).

Misconception 2: Data Must Be Comprehensive to Be Useful

It's logical (and true) that, if there is *no data*, then there is nothing to be analyzed. However, it is *not* true that an imperfect and incomplete data set has little or no value at all.

Time and again, we have watched organizations that feel they are not getting meaningful value out of their data decide that the problem is that *they must not have enough data*. Or their data are not sufficiently integrated across data sets. Or their data have inaccuracies or gaps. All of this may be (or, almost certainly, *is*) true. But that doesn't mean that the *most important thing* is to address those gaps.

The reality is that the data will *always* be incomplete and imperfect, but that doesn't mean that it is not useful. "Letting the perfect be the enemy of the good" is endemic when it comes to data within organizations. Yet, if we take a small step back and consider non-"business" applications of data—public policy research, social sciences, econometrics, political science, etc.—we find a landscape strewn with examples of imperfect and incomplete data that, with appropriate expectations and rigor applied, has been put to effective use!

"Small Data" Can Be Just As Effective As, If Not More Effective Than, "Big Data"

One relatively famous example[6] had to do with economists in the mid-1990s trying to determine the effect of increasing the minimum wage on the rate of employment growth: "If employers are forced to pay their lowest paid workers more, will they hire fewer employees?" Running a true field experiment of setting the minimum wage at different levels was not an option.[7] Simply comparing the employment rate for states that had different minimum wages was problematic, too—if the minimum wage was $2.65/hour in Kansas and $4.27/hour in Connecticut, well, the fundamental differences in their state economies and economic drivers might be a bigger factor in their hiring decisions than the minimum wages they were required to pay.

A couple of clever economists[8] realized that Connecticut was about to *raise* the minimum wage from $4.25/hour to $5.05/hour. Just like comparing different states was problematic, simply comparing the before/after employment rate in Connecticut was problematic: macroeconomic forces could very well be at play that were impacting the employment rate as much (or more) than the change in minimum wage.

But the economists realized that they could combine both of these ideas in a way that was significantly less problematic. Since Pennsylvania butts up to New Jersey, it would be reasonable to treat the economies on either side of

---

[6] "Famous" is a relative term here. In the right circles—a circle of economists in this case—referencing "New Jersey raising the minimum wage in 1992" will lead to a bunch of knowing head-nods!

[7] Imagine telling the owner of a bunch of companies that, yes, they had to pay their workers more than their competitors, but that that was okay because, ya know, it was "for science."

[8] David Card and Alan B. Krueger. You can read the full details of their work in their paper on this topic: https://davidcard.berkeley.edu/papers/njmin-aer.pdf.

the Delaware River—Pennsylvania and New Jersey—as comparable. So, they surveyed 410 fast-food restaurants (which have a pretty standard business model) in eastern Pennsylvania and in New Jersey and, among other questions, asked them how many full-time employees they had. They conducted this survey twice: once a couple of months before the minimum wage change, and then again 6 months after the change. Then, they compared the *change* in the number of employees for each state from the first survey to the second survey.

The result: they concluded there was no meaningful near-term effect on employment as a result of the change in minimum wage. This is an example of what is called a *natural experiment*, and it did something that is foundationally important, in that it worked to "control for all other factors." We'll touch on this idea later in the book in Chapters 7 and 9, but for now, just take away that, even with their cleverness, the results were not unarguably definitive and broadly applicable. But the findings—based on imperfect data, rigorously considered—were still very useful in advancing an understanding of one impact (or lack thereof) of raising minimum wage levels.

Fighting the urge to constantly chase "more and better data" is key! Opportunity costs are real: if all of your energy is devoted to data collection, you won't have the capacity to actually *do* anything with that data. The key, as we discuss in the coming chapters, is the ability to analyze the data you gather in combination with the theory you develop to draw conclusions.

Misconception 3: Data Are Inherently Objective and Unbiased

In the executive madness associated with this data gold rush, we have observed over the past few decades the misconception that "the data" broadly construed are superior to the intuition and information that any individual in business has.

At best, data are a tool leaders can use to test ideas they have no preconceptions about, or to discover when their assumptions are wrong. Data can be combined with previously developed knowledge to further develop intuitions and ideas earned through the work of a hard-fought career. When used for good, data can help organizations make better decisions and reduce their uncertainty sufficiently such that they can act rapidly.

What's not talked about is how data can cut the other way. When used for bad—generally not through malicious *intent* but, rather, as the result of confirmation bias—data can help reinforce the ability of individuals to impose their own ideas about what they should be doing on the rest of the company. In a few organizations we have worked with, it is impossible to actually make the case to do anything without having data available to back up the case. Data are used sometimes as a cudgel in meetings, to undermine the claims that an expert makes when the expert does not bring "hard data" to the table besides their expertise or to "prove" the point someone has.

When data are used in this way, they serve the intentions of the individual and their agenda. That is not necessarily a bad thing, as long as those intentions align with the promotion of success for the stakeholders of the business. This use of data becomes problematic when data become a smokescreen behind which individuals advance their own agenda over the interests of the business. This is why it's important to have a broad level of data literacy within the organization—so that data users can participate in a dialogue of equally footed ideas rather than feel pushed to the side by superior force (whether that be an executive's assumptions or the unfairly produced analysis of an empowered colleague).

The belief that the empirical study of the world is superior to our assumption-based approaches, because data are devoid of the biases we bring in our assumptions, has become overly invasive in business today. In reality, the use of data simply reflects the biases we unwittingly espouse in the measurement processes we use to generate them, our selection of the data we wish to expose, and in the uses for which we apply them. The very fact that we address one idea, and not another, reflects a bias toward the type of uncertainty we wish to reduce or the choices we believe we have available to succeed.

Data in and of themselves do not elicit unbiased, objective answers. Rather, properly constructed tests and interpretations of the results gives us information that can help us reduce uncertainty. Using data for good in business means remaining open to the idea that we could be wrong and, culturally, accepting that *being wrong is okay*. The philosophy of *Analytics the Right Way* is aimed toward constructing analyses that help you to act, and in order to know what to do, you need to know what you would do if you're proven wrong. If ever you encounter a colleague who claims any position other than theirs is wrong, because "the data say otherwise," be sure to ask if your colleague had started with a *falsifiable* position—a position that can be disproven, just as much as it can be "proven right."[9]

---

[9] We've put "proven right" in quotation marks because generally, you cannot actually prove something to be universally right. You can only prove that something constrained is wrong. We won't get into the scientific philosophy behind it in this book. Or at least, that's a statement for which the null hypothesis cannot be rejected, which is *exactly* the sort of arcane language we would need to employ to expand on this further. You can thank our editors for sparing you that side trip.

In Private, Data Always Bend to the User's Will

There's an old economist's joke that goes as follows:

> *The CEO of a major company is hiring for an advisory role. A mathematician, a statistician, and an economist show up to interview for the job.*
>
> *The CEO first calls in the mathematician and asks, "What does two plus two equal?"*
>
> *The mathematician replies, "Four, of course!"*
>
> *The CEO asks, "Four, exactly?"*
>
> *The mathematician responds, quizzically, "Yes, four, exactly."*
>
> *Then the CEO calls in the statistician and asks again, "What does two plus two equal?"*
>
> *The statistician says, "Well, on average, four."*
>
> *The CEO asks, "Four, exactly?"*
>
> *The statistician says, "Well, four, give or take ten percent."*
>
> *The CEO finally calls in the economist and poses the same question: "What does two plus two equal?"*
>
> *The economist gets up, locks the door, closes the shade, sits next to the CEO and in a lowered voice says, "What do you want it to equal?"*

We are not by any means trying to say that all economists are dishonest (in fact, that would be an insult against one of the authors). There is an ounce of truth in the joke: with enough torturing of the data, it will confess to nearly anything you wish.

In the scientific community, thought to be the bastion of proper analysis, there is presently a replication crisis. Scientists are able to replicate the results that are published in peer review journals *less than half* of the time. The number varies by field, with a 2016 survey of scientists published in *Nature* reporting failure to replicate in chemistry at 87%.[10] That suggests that the findings published in these journals, which are supposed to be indicative of general conclusions to be drawn and elucidative of natural laws governing the universe, are in reality "cooked up" by whoever did the analysis. This is also not to say that scientists are trying to lie in their publications, and often these results are achieved as a naïve artifact of the honest but particular choices the author made during the analysis of the data. But it does underscore the point: data always bend to the user's will.

---

[10] Read more here: https://www.nature.com/articles/533452a.

One of the methods we are exploring in the scientific community to overcome this replication crisis is *pre-registration*. The pre-registration process begins with the publication of a standard operating procedure for what an analyst is going to do, before they even have access to the data that they are going to analyze. By employing this technique, analysts foster credibility in their results through the public declaration of what they are going to do before they possibly could've been able to "torture the data," as it were.

We do not recommend pre-registration in all cases, but if you watch closely, you will see the business analytics equivalent of pre-registration throughout the later chapters in this book: setting a target for a key performance indicator (Chapter 5) is a form of pre-registration, articulating a clear hypothesis (Chapter 6) is a precursor to pre-registration, and the hypothesis validation techniques discussed in Chapters 7 through 9 all employ a light form of pre-registration, in that they require upfront thought and articulation of *what is expected* before simply diving into the data and crafting a story that fits it after the fact.

Even When You Don't Want the Data to Be Biased, They Are

In even the most well-intentioned analytics exercises for the business, data can inherently include bias simply because they reflect the state of the world in which the business operates. Allow us to share a story from the health care space.

As part of its *AI.Humanity* initiative, Emory University hired a rock star researcher named Professor Anant Madabhushi, who studies among many things the field of *radiomics*—a quantitative approach to reviewing medical scans that aims to detect diseases with computer vision, machine learning, and AI techniques.

Professor Madabhushi's lab found that a class of models meant to predict the presence of prostate cancer recurrence based on medical images were much more effective at predicting prostate cancer recurrence from images of white patients than from images of black patients. This was not the preferred outcome because it means that the models produced in that class would serve one population much worse than the other, creating arbitrary differences in the level of service technology could offer for medical care.

When they dug into the data, the Madabhushi lab team discovered that it wasn't the direct bias of the researchers causing this to happen, or something aberrant happening in the modeling approach. It was actually in the composition of the data set itself. Roughly 80% of the patient pool for the study were white patients, whereas roughly 20% were black patients. That biased the model toward the majority population simply because the most accurate predictions, on average, would be relevant to the white patient pool. Professor Madabhushi's team found that there are variations in the way that prostate cancer cells look in different populations of patients, and if we don't have enough data for the models to recognize different appearances of those cancer cells, then the models will perform worse for populations where we have less data.

The model was fixed by rebalancing the data set. But to rebalance the data set, professor Madabhushi's team had to employ a mixture of new data collection and specialized data balancing techniques. If the study data had originally been collected in a balanced way, the problem could have been avoided. Once they fixed the model, it improved the accuracy of cancer reoccurrence detection in the black patient population by a factor of six.[11]

With the explosion of AI applications, we are seeing a steady stream of examples of biased training data leading to headline-inducing whiffs:

- *New York Times* (2018): "Facial Recognition Is Accurate, If You're a White Guy"[12]
- *BBC.com* (2024): "AI Hiring Tools May Be Filtering Out the Best Job Applicants"[13]
- *MIT Technology Review* (2021): "Bias Isn't the Only Problem with Credit Scores—And No, AI Can't Help"[14]

In all of these cases, it is not that the researchers intended to develop biased approaches. Instead, it was training data that they used that resulted in these biased applications.

When we develop new analytics techniques—many of which are perceived to be superior machine learning and AI techniques, devoid of error—we are subject not only to the biases that we as researchers bring to the table, but to the inherent biases present in the data sets we use for the analysis.

One innovation we have observed in the past decade is the *data review board*. The role of the data review board in your organization is to review the data sets and analytical techniques used at the organization. By including diverse perspectives, the people on the review board can catch biases that

---

[11] Read more here: https://thedaily.case.edu/ai-reveals-differences-in-appearance-of-cancer-tissue-between-racial-populations/.

[12] https://www.nytimes.com/2018/02/09/technology/facial-recognition-race-artificial-intelligence.html.

[13] https://www.bbc.com/worklife/article/20240214-ai-recruiting-hiring-software-bias-discrimination.

[14] https://www.technologyreview.com/2021/06/17/1026519/racial-bias-noisy-data-credit-scores-mortgage-loans-fairness-machine-learning/.

normally would not be caught, like the ones that we discussed earlier in this section. This contributes to a more fair and unbiased analytics approach and reduces downside risks (for example, if a hospital system were to deploy the cancer detection model discussed earlier before it was fixed, the system could be open to a lawsuit, alleging that it was discriminating in the care it offered). The data review board is a good opportunity to reward up-and-coming superstars with higher visibility within the organization while meeting the organizations risk mitigation goals. We believe this innovation could be more widely adopted. The same model can be used in reviewing the solutions created using AI and machine learning technologies.

Misconception 4: Democratizing Access to Data Makes an Organization Data-Driven

We hear terms like, "data democratization" and "citizen data science" often these days. They are indeed powerful:

- "Data democratization" has the power of...alliteration.
- "Citizen data science" has the power of...being clever-sounding.

Both of these phrases have become as popular as an ice cream stand at the beach in the dead of summer. But just like letting a 9-year-old decide that an ice cream stand should provide breakfast, lunch, and dinner, casually focusing on catchy phrases for getting to effective data usage is unhealthy.

Time and again we've seen data teams set their sights on empowering their business stakeholders to be able to self-serve for most of their data needs. And we are by no means declaring that business users should be prevented from accessing data easily and efficiently. The problem, though, is when a mentality sets in—and it almost always does—that, "If the business has access to the data, then they have everything they need to get value from it."

We had a healthcare client once that illustrated the problems with this approach. The analytics team supporting the marketing organization was quite small—just four people and a manager. And the organization had invested in an enterprise business intelligence (BI) platform into which they had spent several years automating data feeds from a wide range of sources.

The marketing team that was using that data (other departments used the platform too, but we're just going to focus on the marketers here) had more than 40 people in it, and many of those marketers worked with external agencies who also had employees who could access the data through the same tool. Unfortunately, the data (and the BI tool) were not particularly user-friendly, and the marketers had no guidance on *how* to go about using the data.

The result? They would pull up a dashboard, click around a bit until they saw a chart that pertained to their campaign, and then they would screen capture it and put it in the reports they delivered out to the hospital and service line administrators they supported.

The marketers regularly reported that they were not confident that what they were doing was either right or particularly helpful. But the analytics team's response was...to continue to integrate more data into the system, to provide occasional trainings on how to click around in the BI tool, and to then direct the marketers to attend weekly "office hours" sessions to get any of their questions answered.

That's representative of a problem we see in many organizations: a mentality on the part of the analytics teams that their responsibility is just to "get the data in the hands of the business." That is like a driving instructor seeing her primary responsibility to be showing her students how to turn the car on and put it in gear. Where those students wind up as they mash on the unexplained pedals on the floorboard, and what property damage they cause along the way...they are just supposed to figure out on their own.[15]

Effectively using data is much more about creative and strategic thinking *before* engaging with the data itself than it is about knowing where to find a particular metric or what that metric represents.

CONCLUSION

Data can empower us with the ability to reduce uncertainty around creative ideas that, if acted upon, can improve our condition. But data in and of themselves are incapable of doing so. It is instead the application of data through analytical techniques that enable us to act productively upon them; only then will we see value from our data-driven insights.

In this chapter, we discussed four misconceptions that we believe have prevented our society from moving past the idea that data are in and of themselves productive of actionable insight. But now that we've pointed them out, how do we proceed? If we've ignored analysis for so long, how do we begin to realign ourselves to the train tracks toward insight?

In the next chapter, we introduce one more *big* idea—potential outcomes—that will define the role that a good analytics approach plays in our ability to move forward. It is through analytics that we are able to explore causality and uncertainty related to the decisions we make and the actions we take. Understanding those decisions and actions, and the manifold possible worlds that they may create, are the missing piece to analytics nirvana.

MEASURE THIS CHAPTER

It's time to contribute to the performance measurement of this book by visiting https://analyticstrw.com and answering the two-question survey for this chapter.

---

[15] Self-driving cars for the win. If this analogy makes no sense to you, dear reader, then this book has lived on much longer than we ever imagined it would.

CHAPTER 3

Making Decisions with Data: Causality and Uncertainty

Do you regret any decisions you've made in the past? We've only ever met a handful of people who said they had "no regrets," and universally they had illustrious, 15-minute careers as TikTok stars peddling their personal brand of DGAF canvas bags (just kidding). All of us should stand to eat a little humble pie and admit to decisions we've made that, looking back, weren't the right ones. In fact, we decided to write this book at great expense, effort, and time away from our families because we were absolutely certain it would become a best seller. Perhaps upon seeing the sales numbers, we'll come to regret our decision.

As a society, we're hooked on reducing the level of regret we experience because its uncomfortable, painful, and often linked to real consequences, like the destruction of credibility and trust in a relationship, the loss of a stream of income, or a missed opportunity that might have—just might have—solved our problems. We expend incredible time and effort structuring our lives to avoid the feeling of regret.

We universally look to technology to help us eliminate regret because it has historically been the salvation of our problems. There's something comforting in the cold, hard science of technology that seems impervious to the uncertainty that begets regret.

Good decisions run on good information—the "data" so often mentioned. And the better data we have available for technology to use, the better the information, and hence, the better the decision. In a world with *perfect* information, we think we can *permanently* avoid regret.

But why do we—with powerful cloud computing infrastructure, artificial intelligence technologies, and nearly infinite amounts of data at our disposal—still feel such regret?

LIFE AND BUSINESS IN A NUTSHELL: MAKING DECISIONS UNDER UNCERTAINTY

This idea that, given a sufficient volume of data, we will be able to make perfect (regret-free!) decisions is appealing, and it is tempting to "see" evidence that this is the case—Netflix successfully recommends shows that we like to watch, Amazon suggests complementary products for us to purchase, and even the banner ads we see as we browse the web sometimes (creepily) promote products that we were just talking about with some friends yesterday! But these examples are using truly massive volumes of data (which most organizations do not have), and they are still by no means perfectly accurate. Even in the most controlled manufacturing environment, widgets come off the line with slight differences in their weight and dimensions. If they are enough "out of spec," then they are considered defective. In business, we are typically working with human beings out in the real world—far, far from a controlled manufacturing environment. Arguably, the most critical aspect of any knowledge worker's job is making decisions under conditions of uncertainty. The question is not, "How can I use data to eliminate uncertainty?" but rather, "How can I use data to reduce uncertainty to inform the decisions that I make?"

Annie Duke's first career was as a successful professional gambler. Now she writes and speaks about decision-making—often using examples from poker that can be applied more broadly to life. If you think of poker as being primarily about "reading opponents' tells" and intuition around when you are "on a hot streak" (or "on a cold streak"), then you're not thinking about poker as successful poker professionals approach it. That's because poker is actually a relatively controlled environment, governed by the realities of chance, where human beings have to make one decision after another. As Duke describes it in her first book, poker "is a game of *incomplete information*. It is a game of decision-making under conditions of uncertainty over time."[1] For professional poker players, the *game* is their *job*. Make that one-word substitution in Duke's statement, and you have an accurate generalization of every knowledge worker's day-to-day reality, which "is a job of *incomplete information*. It is a job of decision-making under conditions of uncertainty over time."

Unlike most situations in life, the feedback loop for a poker decision is almost instantaneous. At the end of each hand, the results are revealed to every player. It's tempting to think that the results of each hand, therefore, tell each player if they made "good decisions" or "bad decisions" for the hand: the winner of the hand made good decisions, and the losers of the hand made bad decisions. Right? Actually...this is *wrong*! It's a fallacy that Duke refers to as "resulting"—using the benefit of hindsight to declare if a decision was a good one. In poker, as in business and in life, the results of a decision have two fundamental causal contributors: skill and luck. An amazing poker hand (luck) can still be lost because it is poorly played (skill). A terrible hand (luck) will likely be lost *even if* it is played as brilliantly as possible (skill). The degree to which skill and luck each contribute to a result varies from situation to situation!

When it comes to the application of data in a business context, we are always operating with incomplete information. *Even if* we have complete and perfect historical data,[2] we cannot guarantee that, with proper analysis, every

---

[1] Duke, A. (2018). *Thinking in Bets: Making Smarter Decisions When You Don't Have All the Facts.* Portfolio/Penguin, p. 21.

[2] We *never* have complete and perfect historical data, but billions of dollars are spent each year in its pursuit. Getting from "good enough" to "great" is expensive (see "diminishing returns"). Getting from "great" to "perfect" is impossible (albeit the pursuit of this unattainable ideal is a fantastic way to drain an organization's bank account).

decision will generate a positive outcome. What we need to do is to consider the nature of the decision we're trying to make, the stakes of that decision, and how we can as efficiently apply data within that context.

WHAT'S IN A GOOD DECISION?

In business and life, we want to make good decisions. But how do we know a good decision from a bad one? Folks *feel* like they know a good decision when they see one. A good decision will maximize the probability of a successful outcome: we want to take actions that make it most likely for us to close the deal, to get the new job, to set our kids up for success. But it can also be the case that our decisions, despite our best intentions, result in poor outcomes.

The randomness of nature (or providence, if you prefer) is one reason our decisions may go the wrong way. We may have done our best to ensure that on average the outcome our action will achieve is optimal. But there is always a chance that, due to random reasons, things don't turn out the way that we want them to. For example, we may interview for a job for which we are a great fit, and all of the interviews go great. We send personalized follow-up thank you emails to everyone with whom we interviewed, but the company's email system flags all of those emails as spam for some reason (not something that normally happens with our email), and none of the interviewers see our note. Another strong candidate—not *quite* as strong as we were—follows the same strategy, and his emails get through. When the interview team meets to discuss who to offer the job to, the fact that the other candidate sent a personalized follow-up email and we did not (*appear to*!) follow up with any of them tips the decision in his favor, and he gets the job offer. We made the best decision, but it was essentially random chance that caused the outcome. We cannot control the randomness of nature.

A lack of information is another reason our decisions go the wrong way. We may decide to take an action because the outcome looks on average positive, only to find that there was significant downside risk associated with it that we had not predicted. For example, we may decide to open an establishment for our new "Meat-Eaters" restaurant in a bustling mall, only to find that the customers we thought we would earn don't generally eat meat and don't patronize the new establishment. When we considered the decision, we considered it on the basis only of the large perceived market opportunity, not customer preferences. We lacked information as part of our decision-making process.

Even a good decision may go wrong due to randomness or a lack of information. The implication of this is that it is not the outcome of a decision that determines whether the decision was "good." In any decision, there is a level of uncertainty as to how it will affect the outcomes we see. What makes a decision "good" is whether it minimizes the *regret* we might feel in the future for having made it.

MINIMIZING REGRET IN DECISIONS

We feel regret when we compare the outcome we see based on the decisions we make to the other potential outcomes we imagine we could have achieved.

We generally say we "regret" a decision simply when it produces a poor outcome, but that's not the whole story. Regret also comes from the reason for which the decision turned out poorly. We may rightfully feel regret when we make a choice that we knew, at the time, was likely to result in a poor outcome, even if there was an upside to it. Often, however, we feel unfair regret, due to choices we've made that by chance, or because of missing information that was unavailable at the time of the choice, turned out bad.

In the science of decision-making, machine learning, and artificial intelligence, we use this concept of regret minimization liberally to evaluate potential actions and make decisions. To make AI "artificially intelligent," we have to delegate to it the authority to execute complex, previously human-based, decision-making processes. Regret minimization tends to encourage the machines to make decisions that we, as humans, consider to be "good," allowing the machine to successfully emulate the processes and decisions its human compatriots would have made.[3]

The key to minimizing regret is employing a reliable process through which you gather information on a decision that is good enough such that you know you couldn't have made another, better choice. Although we can't control randomness, we *can* control the amount of information we develop to make good decisions. A reliable process will guide you to collecting the right amount of information to address the right questions. Sometimes, we can even gather information that helps us minimize the influence of random chance on our desired outcomes.

This concept is a stumbling block that lies at the root of many misinterpretations and misuses of data to inform decisions. That stumbling block is best removed by exploring the *potential outcomes framework*. It sounds fancy, and

---

[3] In these computational fields, we often employ a notion from game theory called *minimax*, which prioritizes choices that not only maximize the probability of success and minimize the probability of failure, but also maximize the minimum level of success and minimize the maximum level of failure. In other words, we want not only to know which action is most likely to cause the best expected outcome, we also want to reduce our uncertainty associated with the achievement of that outcome.

there are a couple of fancy words that we'll introduce as we describe it, but the potential outcomes framework is an idea that is just as simple as it is profound. It's also a framework that can be easy to miss when working with data.[4]

THE POTENTIAL OUTCOMES FRAMEWORK

At the core of the potential outcomes framework is the concept of "counterfactuals." We invoke counterfactuals all the time, but we often fail to identify them, name them, and factor them into our thinking.

What's a Counterfactual?

The closing minutes of any contest between two teams in any sport when the score is close is fertile ground for counterfactual discussions between sports pundits and fans. Consider an American football game where, in the final minute of a game, the team on offense is down by three points and is facing a fourth down with three yards to go. The coach has two choices: attempt a field goal, or "go for it" on fourth down. Let's consider the outcomes that may result from each choice:

Attempt a field goal. If it's successful, the game will be tied up and, if his team can keep the other team from scoring in the closing seconds of the game, the game will go into overtime, giving them another shot at winning. There are some downside risks associated with this choice: (a) they miss the field goal, in which case the game is essentially over and they lose; (b) they make the field goal, but the opposing team is able to complete some quick plays in the remaining seconds and kick a field goal or score a touchdown and win the game before time runs out; or (c) they make the field goal, hold the other team from scoring, advance to over-time, and then lose anyway.

"Go for it" on fourth down. If the team successfully converts the fourth down, then they will be able to run a few more plays to (hopefully) score a touchdown, but if not, then at least kick a field goal from a shorter distance before time expires. *This* option has the following downside risks: (a) they

---

[4]The potential outcomes framework was generalized by Donald Rubin, now an emeritus professor of statistics at Harvard University, in the 1970s. For an accessible (but technical) scientific restatement of the potential outcomes framework, see chapter 4 of *Causal Inference: The Mixtape*, by Scott Cunningham, freely available as of the time of writing at https://mixtape.scunning.com. In this book, we tweak some of the concepts of potential outcomes to make points for the business audience.

fail to convert the fourth down, in which case the game is essentially over; (b) they successfully convert the fourth down, but even with the extra plays this gives them, they're not able to score any more points before time expires, so they lose the game; or (c) they successfully convert the fourth down, but still are only able to score points by kicking a field goal as time expires, which sends them to overtime, where they lose the game.

What should the coach do? These days, head coaches have a wealth of analytics and information that tells them the precise probability of success and failure in each case, but they can only actually *do* one thing: attempt a field goal or "go for it."

Once the coach makes a decision and takes action, *all* other scenarios become *counterfactuals*—the "what might have been" conjecture of the commentator or fan.

For example, let's say the coach decides to kick a field goal, the kicker misses, and the team loses the game. A long-time fan watching the game in a bar with friends turns to them and articulates a counterfactual: "Ugh! If the coach had just gone for it on fourth down, we could have gotten the first down and gone on to score a touchdown and win the game!"

Or consider a counterexample. Let's say the coach decides to go for a first down, which is unsuccessful, and the team loses the game. That same fan, in a parallel universe, turns to his buddies and articulates a different counterfactual: "If the coach had just kicked a field goal, we would have tied the game up and then almost certainly have won in overtime."

Armchair quarterbacks (many of whom have found moderate success in their business careers and take great pleasure at critiquing leadership decisions) find nothing more pleasing than to go for a dip in the Counterfactual Pool. As it happens, *any* form of second-guessing of a decision is a swim in the Counterfactual Pool, and that pool is infinitely wider and deeper than the Actuality Pool: when it comes to each passing moment in our lives, we can only *do* one thing, and there are countless things that we *could* have done instead. Some of those other things would be consequential. Some would not. But they are all *counterfactuals*.[5]

This is known as the Fundamental Problem of Causal Inference: we cannot go back in time to try something else and discover what would have happened. Instead, we can only try to *predict what would have happened.*

Uncertainty and Causality

While this may feel like abstract theorizing that doesn't apply to the day-to-day business world, it is a critical concept! It's the key to understanding *uncertainty and causality*, which are at the root of effectively using analytics to make decisions (by validating hypotheses):

> **Uncertainty:** Principled appreciation for the range of outcomes that are likely to occur due to random chance and incomplete information.
> **Causality:** Strong knowledge that if you take an action associated with a hypothesis, it will likely result in a particular outcome (ideally, a beneficial outcome).[6]

---

[5] Relatedly, the "many worlds" theory within quantum mechanics posits that the universe splits every time anyone makes a decision, and *all* possible outcomes then live on in their own parallel universes. This is either mind-bendingly profound and cool (and makes the Marvel Comics Multiverse seem quaint) or depressing ("So, it doesn't matter what I do? I'm doing the other thing in a parallel universe? What's the point?!!!" Eeyore, perhaps, was just secretly embracing the many worlds theory and that was the root cause of his gloomy disposition?).

[6] Note that we said strong knowledge, not definitive knowledge. It is important to distinguish causality in the business and social context from causality in the study of the natural sciences, like physics and chemistry. When working in the social context, various subcontexts can influence the relationship between the cause and the effect.

The concept of uncertainty is useful because it forces us to accept that, even despite our best efforts, an action may not produce the outcome that we wanted. The concept of uncertainty can, in fact, help us to couch the actions that we might take by revealing the potentially large downside risks associated with a decision.

Furthermore, when we have high levels of uncertainty, it is hard to demonstrate causality, because the result we observe after the action is taken could simply be one of the results we would have observed by chance. To demonstrate causality, we have to show that the result we produced is unlikely to have happened by chance. We also have to show that no other thing could have caused the outcome to happen other than the thing that we think is responsible.

Consider the potential outcomes framework in the context of historical data. Looking at historical data, we know what we did and what happened, but we don't know *what would have happened* if we had done something different.[7]

Let's say that, as a response to some moves by our top competitor, we decided to do an across-the-board price cut of 10% for all of our products at the start of June. It's now the end of the year, and we realize that, really, we had an unstated hypothesis back in the spring that, if we dropped our prices, we would see an increase in revenue, as we would be more price-competitive with our top competitor, which would increase demand for our products.[8] You take a look at the data and see the results shown in Figure 3.1.

It can also be the case that a result generated at time period one does not hold in time period two because humans are constantly changing. In physics and chemistry research, causality is definitive because the relationships among atoms, temperatures, thermodynamics, etc. are not subject to the vagaries of social dynamics.

[7] If it feels like we're belaboring this concept, we are. We had to make a choice between touching on it lightly and having the reader skim past it and, as a result, not understand how foundational it is to the remaining topics in this chapter *or* we could come at it from a few different angles so that we were confident that we had covered it so thoroughly that only the most aggressive skimmer would miss its import. We decided to make the first option our counterfactual. If you understood the last sentence, you're getting it!

[8] Stated formally using the hypothesis formulation framework in Chapter 6: "**We believe that**, if we drop the price for every one of our products by 10%, then we will see an overall increase in revenue **because** that will put us at or slightly below the price for comparable products as sold by our top competitors. **If we are right**, we will maintain that lower price and monitor our competitor's pricing so that we can react more quickly to any future price changes they make." We'll put aside the risks of pursuing a competitive pricing strategy like this, as that's not relevant for the sake of this example.

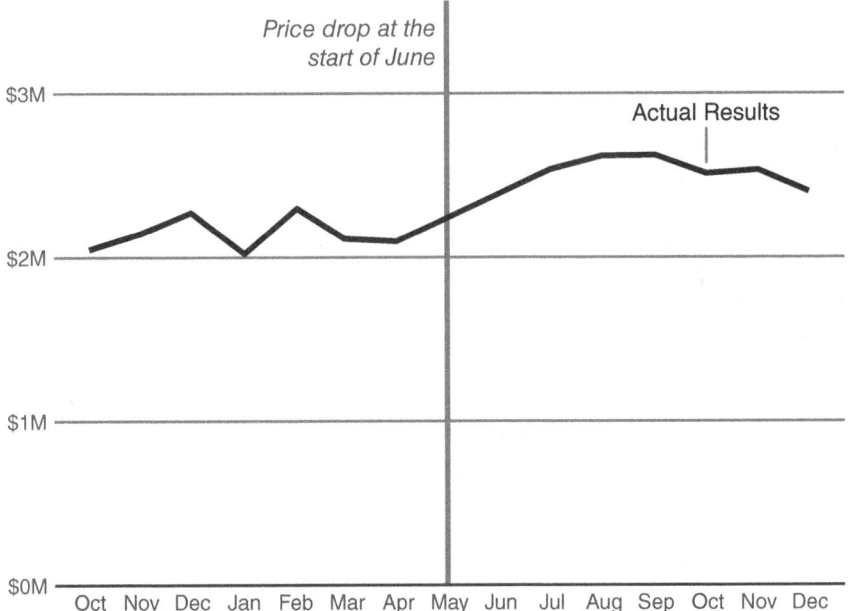

FIGURE 3.1 Revenue results after a price drop

Was our hypothesis validated?

Before we try to answer that question, let's first get more explicit with where we triggered the relevant counterfactual. The price drop was at the start of June. If the plotted data represents what *actually* happened, the *counterfactual* of interest—the potential outcome *not* realized—is what *would have happened* had we held prices the same. *This is not explicitly knowable in this situation*, but we will pretend for a minute that it is and add it to our original chart. See Figure 3.2.

Now that we can see both the actual outcome and the counterfactual outcome, it's clear that the drop in our pricing *did* lead to an increase in revenue. Hurray! Of course, we can only see this because we've entered a fictional world where we can see both actual outcomes and potential outcomes (counterfactuals).

Now, imagine that, due to a mistake, the potential outcome we showed in Figure 3.2 was *incorrect*. We've corrected that, though, and Figure 3.3 now shows the *correct* counterfactual revenue for what *would have happened* had we held firm with our prices rather than dropping them.

Egad! Now things look quite different. Even though overall revenue increased slightly after we dropped our prices, revenue would have increased *even more* if we had kept our prices at the original levels.

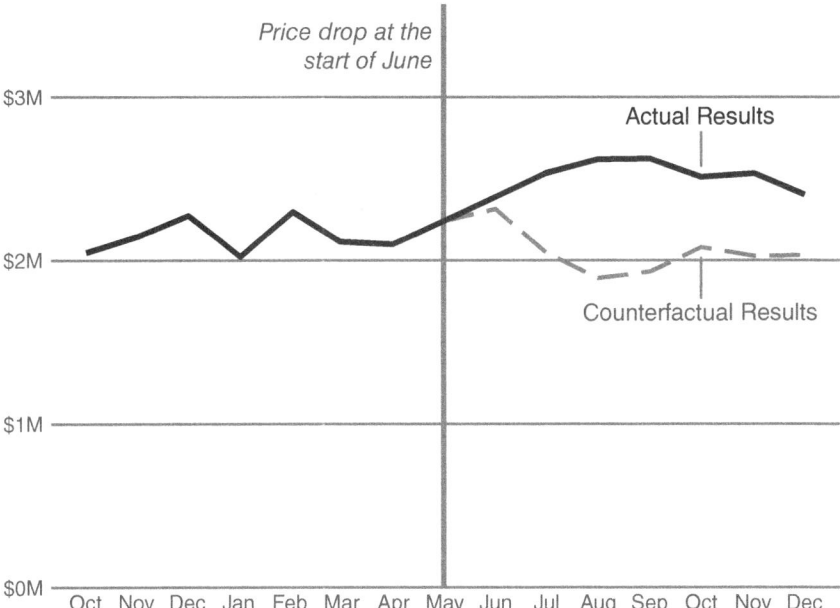

FIGURE 3.2 A counterfactual: what revenue would have been if there had been no price drop

The basic point here is that it is dangerous to simply look at a set of data over time (Figure 3.1) and draw conclusions without identifying the contours of the counterfactuals involved. Going back to the idea of uncertainty and causality, we can offer some intuition around the contours we would want to nail down in this case:

Uncertainty: If we had not cut prices at all, what is the range of outcomes we might have observed? Assuming we did cut prices, what are the worst and best case scenarios we would have expected?

Causality: Is the outcome we observed after cutting prices significantly different from the average outcome we would have observed if we had *not* cut prices? Is the price cut the *only* thing that could have affected the result, or did something else simultaneously happen at the time of the price cut that was actually the cause?

Figure 3.4 shows a scenario where the result we observed is *contained* in the set of outcomes we knew we were likely to observe had we simply maintained the status quo (*not* dropped our prices). This set of potential outcomes could be estimated through a range of different techniques into which we're

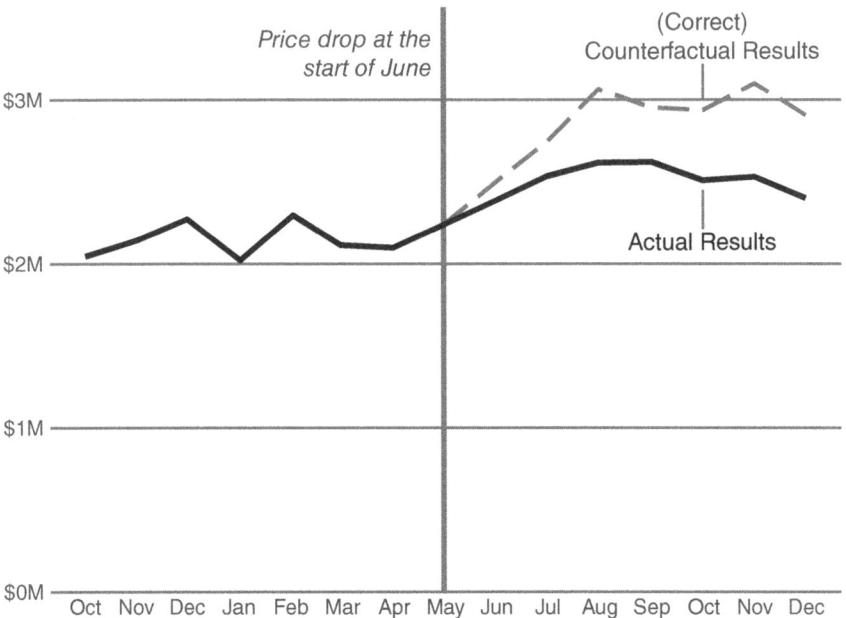

FIGURE 3.3 The corrected counterfactual: what revenue actually would have been if there had been no price drop

not going to go into detail, but think of them as forecasts that could have been created back before the price drop was put in place that were based on *not* changing pricing.[9]

In this scenario, we would *lack* evidence that the price intervention caused a change in revenue, even though some of the outcomes are better, and some of the outcomes are worse, because the *actual observed results* fall within the range of results that we estimated we would have seen if we had *not* dropped our prices.

Figure 3.5 shows a scenario where the result we observed was *not* contained in the set of outcomes we estimated we would have seen had we not

---

[9]The charts here are showing discrete dashed lines for each "estimated potential outcome." These could be the result of different forecasting models being run or a range of simulations being run that each generated a different forecast. Other techniques would return a "range of potential outcomes" represented more as a "band" or a "ribbon" around some base estimate. The interpretation is the same either way: do the actual observed results fall inside or outside an estimated range?

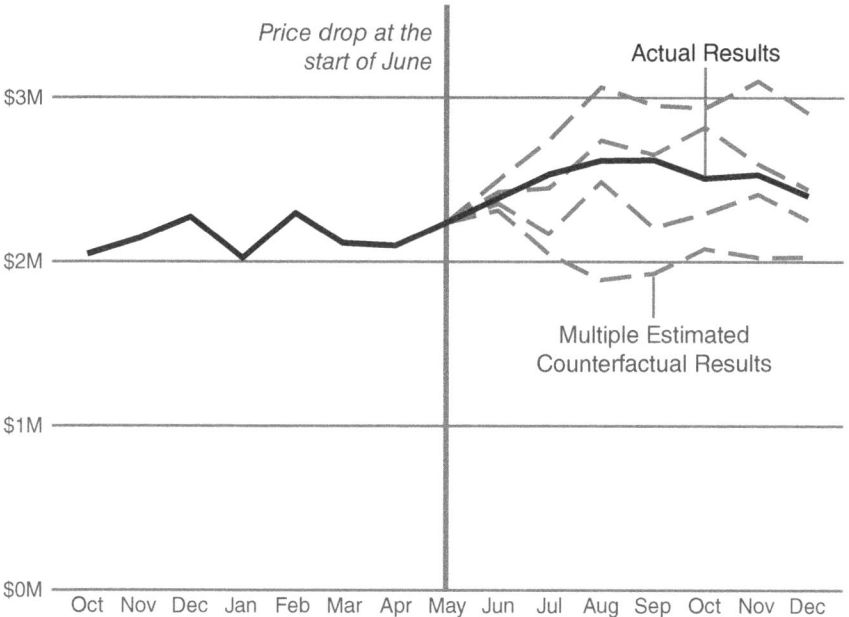

FIGURE 3.4 The distribution over expected counterfactuals vs. the actual results (no causal effect)

dropped our prices (we're showing the same actual results as in the previous scenario, but showing a different set of estimated potential outcomes; in the real world, we only have one set of estimated potential outcomes).

In this scenario, we would have evidence that the intervention *did* cause a change in revenue. The important thing is that the outcome we saw was greater than or equal to the bulk of the outcomes we would have expected by chance.

However, even given the analysis in Figure 3.5, we did not *prove* that it was the price change alone—and not some other factor that happened at the same time as the price change—that increased revenue. To draw the strongest possible conclusion that the price change increased revenue, we would need to go one step further and conduct a scientific analysis to eliminate the possibility that anything else may have confounded the result.[10]

---

[10] If you are...confounded...by what we mean by "confounded" here, don't worry. It is a really important concept, and we will get into it in more detail later, but you can gloss over it for now.

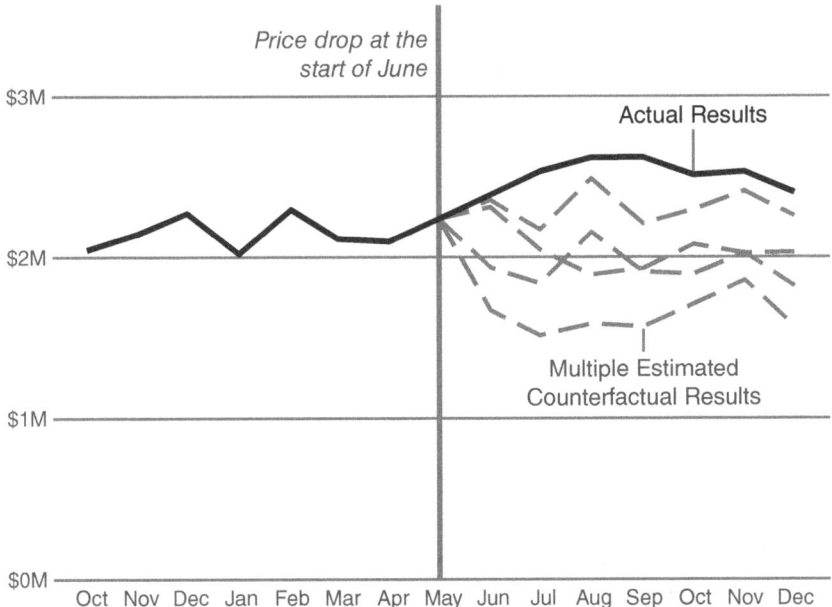

FIGURE 3.5   The distribution over expected counterfactuals vs. the actual results (had a causal effect)

Causal evidence about the relationship between an action and an outcome is the highest quality information we can get when making decisions. When we make important decisions, we want causal evidence—for instance, if we were considering making this same price-cut decision again, despite our cavalier attitude the first time, we would want strong scientific evidence to support it. We discuss the scientific analysis techniques we can use to produce this evidence in more detail in Chapter 9.

Potential Outcomes in Summary

The potential outcomes framework is an umbrella term for examining (to the extent possible) the difference between what happened after some action was taken and what *would* have happened if a different action had been taken (the "counterfactual scenario"). This approach stands in opposition to the usual "off the cuff" predictions and suppositions that armchair quarterbacks make. Indeed, in a world without the standard methodologies we introduce in Chapters 6 through 9, all claims that armchair quarterbacks make seem equally credible.

The key to good hypothesis validation, which we develop in this book, is using reliable methodological techniques to generate good predictions for what would have happened or what could happen. But not all decisions have the same weight, not all decisions lack clarity in what is expected, and not all decisions can garner the investment required to be supported with the "strongest grade" of evidence. We explore these trade-offs further in Chapter 6.

SO, WHAT NOW?

When we introduce the potential outcomes framework to our audiences, it's usually a little mind-bending, and it can take some time for it to sink in. But you'll find yourself wondering more often what the outcome *would have been* had you done something differently. This is the one key learning that we ask you to internalize for the remainder of the book: good analytics for the purpose of good decision-making is about properly estimating all of the ways that *things might end up*, so that you ultimately can choose the option that best advances your cause. When we use historical data, we do the same: we try to estimate how things *might have ended up* had things gone differently so that we can learn what we should do today.

MEASURE THIS CHAPTER

It's time to contribute to the performance measurement of this book by visiting https://analyticsrw.com and answering the two-question survey for this chapter.

4

A Structured Approach to Using Data

As we discussed in Chapter 2, one of the *misconceptions* about data is that, given sufficient data, "the truth" is knowable: uncertainty can be eliminated from business decisions! This is a seductive idea, and the business world would be a lot simpler to navigate were it true: simply keep collecting data until every decision can be made with certainty! Alas! This is *not* true, and it behooves us to remind ourselves of that on a regular basis.

Ironically, we can be *absolutely certain* about one thing: uncertainty *cannot* be eliminated! Once we accept that, we can slow our endless pursuit of data in the hopes that the next gigabyte of detail about our customers, our competitors, our marketing campaigns, or our internal operations will *finally* lead us to deterministic nirvana. We can shift our energies to adding structure and clarity to how we *use the data we already have* (and, yes, occasionally expand what we collect and integrate, but with focus and discipline).

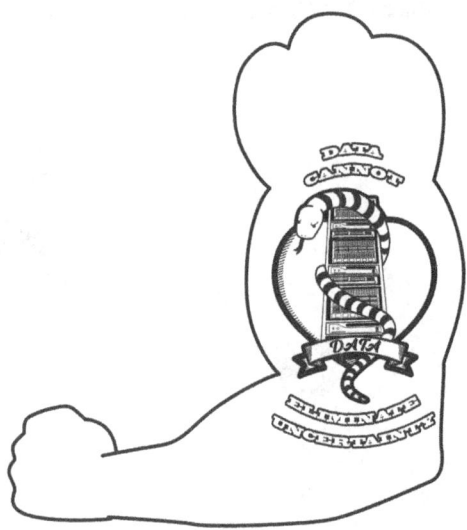

Implementing a structured process for using data would be relatively straightforward if not for the need to break through various misconceptions and inefficiencies that have become generally accepted practices in the corporate world.

When Tim worked for a creative agency less a decade into his analytics career, he had an experience that illustrates this challenge. The agency had recently landed a major mattress brand as a new account, and the account team flew up to the client's headquarters to spend a couple of days kicking off the engagement. No analysts were part of that initial meeting, which was customary at the agency. But when the team returned to the agency's offices, the lead account manager stopped by Tim's cubicle as soon as they returned and excitedly announced, "You are going to love this client. They are alllll about the data and are totally data-driven! They actually have thick binders of reports printed out that they brought to our kickoff meeting!" Tim's immediate response was...a quizzical expression as he contemplated exactly what was being done with a *thick printed binder* of reports. The account manager triumphantly followed up: "Their problem is they don't know what to *do* with all of that data! We told them that you can tell them!" This seemed odd then and it seems odd now: an organization (and their recently hired agency) apparently able to embrace cognitive dissonance by seeing the presence of piles of data as being simultaneously "evidence of being data-driven" *and* "evidence that we're rarely or barely *actually* using the data to drive *anything*."

What was missing in this situation is all too common: a clear and useful approach for connecting those piles of data to their productive application to the business. In this chapter, we will introduce an approach that does just that!

AN OVERARCHING FRAMEWORK FOR DATA USAGE: MAKING DECISIONS VS. OPERATIONALIZING THE USE OF DATA

Making decisions can be boiled down to two fundamentally different types of work:

> **Measuring performance** ("Are we achieving what we set out to achieve?"), which we will explore in Chapter 5
> **Validating hypotheses** ("Given different ideas and options for what I do next—strategically and tactically—which one will likely deliver the best results?"), which we will dig into in Chapters 6 through 9

Separate from making decisions, data can be put to **operational use**—as a stream of information flowing into a system (a customer relationship management (CRM) platform, a marketing automation platform, an enterprise resource planning (ERP) platform, etc.) or process that then triggers some action by the business or the system itself. These triggers can be rules-based: "A user placed an order, so it now needs to be fulfilled." "A user submitted a form on our website, so the appropriate salesperson now needs to follow up with them." Or they can be model-based: "Based on what we know about this user, this predictive model will automatically determine what the next best action for us to take is and will automatically trigger that action." This is the subject of Chapter 10.

These three different uses of data are illustrated in Figure 4.1. Every organization does all three, whether they are consciously aware of it or not.

While these are distinct ways of using data, they are also often interrelated. For instance, if performance measurement highlights an area where the business is missing expectations, then the team will want to know why and what they should do about it, which they should answer by identifying, prioritizing, and validating hypotheses. And once they've found one or more root

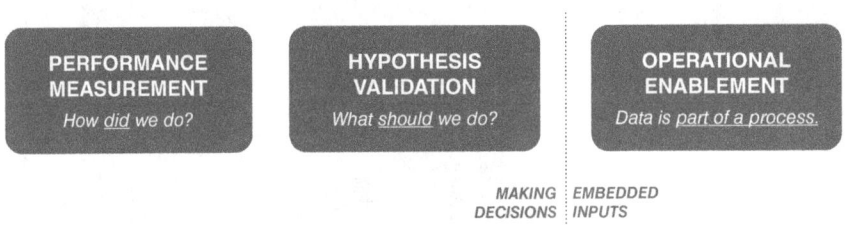

FIGURE 4.1   There are three fundamentally different ways businesses use data

causes that they can act upon, then they will want to measure whether the performance has improved. Figure 4.2 shows how performance measurement and hypothesis validation can be connected in this way.

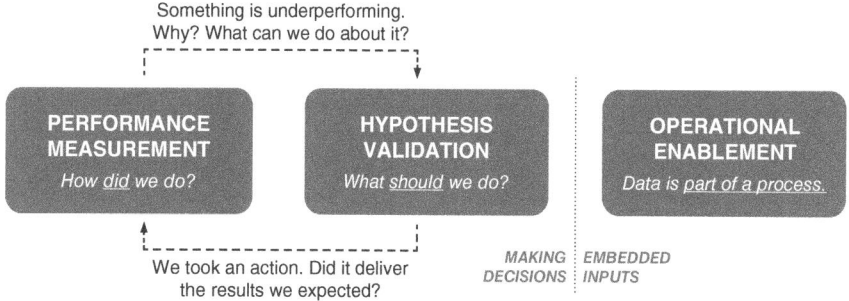

FIGURE 4.2   The interconnected nature of performance measurement and hypothesis validation

This interaction is by no means the *only* way that either of these uses of data operate. They can—and often are—each applied independently. The same is true for operational enablement, although both performance measurement and hypothesis validation *should* play a part in the creation, implementation, and ongoing maintenance of any process. Consider the social media marketing team at an organization that is excited about the potential for generative AI to help them produce better content for them to post, as well as to enable that content to be produced more quickly and more often:

- The process in question is the social media content development process.
- The idea being considered can be viewed as a hypothesis that generative AI will produce two positive business outcomes: (1) better performing content and (2) a lower production cost for that content.

Rather than simply diving into using generative AI in this process, the team can consider how they can best *validate* that its use will provide the expected benefit. This could be as simple as committing to a period of alternating content that is AI-generated (and human reviewed and edited) with content that is created without any assistance from AI. And including in that commitment a plan to both track how much time and effort is required for each post, as well as how each post then performs. This is a pretty basic hypothesis validation exercise, but a useful one! For the sake of illustration, let's say that this plan validated that incorporating AI was, indeed, a good idea.

AI is then going to be instituted as part of the social media team's standard operating procedure for content development. How is the impact of social media content measured? If AI appears to be a productivity and performance enhancer, should the bar be raised a bit on the expectations for that content? This is a *performance measurement* exercise—the validation of a hypothesis regarding an operational process feeding back into the measurement of performance. Figure 4.3 completes our overview diagram by showing how operational enablement interacts with the decision-making uses of data!

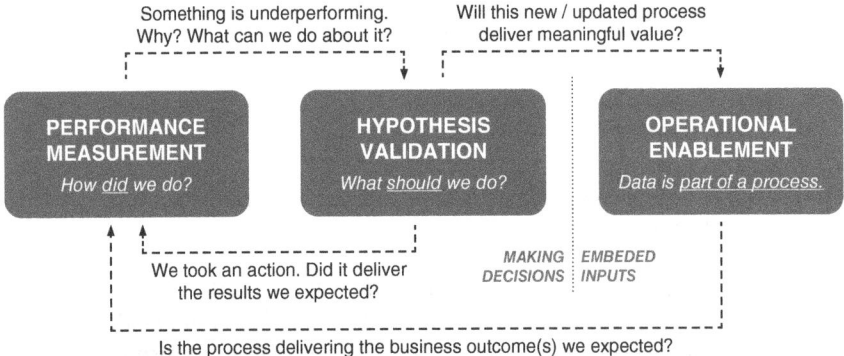

FIGURE 4.3 The interconnected nature of operational enablement with performance measurement and hypothesis validation

While all three of these uses of data can interact with each of the other two, they are distinct in both what they are doing and how they are carried out:

> **Performance measurement** lends itself to a defined planning exercise followed by a regular cadence of actually doing the measuring piece, often as manifested in an automated or semi-automated dashboard or report. We will explore the "two magic questions" of performance measurement in Chapter 5, which are a useful way to conduct that planning.
>
> **Hypothesis validation** is an inherently ad hoc exercise. Some hypotheses can be validated almost immediately with very little effort by analyzing historical data. Some hypotheses warrant the application of advanced statistical methods. Some hypotheses are best validated by running an experiment (an A/B test or some other form of randomized controlled trial). Some hypotheses can be validated by conducting a survey of customers or some other form of primary research. Regardless of *how* a hypothesis is best validated, how it gets articulated in the first place can follow a straightforward fill-in-the-blank construct, which we will dig into in Chapter 6.

Operational enablement is, among other things that build organizational capacity, about defined processes that have data flowing into them as necessary inputs, which means they are typically ongoing (even if the process isn't fully automated or the data feeding into the process is not fully automated). AI, typically, is part of operational enablement, but we will cover different flavors of this use of data and how to approach them in Chapter 10.

Once we have a deeper understanding of the what, why, and how of each of these uses of data, we will revisit their interrelationship, which we've only scratched the surface of in this chapter. At that point, we hope you will go through every day seeing each of these three uses of data underpinning all of your and your team's work. You will be excited when a colleague approaches you with a binder full of data (be it physical or digital) because you will be ready to start probing with the tools and techniques outlined in this book to help them put that binder to meaningful and purposeful business use. You *may* be a bit dismayed that some of your colleagues will be resistant to your questions—wondering why "actionable insights" cannot simply spew forth from your organization's IT systems. Be patient with them!

MEASURE THIS CHAPTER

Once again, it's time to contribute to the performance measurement of this book by visiting https://analyticstrw.com and answering the two-question survey for this chapter. Hopefully, you are starting to see more clearly what role those two questions are playing—both to enable us to measure the performance of the book and the impact it is having, but also as a mechanism to help you pause for a few beats to reflect on how it is performing for you personally.

Making Decisions Through Performance Measurement

One of the simplest ways we expect to use data to make decisions is through performance measurement. "The weekly report" or "the real-time dashboard" are, at their core, intended to show "what's happening with the business." Simple, right? So, why do weekly and monthly reports so often tend to grow into cumbersome monstrosities? Why do dashboards seem to have a lot of information on them without illustrating what is going well and what is not? The answer is that, while measuring performance seems simple, it requires several key elements that can feel messy and intimidating, and human nature, as a result, pushes us to skip them.

A SIMPLE IDEA THAT TRIPS UP ORGANIZATIONS

Put simply, performance measurement is defined as follows:

Objectively and quantitatively measuring where we are today relative to where we expected to be today at some point in the past.

This is an exercise in looking at the past to the present: marking the current point in time, where key metrics stand, and how those metrics compare to the expectations of our past selves.

When it comes to measuring *people* and *teams*, specifically, there are a number of established frameworks for performance measurement: management by objective (MBOs); objectives and key results (OKRs); balanced scorecard; and objectives, goals, strategies, and measures (OGSM) to name a few. In our view, these are *all* different flavors of performance measurement. They have different strengths and different cases can be made and debated by others as to which form is "the best." We are not going to take a position on that, specifically, other than to say that we are fans of any measurement process that is well thought-out and well executed. We are not introducing anything here that conflicts with *any* of these frameworks. Rather, we are providing a perspective and a technique that can be incorporated within any of these frameworks and, furthermore, can be applied to *any* project or initiative (rather than just to individuals and teams)—a marketing campaign, an update to the sales process, the rollout of a customer-facing AI-driven chatbot, or even the publication of a book!

Think of performance measurement as being something of a time machine, in that we build a process where we think about the results that we expect to have in the future, and then, in the future, we compare the actual results to those expectations. We're going to come back to this analogy a lot in this chapter, so travel back in time to that last sentence and read it again if you glossed over it!

To illustrate this with a simple example, consider a business-to-business (B2B) lead generation marketing campaign that has been running for 6 weeks. A key metric is the number of qualified leads from the campaign. Six weeks in, a report lands on our desk showing that the campaign has garnered 1,500 qualified leads (see Figure 5.1).

FIGURE 5.1   A marketing campaign result without context

Given this data, how is the campaign doing? Think about that for a minute. Can we say one way or the other? Before we go further, ask yourself if this example reminds you of any real-world situations you've run into. Have you had a project, initiative, or campaign for which you've checked the progress, and despite getting the results for one or several key metrics, you still don't know if the effort is performing well or not?

When this happens, the question that automatically gets asked of the analyst (or whoever delivered the information) is, "Is that result good?" (See Figure 5.2.)

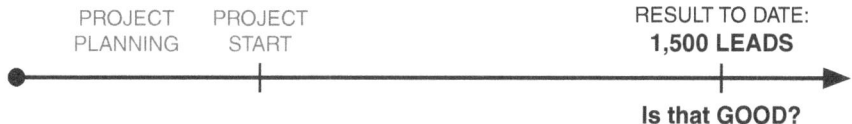

FIGURE 5.2   The natural question asked in the absence of context: "Is that result good?"

Experienced analysts get a sinking feeling when they hear this question because they recognize the question as an indication that there has been a miss in their performance measurement, and it is likely too late to address it. But they ask a question in return on the outside chance that all is not lost: "Well, what did we expect?" (See Figure 5.3.)

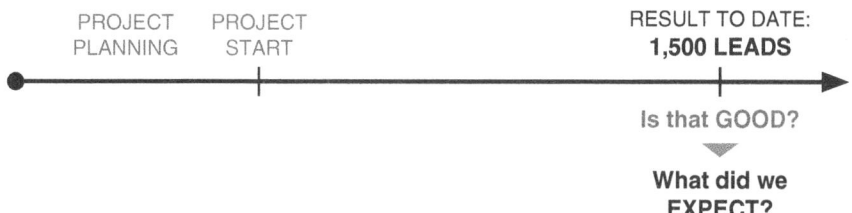

FIGURE 5.3   "Good" is determined based on expectations

Logically, that question leads to why this process is an exercise in building a time machine. "What did we expect?" means we need to travel *back in time* to when we were planning the campaign to find out what our expectations were at that point (see Figure 5.4).

FIGURE 5.4   Expectations must get set during planning

Where many organizations fail is that they open that door to the past only to discover that they are staring into an empty void: they had not set clear expectations before they launched the project! They might have *thought* they set expectations because they remember very clearly asking and answering the question, "What are our key performance indicators (KPIs) for this effort?" Maybe they even find that they had listed out a set of metrics, and one of those metrics was "the number of qualified leads." But that was only half of the answer—it did not include the step of quantifying *how many* qualified leads they expected from the campaign.

Setting these expectations can feel daunting, but it doesn't have to be. And without setting those expectations—without using them to build a metaphorical time machine—performance measurement cannot be effective (see Figure 5.5).

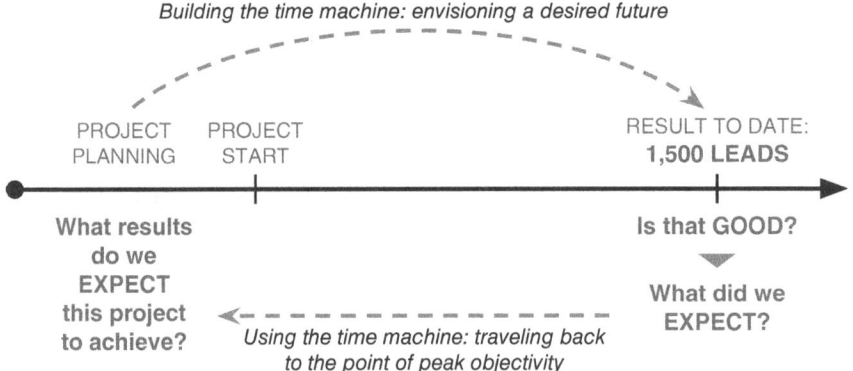

FIGURE 5.5   The performance measurement time machine

This all seems simple enough, right? Or if not simple (organizationally committing to setting expectations—targets—for meaningful key measures takes real commitment and, often, a fundamental mindset change), at least it is clear and logical.

Before we dive into tools and techniques for building a performance measurement time machine, let's do a quick review of some things that performance measurement is *not*:

- Performance measurement is *not* about "how did we get here?"
- Performance measurement is *not* about "what did we learn along the way?"
- Performance measurement is *not* about "insights."

Keep performance measurement's purpose clear and concise:

Objectively and quantitatively measuring where we are today relative to where we expected to be today at some point in the past.

The value of performance measurement comes from allowing the organization to focus on *specific areas where performance is below expectations* (that focus then leads to hypothesis validation, which we will cover in the next several chapters).

As organizations have steadily adopted more and more reviews of more and more of their data, combined with the proliferation of both business intelligence (BI) platforms (Power BI, Tableau, Qlik, Looker, etc.) and the ubiquity of presentation software (PowerPoint, Google Slides, Canva, Keynote, etc.) as a way to create regular "reports," it is now often an accepted practice that each key metric for a project or initiative must be reviewed, drilled into, and explained during each reporting cycle. *This is an inefficient use of time and resources.*

By way of a relatable example, consider a scenario where we have decided that we would like to lose 10–12 pounds. We've worked with a trainer or a nutritionist to lay out a plan of diet and exercise that should help us shed those pounds steadily over a 3-month period. We weigh in once per week, and every week, we have dropped 0.8 to 1.2 pounds. This means we are *right on target* for your 3-month goal.

Given those results, would we spend an hour or two after every weekly weigh-in doing a detailed analysis of what and when we ate and drank, what exercises we performed, and the details of our sleep schedule? No! *If we are achieving the results we expected, then it makes little sense to dive into why we achieved those results. They're exactly the result we were seeking!*

Even in this simple example, it's possible that the weight loss was not actually caused by the diet and exercise. It's *possible* that little green aliens were putting us into a nightly trance and extracting little bits of fatty tissue undetected. It's *possible* that we were exposed to a hitherto unknown virus that causes exposure to the sun to gradually reduce the mass of our body. It's possible, but Occam's razor states that, when given multiple possibilities, the simplest explanation is the most probable. We will discuss some of the complexities of causation later, but when it comes to finite resources, a clear plan, and an outcome that was expected as a result of that plan, it rarely makes sense to dig deeply into the data to prove that the hoped-for cause-and-effect was the definitive driver of the expected outcome in the context of performance measurement.

This is often a cultural hurdle that organizations need to overcome, but the logic is clear and unambiguous: given limited resources, if results meet expectations, then it's unwise to devote resources to explaining why and how those results were achieved!

"WHAT ARE YOUR KPIs?" IS A TERRIBLE QUESTION

In theory, performance measurement is "just" a matter of nailing down KPIs. If we lived in a theoretical world, though, then we could easily lose weight "just" by eating healthier and exercising. That's the problem with theories: putting them into practice can be *hard*!

KPIs are absolutely the cornerstone of performance measurement, but identifying appropriate ones and setting meaningful targets for them can be challenging. Excitement is in the air as a project kicks off: it's funded, and it's going to do something new and interesting! The vibe in the kickoff meeting is positively electric! Then, as the ideas are flowing and everyone is nodding their heads, along comes the analyst with a question: "What are the KPIs that we will use to measure the success of this effort?"

All discussion stops.

Everyone stares at the metaphorical wet blanket that has been tossed squarely on top of the conversation.

And then, collectively, to get past the awkwardness and back to Exciting Things, everyone starts speaking at once. They know what KPIs *are*. And they understand they are *important*. So, they immediately begin rattling off— spewing, even—metrics. The analyst furiously takes notes.

Once the stream of metrics has slowed to a trickle,[1] all eyes turn back to the analyst, who looks down at their notes, sees a long list of metrics, looks back up at the room and (correctly) reads the facial expressions as saying, "Is that enough? Can we move on now?!"

And that's it.

The problem with this scenario is that it's not so much an exercise in identifying how the results of the project will be assessed as it is a list that includes the following:

- Various metrics that were included in the reporting on previous projects (whether they were useful or not)
- Metrics that "someone will want to see" (regardless of whether they are fundamentally an indicator of whether the project is successful)
- Metrics that are known to be readily available (again, regardless of whether they will be useful)

Time and again, though, this is how we see organizations operate in their KPI planning, and the result is depressingly predictable: during or after the actual execution of the project or campaign, a sea of metrics flood the room in the form of an incredibly dense or multipage dashboard, as a 40-slide deck, or

---

[1] Or, possibly, simply to dry heaves? We agree. This footnote just pushed a visual analogy too far. We apologize for that.

as both! There is a *lot* of data shared, but a frustrating inability to answer the question as to whether the results are good or bad!

Does this scenario resonate with you? Can you swap out a few words in the description of these examples and find a pretty clear picture of how your organization "measures performance?" If so, then the good news is that the rest of this chapter is devoted to specific tactics for breaking that cycle.

TWO MAGIC QUESTIONS

One way to avoid this deluge of metrics that turn out to be ineffective at quantifying whether what we are measuring is performing at, above, or below expectations is to employ what we call the two magic questions. Will they seem earth-shatteringly brilliant once we reveal them? Probably not. Can't the same be said of most magic tricks, though? They can be incredibly effective and mystifying when performed well, but once we find out how they're done, "the trick" seems obvious.

In this case, that's actually a good thing because these questions are simply prompts to provoke focused thinking and alignment between us and the key stakeholders for the initiative, project, or campaign that is in the works.

There are three *absolute requirements* with these questions:

- They must get asked and answered *while the project or initiative is being planned*. We are never more objective about what we might achieve than before we set out to achieve it! So this exercise is part of the planning process—it cannot be done after the fact!
- They must get asked and answered *in order*. It can be tempting to jump to the second question prematurely, and that is almost always counterproductive.
- The answers to the questions must be *written down*. This requirement provides the nuts and bolts that hold our time machine together; it ensures everyone is clear and aligned on the expectations for the project, and the act of documenting the answers with written (or typed) words reduces the risk of ambiguity that comes when simply relying on undocumented discussions and the memories of the participants!

Enough with the buildup! Let's get locked into the box and start sawing it in two! The first magic question is:

Magic Question 1: What are we trying to achieve?

"That's it?!" you exclaim! "That doesn't seem magical at all!" Maybe not, but it is! This question forces the discussion and thinking to start *before* the data. Regardless of the project or initiative, *someone* decided that it was "worth doing." Has the rationale behind that decision been clearly articulated and codified? This question ensures that it has been—that the business justification of the investment is clearly captured.

Think about the answer to this question as our elevator pitch for the project: we've gotten on the elevator and realized the CEO is standing right next to us. She asks, "So, what are you working on these days?" We respond, "Right now, I'm really focused on getting Project Hypersnappy off the ground." She then asks a follow-up: "What's that going to do for us as a company?"

The answer to the first magic question is the same as the answer to her follow-up, which means we are aiming for a sweet spot as to what *business-relevant outcome* Project Hypersnappy is intended to deliver. This can be more challenging than it seems at first blush and, surprisingly, *does not need to include any metrics in its answer*. The answer to this first question should be *concise*—just one or two sentences or bullet points—and *clear*—something that all of the relevant stakeholders would interpret the same way while also agreeing with the answer.

To illustrate with a simple example, let's say that Project Hypersnappy is a marketing campaign that is announcing our company's acquisition of another organization. The acquisition will expand the services that our company is able to offer to our existing clients, as well as provide an entry point with prospects that, historically, we have not been able to successfully turn into clients.

What are we trying to achieve with the campaign? Let's consider some possible answers that would be less than ideal:

Possible Response	Why the Response Is Problematic
"We're trying to achieve an email clickthrough rate[2] that exceeds our historical benchmark for emails."	This is a common (and readily available) metric for measuring whether emails are resonating with their recipients, but there is *no inherent business value* in any given email clickthrough rate. This response would be too far into the tactics of the campaign.
"We're trying to achieve two million impressions with the advertising that we run."	"Impressions" is another common metric for measuring paid advertising—an attempt to count how many times ads were shown to people. They are one option for approximating the scale or "reach" of a campaign, but, again, there is *no inherent business value* in an impression: the *company* is not trying to *achieve* impressions.
"We're trying to drive revenue."	On the surface, this seems like a great answer, but in general, it has the opposite problem of the previous two responses. There is definitely business value in revenue, but this campaign seems to be more nuanced than simply immediately and directly driving revenue. *Eventually*, it should be setting the stage for (profitable) revenue, but the CEO may feel you are pandering (and you may be). Of *course* everyone should be supporting efforts to drive revenue in some way, be it directly or indirectly. We *haven't* actually given her information as to what this campaign specifically is geared toward doing to support that.

It is easy (and, as a result, tempting) to answer this question with something too narrow (the first two examples) or something too broad (the last example). But these are problematic because they don't concisely and unambiguously capture *why* the campaign is a worthwhile investment of the company's resources.

---

[2] The definition of this metric is not really relevant for making the point we're trying to make here, and different email platforms calculate it differently, and different marketers will happily bend your ear—or send you emails, ironically—debating the relative merits of a straight-up clickthrough rate (CTR) versus a click-to-open rate (CTOR). But, if you're a stickler for definitions, then we'll meet you halfway and say that, generally speaking, the clickthrough rate is the number of people who clicked on a link in the email divided by the number of people to whom the email was delivered.

What might be a better answer to the question of what the campaign is trying to achieve? We haven't provided enough detail to definitively answer that, but that too starts to reveal the magic of this first question: it forces an interrogation of the underlying rationale for the campaign!

One possible answer to the question could be this:

We are trying to ensure that our existing customers are aware of our expanded service offering. This should do two things: (1) some of them will reach out to our account teams to learn more, and (2) when our account teams bring up these services, the conversations will be more productive. Separately, we want this campaign to put us into the consideration set for companies that have historically dismissed us because they knew we did not offer these services.

Is this the "right" answer? Before we proceed to the second magic question, it needs to be agreed upon that it is! It could be that this is a first draft, and after reviewing it, the team (possibly including the CEO once it's been floated to her on the elevator!) could decide that this is too much—that the focus for the campaign should just be on existing customers or on prospects, but not on both. There are two key things going on here:

- There are *no metrics* included in this answer. There certainly can be metrics included, but it's not a requirement. Answering this question is all about capturing why we're making this investment without being encumbered by the tyranny of what data or metrics we know or think will be readily available.
- The response to this question, when done well, becomes a guiding light for the duration of the project. It is a straightforward way to ensure everyone's eye remains on the same ball, and it's the first thing we will see when we step into our time machine in weeks or months when we're looking back to what our expectations were for the campaign. It is wildly more desirable to invest in uncomfortable discussions ("I don't think we're on the same page as to why we're even doing this!") and wordsmithing up front than waiting until the costs of the project have been fully sunk, only to find out that the crew was not actually in agreement as to where they were trying to sail the ship!

Answering that first question effectively is critical, but answering the second question is where the rubber really hits the road. The second magic question is this:

Magic Question 2: How will we know if we've done that?

To reiterate an earlier point, the second magic question is *not*:

- What data or metrics do we think we might want to review when analyzing the results of the project?
- What data or metrics have you seen in reports about past projects that were similar to this one?
- What data do you know will be readily available that is related to this project?

Let's add some necessary emphasis to the second question to bring it more into focus:

How will we know if we've done **that***?*

"That" is the operative word here, and it is a direct reference back to the answer to the first question (All together now! What's the first question? "What are we trying to achieve?!"). The answer to the second question does incorporate metrics, as well as targets for those metrics. The question could be written out much more verbosely as follows:

What outcome-oriented metric (or metrics), and with what targets, will we use to either directly or indirectly (as proxy measures) determine if we are achieving what we said we expected the project to achieve?

In some cases, the answer to this question is obvious. If that's the case, great! More often, though, answering this second question requires further discussion and research and, often, some creativity. It may even uncover that there is additional data that will need to be collected that no one realized, and for which it would be too late to collect after the fact![3]

Let's tackle this second question with our last example. As a reminder, our answer to the first question for that example was this:

We are trying to ensure that our existing customers are aware of our expanded service offering. This should do two things: (1) some of them will reach out to our account teams to learn more, and (2) when our account teams bring up these services, the conversations will be more productive. Separately, we want this campaign to put us into the

---

[3] We know. We railed about the downsides of overemphasizing the collection of data earlier in this book. And, we stand by that! What we're describing here is very focused collection of data with a very clear purpose rather than the travesty of collecting data because we can and assuming that it will reveal itself as valuable at some later date.

consideration set for companies that have historically dismissed us because they knew we did not offer these services.

What metrics could we use to measure if we are achieving all of this? It certainly seems like it's going to be more than one! We can break down our answer to the first question and consider some options:

What are we trying to achieve?	How we might measure that?	Feasibility	Use This?
"...ensure that our existing customers are aware of our expanded service offering."	Conduct a weekly survey of all of our existing customers to track awareness over time	**Low:** This would be expensive, may annoy customers, and likely would have a very low response rate.	No
"...[existing customers] will actually reach out to our account teams to learn more [about the new offering]"	Conduct a weekly survey of account teams: ask for a list of customers who contacted them about the new services	**Medium:** Account teams may not comply with the request, so this would require buy-in from their leadership.	Maybe
"...when our account teams bring up these services, the conversations will be more productive."	Conduct a weekly survey of account teams: ask for a list of customers whom *they* contacted to discuss the new services and, for each customer, rate the receptiveness of the customer	**Medium-High:** Account teams may not comply with the request, but this is an opportunity for them to provide feedback about the campaign and how well it is working for them.	Yes
"...put us into the consideration set for companies that have historically dismissed us because they knew we did not offer these services."	Count the number of opportunities from new prospects in the company's customer relationship management (CRM) that are flagged as having interest in the newly available services	**High:** This data should be generated as part of the normal operations of the business, and it can readily be pulled from our CRM platform.	Yes

None of these metrics would be perfect, direct measures of what we're trying to achieve, but they are all reasonable proxies for the different outcomes that we're trying to deliver with the campaign. We've already identified that measuring the awareness of our existing customers over time is not particularly realistic, but we theorized on how we might measure it, which might trigger further discussion.

We've identified a couple of measures that would require engaging with our account teams. What are the organizational dynamics that will enable us to do that? As is often the case in the real world, these will likely be more effective if communication with the account teams about this data collection occurs early and often. Simply waiting until mid-campaign and dropping a survey in their inbox will almost certainly negatively impact the quality of the data we get back.

Even the data we expect to get from our CRM platform requires some additional thought and, possibly, internal research. We've *assumed* that the appropriate fields are being updated in the CRM to reflect our new service offerings, but assumptions are dangerous. Is the operations team looped in and planning to make that happen? Maybe we typically get our data from the data warehouse, which pulls data in from the CRM on a nightly basis. Are we confident that the updated fields will come through there? That's another assumption that we need to check!

While all of this thought and research and assumption-verifying may sound like a lot of work, it doesn't have to be! And, hopefully, this example illustrates why it's so important and how useful this process is on two fronts:

- It's the foundation of our performance measurement time machine—if we don't figure out what our expectations are and how we'll measure them, then we will have no way of answering the question, "Is this good?" when we start reviewing the performance during the campaign.
- It is the most effective way to ensure that everyone's expectations are aligned! By focusing on the specifics required for measurement, all of the stakeholders are able to unambiguously consider what they would view as success for the effort.

So, we're done, right? We've answered the two magic questions: (1) What are we trying to achieve? (2) How will we know if we've done that?

Alas! We have not fully answered the second question! All we have done is nail down what metrics we will use, but *we have not set targets for them yet.*

Outputs versus Outcomes

Throughout this chapter we have—and will continue—to refer to *outcome*-oriented measures. This is in contrast to *output*-oriented measures. If you are already vigorously nodding your head because you recognize and embrace the power of the distinction, then feel free to just return to the main text. If, though, you are wondering if this is some sort of alliteratively pedantic semantics, then bear with us for a bit.

Outputs are directly impactable and countable things: how many emails were sent, how much traffic came to a website, how many "impressions" a digital advertisement garnered, how many steps were taken in a day (yes, we're belaboring the weight loss example; "calories consumed" is also an output metric, although we'll admit that it feels like more of an *input* metric! In this context, it's an output!), how many pages of a book about analytics get read, etc.

Outcomes are things that truly matter at the end of the day: how much revenue was generated, how many prospects are considering purchasing a brand's products or services, how healthy a person is, how effectively and efficiently an organization is putting its data to use, etc.

Generally, we expect one or more outputs to lead to a meaningful outcome:

- More traffic to our website (output) will lead to more revenue (outcome).
- More ad impressions (output) will lead to increased consideration for our products/services (outcome).
- More daily steps (output) and a reduced caloric intake (an input-y output!) will lead to improved health (outcome).

As a general rule, outputs are easier to directly impact and easier to directly measure than outcomes, so it's easy to default to measuring outputs. *This is problematic*, since outputs are generally just a hoped-for means to an end rather than the end itself. If the outputs do not actually drive the outcome, or if the output is subject to manipulation, we wind up with a situation where the "results" are reported as positive when the organization is not actually realizing value from the project or initiative. An extreme example of this is in digital advertising where bots, ad fraud, and absolute garbage "listicle" sites abound because marketing agencies are driving as many "clicks" as possible on behalf of their clients.

While this explanation implies that the output/outcome distinction is simple and clear, the line between the two can be fuzzy. Consider "qualified leads" as a metric. For a marketing organization, the area of influence may truly end at the leads they hand off to the sales team. Qualified leads are certainly *more* of an outcome than "website traffic" or "product views" or even "lead form completions" or "leads." But it's also not as much of an outcome as "closed business" or "revenue." The simplest way to think about this is to be *as outcome-oriented as possible when choosing metrics.*

Outputs versus Outcomes (cont'd.)

Outputs versus Outcomes (cont'd.)

> The two magic questions are set up specifically to drive a focus on outcomes over outputs. Does this mean *never* use output metrics for performance measurement? Alas! Like many topics in data and life: there are no absolutes! But adopting a *bias* for outcome-oriented measures is a must!

A KPI WITHOUT A TARGET IS JUST A METRIC

Returning to our example (we won't belabor it too much more, we promise!), let's look at just that last measure (what follows applies to all of them, so any of them will do):

The number of opportunities from new prospects that are flagged as having interest in the new services

Now, let's imagine we're halfway through the campaign and we see 100 opportunities that match this scenario.

Is that good?!

If you're thinking, "It might be. You haven't provided enough information about the campaign or the company. How much is being spent? How much do these services cost? How many total opportunities (for any and all services) even get created in a typical month?"

These are all fair questions. But even if you had the answers to all of them, there is only *one* question you need the answer to answer the "Is that good?" question.

And that question is: "How will we know if we've done that?!" To answer that question, we need the metrics *and targets for those metrics.*

Imagine that we had set a target of getting 1,000 opportunities per month that matched our criteria for the metric. If we had only gotten 100 opportunities, then the answer to the "Is that good?" question is a resounding, "No!"

Alternatively, imagine that we had set a target of getting 10 opportunities per month that matched our criteria. If we'd gotten 100 in the first month, then the answer to the "Is that good?" question is a fist-pumping, emphatic, "Yes!!!"

If companies regularly struggle to identify appropriate metrics to use to measure meaningful outcomes for their projects and initiatives, they outright and overtly fail to set targets for their KPIs. Why is this? Unfortunately, it's human nature. It feels scary. The data-abundant world in which we live has us conditioned to having a cornucopia of historical data at our fingertips. That data may not be perfectly accurate, and often

enough, our fingertips get worn raw during the process of accessing the data because the data access tools are clunkier than we would like. But, still, *the data are there.*

When it comes to setting targets, though, we're trying to envision and predict the future. What *will* happen? Or more accurately, what do we *want* to have happen? This is uncomfortable. Whether consciously or subconsciously, we wrestle with the ramifications of setting targets, as we perceive various negative outcomes if we do:

- If we set a target that is too high and then miss it, it will be a black mark on our Permanent Professional Record! We will be viewed as failures! We'll never get a promotion or a raise again, and we might even be fired!
- If we set a target that is too low, then we'll be accused of sandbagging! Why, the powers-that-be might just cancel the whole project because we lowballed our expected results. We will be viewed as either being unduly timid or manipulative. We'll never get a promotion or a raise again, and we might even be fired!
- If we exactly hit the target, well, that would be amazing! But that means we have to be able to see the future in perfect clarity, which we can't do (our time machine only travels back in time, not forward)!

Once again, we have a conundrum: we know it's critical that we set appropriate targets for meaningful, outcome-oriented KPIs, but the prospect of doing so is terrifying and (conveniently!) easy to skip at the time we need to set them.

Let's first dispel the fears we just described and then dive into some simple and unscary techniques for setting targets.

First, we'll confront the fear of getting fired (or, at least, having some sort of black mark on our professional record) if a target gets missed. In most cases, this fear is simply unfounded. Consider reporting the following after a process change has been rolled out to streamline some aspect of our call center's operations: "We expected this project to deliver 100 hours of time savings across all of our customer service representatives each week, and, so far, it is only saving 45–50 hours a week." This target could be missed for three different reasons:

Why the Target Was Missed	Why This Is Still a Positive
The rollout of the process did not go exactly as planned, but we have ideas for additional adjustments that we expect to improve the results.	There is no debate or "spinning" of the results. Rather, there is an objective admission that the results have fallen short of the organization's expectations (not just our personal expectations). But we have ideas as to how to close the gap, so there is no need to panic, everyone is informed, and we've demonstrated that we are responsibly managing the effort. (These ideas, by the way, are actually hypotheses, which we'll dig into in the next chapter.)
The process rolled out pretty much exactly as expected, and we still feel like it *should* be able to achieve the target, but we're currently baffled as to what else needs to happen to get there.	This is similar to the previous possibility, but it's a little tougher, as we don't actually have ideas for a fix. But, again, rather than getting caught up in a debate or pointing fingers, the objectivity of the "target vs. results" means the discussion can immediately pivot to, "Let's brainstorm as to how we can get improved results." (Again, this leads to hypotheses! See the next chapter!)
As the project rolled out, we realized that expectations (targets) were overly optimistic, and the 100 hours/week time savings wasn't realistic.	This is unfortunate, and it's possible that the project would not have been undertaken at all if a target of 50 hours had been set. But as an organization, we've gotten some great practice when it comes to setting targets, and that is a skill that will absolutely carry forward to future projects. This may feel like a hollow positive, but in our experience, within just a couple of cycles of appropriate target-setting, organizations get much, much better at setting realistic targets.

For business leaders who are focused on continuous improvement, missing a target is an opportunity. Setting targets is a way to sidestep the conversational circles that are triggered by the "Is that good?" question when reviewing project results and getting straight to productive, "What do we do next?" discussions!

Consider the second fear just outlined: that a too-conservative target will be perceived as sandbagging. Again, this is an unfounded fear. If a conservative target is set, and the project is *still* a compelling investment, then that's great! The expectations have been set low, but they've been set. If the project dramatically exceeds the target, then that's just added value that has been delivered. If, though, a conservative target leads to a questioning of whether the project even makes sense to undertake, then *that is good too!* The target has opened the door for an immediate and productive discussion: if the target seems too low, what would a reasonable target for the metric be? And if the target gets raised, is it realistic that it can still be hit? These questions and the resulting discussion and cogitation are the sign of a healthy business—an open assessment of why an investment is being made and what outcomes need to be delivered to make it worthwhile.

But here we've wandered into the territory of the third fear: the fear of the unknown. Target-setting is inherently an exercise in predicting the future. It's a search for a number that can be written down, and while that may feel very similar to the numbers that we've seen in reports and dashboards of past performance, those numbers were simply extracted from a database somewhere. They were *real* numbers. Targets are *future expectations* that don't yet exist anywhere in a queryable database. That is... unsettling!

Using our weight loss example again, our doctor's office may be able to provide facts about how our weight has changed over time *historically* based on the measurement they took each time we visited for an annual checkup, but they cannot provide any hard data about what our weight should be by the end of next year. We can pick a target, and our doctor can *weigh in* (yes, we know what we just did there) on our target, but that is an exercise in setting expectations—how much are we planning to alter our diet and exercise regimen, and what is realistic and healthy to expect as a result? Setting a weight loss target can be motivating, but it can also be scary, and setting one is by no means a guarantee that it will be achieved!

This leaves us with something of a conundrum: setting meaningful, outcome-oriented targets is critical, but thus far, all we've done is acknowledge that it is daunting to actually do so. We haven't really discussed how to go about setting targets yet, but we will rectify that now by outlining three distinct techniques for target-setting. As you will quickly discover, the most challenging part of setting targets is starting the process—getting past the fear and jitters that we have now belabored to the point that we've exceeded our word count target for this background by 60%. (And yet, the world did not end. The book still got published, and you are still reading it!)

Setting Targets with the Backs of Some Napkins

When it comes to setting targets, our tendency is to feel that we are starting entirely from scratch: we've never done *this* project before in *this* exact business or competitive environment, so it feels like we're just stuck *guessing!* And we are! But our guess can be an *educated one*, and we can incorporate the wisdom of the crowds to productively refine that educated guess.

This technique works as follows:

1. Gather the key stakeholders (in person or virtually) and ensure that everyone is aligned on the importance of having outcome-oriented key metrics identified, as well as having targets set for them.
2. Identify the metric(s) that will be used for the project or initiative (the two magic questions!).
3. Have each stakeholder develop a proposed target for each of the metrics to share in the next meeting.[4]
4. Race to the door to block it as everyone tries to make a hasty exit rather than committing to the assignment.
5. Remind them that everyone will be doing the assignment. They do not need to spend a lot of time on it, and they will simply be providing one data point of many with whatever they come up with.
6. At the next meeting, for each metric, have everyone share their proposed target.
7. Discuss the proposals and align on a target!

Wait. What? Did that last step seem too simple? That really is all there is to it.

---

[4]This can also be done in the same meeting. For smaller, lower stakes efforts, it's often feasible to set the targets immediately following the identification of the metrics that will be used as KPIs.

What almost always happens with this technique is that the fears of target-setting get blunted by the process itself: no individual is put on the hook for setting the targets, as it's a collective process. And there is a little bit of the social theory of groups at play: knowing that everyone is doing the same exercise inherently pushes each stakeholder to apply some form of creative thought to their own process so they don't look lazy when they share their work and their rationale.

While a true "wisdom of the crowds" approach would simply average the different proposed targets, this would be a missed opportunity. The wisdom that this technique is tapping into is the wisdom of *approaches to setting the expectation for the results*. Consider a marketing campaign where one of the identified key metrics from the two magic questions is "qualified leads":

- One stakeholder may use her (metaphorical) napkin to look at the last four campaigns that were run, how much was spent on each one, the number of qualified leads attributed to each campaign, and, with some simple math, the cost per qualified lead from those campaigns. Then, based on the budget for the new campaign, estimate how many qualified leads it might generate based on the target.

- Another stakeholder may go through a similar process, but she looks at the campaigns that ran in the same period for the last 3 years rather than the most recent campaigns. She then increases the target by 25% from what that exercise returned because she thinks the new messaging being used, along with how much better they've gotten at targeting their advertising to the appropriate audiences, should deliver discernibly better results.
- Yet another stakeholder may simply do a thought experiment based on the budget for the new campaign and what they would feel good reporting to the chief financial officer as to the number of qualified leads the campaign delivered.

None of these approaches is a sophisticated application of advanced statistical techniques. None of them take an enormous amount of time or effort. None of them are objectively better or worse approaches. But, *all* of them prompted the individuals who came up with them to think about *what expectations are reasonable for the campaign.*

When the group[5] reconvenes and shares their proposals, *typically* there will be a cluster of similar proposed targets, with at least one fairly extreme outlier. The cluster of similar ones warrant discussion: were fundamentally different calculations conducted that all triangulated around a similar number? That is powerful! But, it doesn't mean the outlier(s) should be discarded. What approach—what assumptions—were used on those metaphorical napkins? Sometimes, the group may decide that aspects of those outliers are worth incorporating in their expectations.

This exercise almost always reveals that there is a wealth of historical information, perspective, and knowledge that is invaluable. The discussion—along with some additional on-the-fly updating of napkins—turns the target-setting exercise into a collaborative alignment on expectations, which is the most critical task when it comes to the assembly of a functional performance measurement time machine!

Setting Targets by Bracketing the Possibilities

While the group consensus from the back-of-some-napkins approach is generally preferred—it taps into individual experiences and fosters collaboration and alignment on expectations—it is not always feasible. The timing of the initiative's planning may preclude the "meet, then go away and think, then meet again" process. Or stakeholders may dig their heels in and insist that

---

[5] The group can be as small as just three or four people or as large as 15–20 people. There is no statistical magic here: we're just trying to get the key stakeholders thinking about their expectations in a way that is tangible and, ultimately, alignable.

they simply *do not have enough information* to establish realistic targets for the key metrics. Perhaps even you, dear reader, are skeptical that a target can be set in situations where a never-before-used metric has been identified (see the sidebar earlier in this chapter about outputs versus outcomes—outcome-oriented measures often wind up, initially, as metrics that have never been captured or tracked by an organization)! These are all scenarios where a technique we've dubbed "bracketing" can be useful.

For the sake of illustration, let's return to our earlier example of a marketing campaign where "qualified leads" has been identified as a key metric. The stakeholders are completely aligned that this is a great metric for the campaign. Unfortunately, they are equally aligned on the fact that it is going to be *impossible* to set a target for the number of qualified leads they expect the campaign to generate.

Alignment is generally a good thing, but alignment on skipping the setting of targets is terrible! Buck up! Push back! Bracketing is a technique for getting over that initial hurdle of "No!" to start the process of thinking about expectations for the project. An inability (or unwillingness) to set a target is, implicitly, a declaration that we have *no expectations* for what the campaign will deliver. The range of potential results in such a universe can be visually displayed on a number line[6] as shown in Figure 5.6.

FIGURE 5.6   The range of possible qualified leads resulting from a campaign

If the team truly has no expectations for the results for this campaign, then any result from zero to infinity would elicit an identical response: a shrug. And clearly, that is ridiculous. Or if it's not yet clearly ridiculous, then let's play it out a bit, as bracketing tests that purported lack of expectations (the shrug) by picking two possible outcomes: an absurdly low one and an absurdly high one, as shown in Figure 5.7.

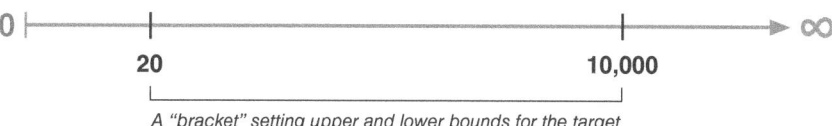

A "bracket" setting upper and lower bounds for the target

FIGURE 5.7   An absurdly wide range of possible results

---

[6] If you have young children, now is the time to call them over to show them that you're reading a book that uses number lines—a concept generally introduced early in grade school. Do *not* let them look ahead, though, as we're about to go very much "not to scale" with our labels on this line!

Conversationally, this would go something like this:

You: "So, what if the campaign generated a total of 20 qualified leads? Would we be okay with that?"

The Team: *[leaning over to sniff your coffee mug as a casual sobriety check]* "Of course not! We're spending $100,000 on this campaign. If we only generate 20 qualified leads, we would be ridiculed by the sales team. We had better drive way more than 20 qualified leads!"

You: *[maintaining a straight face as you internally high-five yourself as The Team plays right into your hands]* "Ah. Okay. So, what if the campaign drove 10,000 qualified leads? We would be thrilled by that, I assume?"

The Team: "That's not even possible! The total addressable market for the product is only 8,000 companies! There is no way that we'll generate 10,000 qualified leads!"

You: "Perfect. Let's start there. We thought we had *no expectations at all*, but we can at least say that we expect the campaign to deliver somewhere between 20 and 10,000 qualified leads!"

What you shouldn't say—no one likes a smartass—is that, while this is still too broad of a range to use as a target, a nearly infinite number of possible targets have now been eliminated! Replacing "infinity" with a hard number is useful!

More importantly, in this brief exchange, you've already started the process for aligning on expectations for the campaign. The team has experienced immediate reactions to two numbers (it is *really important* that both numbers be quickly dismissible by being fairly extreme), and that has sparked the same sort of thinking that you would have had them employ independently if you were using the backs-of-some-napkins technique from the previous section!

The next step is to build on that momentum by working up from the absurdly low number as shown in Figure 5.8.

You: "We said 20 was ridiculously low. What if we set the target at 40 qualified leads?"

The Team: "That's pretty much just as ridiculous!"

You: "80 qualified leads, then?"

The Team: "Hmmm. That would mean, what, that we spent $1,250 per qualified lead? I wouldn't want to defend that as being successful. We only see ~$3,000 of profit from the average new customer."

You: "What if it was $500 per qualified lead? That would be....let's see....200 qualified leads."

The Team: "Well...maybe. That still feels a little high, but we've already agreed that we have no idea just how much traction we'll get with this campaign. I don't think we'd want that high of a cost per qualified lead over the long haul, but we could probably justify it as, if not a shining success, at least as being decent enough results to have validated trying out the entirely new approach we're trying with this campaign."

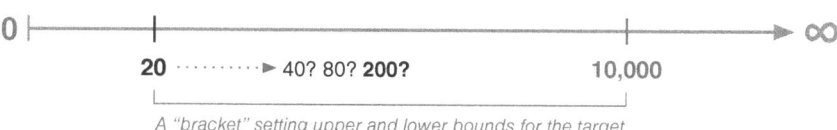

A "bracket" setting upper and lower bounds for the target

FIGURE 5.8 Work up from the lower bound

Once you get to the point where there is a lot of squirming—maybe even some irritation that you seem to be pushing for expectations when the team has already made it clear that there is a high degree of uncertainty (!)—stop pushing! Shift gears and go through the same exercise, but starting with the high number and working downward[7] as shown in Figure 5.9.

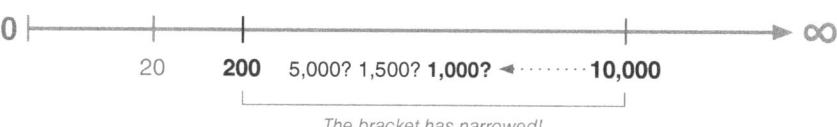

The bracket has narrowed!

FIGURE 5.9 Work down from the upper bound

This "come at it from both directions" gently forces some cognitive shifts—reframing the question from a few different angles to get the team to probe (and voice) their expectations. While this may seem obvious and formulaic, in practice, the exercise generates the exact sort of thought and discussion that is needed to build our performance management time machine.

---

[7]We wanted to include the dialogue for this, too, but the editors were concerned that we might abandon this project as a book and decide, instead, that it really needed a full treatment as a screenplay.

The result will be a *narrower* bracket of expectations, which we can semantically reframe as a "base target" and a "stretch target," as shown in Figure 5.10.

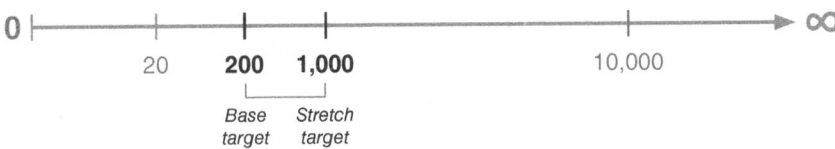

FIGURE 5.10   The bracket is now a "target range"

It's okay if this target range seems overly broad—it's still infinitely narrower than not having any target at all! When the target is a range, it is generally even more important to socialize the key metrics and their targets to a broader audience—if an extended stakeholder has a negative reaction to the breadth of the target range, then by voicing that reaction they have explicitly (even if unintentionally!) volunteered that *they* have expectations for the campaign. And as we've belabored at this point: identifying and aligning on those expectations at the outset is critical!

Setting Targets by Just Picking a Number

One final technique for setting a target we call (just a little bit cheekily) "just pick a number." Essentially, this approach combines and shortcuts the previous two techniques discussed. It works as follows:

1. One person (it could be you) does a back-of-the-napkin calculation to come up with a proposed target.
2. That proposal gets shared with the key stakeholders.
3. It then gets discussed, adjusted, and agreed to.

What makes this a *less ideal approach* is that it puts all the downsides of "anchoring bias" front and center to the process: whatever that initial proposed target is will get undue weight as everyone assesses it. Rather than independently assessing their expectations, each stakeholder will be inclined to think about whether the proposed target is a *bit high* or a *bit low*, even if they would have come up with a dramatically higher or lower target if they had independently set a target.

This approach also runs the risk of stakeholders being able to simply skip over the exercise—to see that a target has been proposed and then metaphorically (or literally) shrug and say, "Sure. That works." Metaphorically, this means they're coming up on the construction of our time machine, seeing that someone is working on it already, and just walking right on by. When it comes time to *use* the time machine down the road (to answer the question, "Is this good?" when seeing the reporting on the initiative's results), they will be able to just as easily shrug and say, "Oh. Well, I guess the time machine wasn't built very well. Someone else was working on that, though, so it's not really my concern."

If you're getting the impression that we're including this as an option because, although it's not our preferred technique, we're realistic pragmatists and have been in the position of falling back to this option in our work with clients, then you are perceptive! While this is *not* an ideal approach, it certainly can work, as it is still documenting an expectation and giving stakeholders something to react to and discuss: it's wildly better than not setting a target at all! And if it turns out the integrity of the time machine gets questioned down the road, that can be used as evidence for why the organization should use one of the other techniques the next time targets need to be set!

Forecasting As a Way to Pick a Number

While we have referred to doing quick, back-of-the-napkin calculations several times to this point, we don't want to be overly dismissive of the rigor that *can* go into setting targets, so we are stepping aside here for a brief word about forecasting.

As we have noted in this chapter, setting targets is all about setting expectations for what *will* happen in the future. When we are planning a project or initiative, we are also trying to *influence* the future. What actually happens in the future will be a combination of two things: (1) things we can affect and (2) things that we cannot! By definition, then, the target for a key metric cannot be set *just* by using historical data to forecast a future result.

Rob J. Hyndman and George Athanasopoulos break out four distinct factors that influence the predictability of a future value for a metric:

- How well we understand the factors that contribute to the metric
- How much historical data we have available for those factors
- How similar the future is to the past with respect to the metric
- Whether the forecasts themselves can affect the metric we are forecasting[8]

---

[8] Hyndman, R.J. and Athanasopoulos, G. (2021). *Forecasting: Principles and practice*. 3rd ed. OTexts: Melbourne, Australia. https://otexts.com/fpp3/what-can-be-forecast .html

We'll add a fifth item to this list:

■ The extent to which we expect our actions to influence the metric we are forecasting

This may start to feel like we're getting overly academic, but this really is a useful lens through which we can consider our expectations for the results we are trying to deliver: if we did *nothing*, what would we expect our key metric result to be (e.g., how much revenue would be generated if we didn't run the marketing campaign at all?); by *doing something*, how much *different* do we expect the key metric result to be?

Forecasting techniques can be useful for digging into these questions and, ultimately, setting targets. But they still should be complemented by asking the question, "What result would we need to see to make the investment even worthwhile?" If the forecasting exercise results in a best-case estimate of the campaign delivering 250 qualified leads, and it wouldn't be worth running the campaign if it doesn't deliver at least 400, then stop the presses and have a serious alignment discussion!

DASHBOARDS AS A PERFORMANCE MEASUREMENT TOOL

Before we wrap up this topic, we need to spend just a few minutes on the subject of dashboards. Many organizations have separate groups that have contradictory perspectives when it comes to the dashboards that are produced and maintained in the organization:

The team that creates and maintains the dashboards[9] sees them as incredibly powerful—they are well-designed, automatically updated, interactive gateways to the rich set of data that the company collects and manages! They are portals to deep and powerful insights that business users can hop into and quickly and easily navigate to answer any and all of their questions so that they can make deeply impactful data-driven decisions!

---

[9] This team often includes member of the analytics and/or business intelligence (BI) team, members of IT who support the technical implementation and maintenance of the dashboard tool(s), representatives from the BI tool vendor itself, and even consultants who have been hired to support the maintenance of the platform and the development of new dashboards. This team, in short, can be a small and formative army that has dug pretty deep trenches in support of their position!

The business users who are the intended consumers of the dashboards see them as overwhelming and clunky—dumps of data that looked really exciting the first time they saw them, but somehow never seem to *quite* have the information they're looking for and that generally leave them scratching their heads asking, "So what? What am I supposed to do with this?"

What is going on here? This is something of a callback to Chapters 1 and 2, but it bears repeating here: the tool vendors that produce the technology that generates dashboards—be they straight-up BI platforms or some other platform that generates, collects, or processes data and has "custom dashboards" as a feature within the tool—are strongly incentivized to over promise on their value. That overcommitment then trickles down to the team that manages the platform within an organization, as well as to the consultants who support them!

This is not to say that dashboards are not useful. They absolutely are! But they are most valuable as *performance measurement dashboards*. By adding those qualifiers, the focus of the dashboards gets narrowed considerably. Remember, performance measurement is *just* about getting an objective and quantitative assessment of how something is performing against expectations. An effective performance measurement dashboard has some very specific characteristics:

It is structured (designed) around "the two magic questions"—it provides a clear reminder to the viewer as to what the initiative or project it is showing data for was intended to achieve for the business.
Key metrics and their performance against targets are the dominant elements—only showing the actual value for the key metric sparks the "Is this good?" question, so even though it can be technically tricky, it is an absolute requirement that the targets and how the metrics are progressing against them be included on the dashboard.
It incorporates data visualization best practices—the information is clearly presented so that the user can assess the results at a glance.[10]

---

[10]This is a massive topic in and of itself, and an enormous amount of neuroscience and psychology research has been devoted to the subject, which has resulted in very practical tactics for improving the impact of data visualizations. Absolutely fantastic and readily digestible content is available from Cole Nussbaumer Knaflic, Stephen Few, Alberto Cairo, Lea Pica, Brent Dykes, and Nick Desbarats if you want to dive into the topic further.

Only limited supplemental/contextual information is included— in many cases, if a key metric is missing its target, a handful of "first things to check" can be identified at the outset of the planning of the dashboard. This may be breaking the metric down across a couple of specific dimensions, assessing a few underlying metrics that, collectively, compose that metric, or something else. These can be included, but they need to be visually secondary to the key metrics themselves.

After reading this chapter, these may seem like somewhat obvious requirements. Consider the dashboards you currently have in place. How well do they conform to these characteristics?

If you're thinking, "I get what you're saying here, but what about *all of the other data* I and my team have access to on our dashboards? Are you saying that all of that data would just go away and not be available to us?" Well...yes and no:

- The "yes" is that, hopefully, you're not reading this book if you feel like your dashboards are throwing actionable insights your way at every turn.
- The "no" is that BI tools like Tableau Software and Microsoft's PowerBI can, with training and practice, be a great way to democratize access to data within an organization. Beyond having "dashboarding" features, they have powerful "ad hoc query and visualization" features that can provide a visual, drag-and-drop interface for interacting with data. But the "with training and practice" aspect is key—experienced users of these platforms will strongly believe that they are easy to use and intuitive, and they are...*once a certain level of comfort has been developed that only comes with practice*. There simply is no shortcut of "build the perfect dashboard, and access to all of the data will be easily available to all casual users."

Dashboards are great as performance measurement tools that allow some limited additional context beyond the key measures. They're *not* the Grand Solution for providing simple, intuitive, on-demand access to all of the data.

SUMMARY

Performance measurement is all about objectively and quantitatively answering the question: "Where are we today relative to where we expected to be today at some point in the past." We can think about this as though we are building a time machine when we are planning a campaign, project, or initiative. At some point in the future (and, likely, multiple times in the future), we will be looking at the results of our work and asking the question, "Are these results good or bad?" To answer that question, we'll want to step into our time machine and visit our earlier selves—bringing the actual results back in time and asking, "What do you think? You haven't started the work of actually making this initiative happen yet, so you're pretty objective about it. If this is what you get as a result, how will you feel about it?"

While in theory performance measurement is "just" an exercise of identifying appropriate KPIs and setting targets for them, in practice, organizations often simply identify metrics that are readily available as their KPIs, *and* they neglect to set targets for them. This winds up being not useful at all, so instead, we can use two magic questions—asked in order and with the answers written down and socialized across the entire team:

> **What are we trying to achieve?** This does not need to include any actual data in the answer, but it does need to be a concise explanation of *why* we are undertaking the project. It needs to represent some degree of business value that the investment in the effort is expected to deliver.
>
> **How will we know if we've done *that*?** Given the answer to the first question, what measure(s) can be used—as direct measures (ideally) or as imperfect proxy measures (often)—to determine whether we've achieved what we set out to? The answer to this question must include one or more (but not too many!) metrics *and targets* for each identified metric.

Setting targets for key metrics is intimidating, and because those targets don't actually get used until some point in the future, the exercise of setting them often gets glossed over or skipped entirely, which then breaks the entire process of effective performance measurement. There are three techniques for setting targets:

> **The backs of some napkins**—have all of the key stakeholders *independently* come up with proposed targets for each metric, and then compare, discuss, and align on a final target. This is as much about getting everyone mentally engaged with their expectations for the results of the initiative as it is about setting the "perfect" target.
>
> **Bracketing**—picking an absurdly low number for the target and an absurdly high number for the target, ensuring everyone agrees that they are...absurd...and then working progressively up and down from each of those numbers until we hit a collective, "We just don't know! This might be reasonable!" point for each one. This generally results in a target *range*, which is fine (even if it seems rather broad): one end of the range is the "base target," and the other is a "stretch target."
>
> **Pick a number**—this is the technique of last resort, as there is a very real risk of anchoring bias introducing undue influence on the selected

target. It is simply *one* person proposing a target (through a back-of-the-napkin calculation or through other means) and then discussing that proposal with the full team and adjusting it based on the discussion.

Dashboards are *most* effective as a performance measurement tool, despite rampant overpromising by many tool vendors and consultants that they are the source of deep insights. The most effective performance measurement dashboards are structured to reflect the two magic questions—including the "why we're doing this" behind the initiative—and reflecting performance against the targets set for the key metrics that were identified in the answer to the second magic question. There may be some limited "one level deeper for context or an initial exploration" included on the dashboard, but adding additional data can quickly make the dashboard unwieldy to the point of unusability.

MEASURE THIS CHAPTER

And now, it's time to contribute to the performance measurement of this very book by visiting https://analyticstrw.com and answering the two-question survey for this chapter. You will then get to see how this chapter performed against the targets we set for our key metrics and, hopefully, pause to reflect on the results as a direct application of what we have explored in this chapter.

CHAPTER 6

Making Decisions Through Hypothesis Validation

Performance measurement, which we discussed in the previous chapter, is inherently *backward*-looking: it's about the expectations for an investment that were set in the past, and then comparing those expectations to actual business results in the present. Hypothesis validation, on the other hand, is inherently *forward*-looking. It's about making the best decisions possible given imperfect, incomplete data and a finite amount of time.[1]

A useful starting point for exploring hypothesis validation is with a formal definition of the word "hypothesis":

Hypothesis: A **tentative assumption** made, in order to **draw out and test** its **logical or empirical consequences**.

Consider the three bolded elements in this definition. The first is the **tentative assumption.** A hypothesis starts with an *idea*. It does not *start* with data. While it's possible that, in the business context, a particular chart or report might spark an idea, it's also possible that raw critical thought—an instinct, or an observation of a competitor's behavior, or a passing comment by a colleague, or a conversation with Richard Feynman in the middle of a lucid dream, or something else—might spark an idea. Isaac Newton observed an apple falling out of a tree, wondered why it was that the apple fell to the ground rather than falling upward or sidewise, and hypothesized that there must be some sort of invisible force at play. Tentative assumptions are a key component of the scientific method because they allow us to articulate ideas that we can generalize. Newton's hypothesis ultimately informed his theory for the behavior of celestial bodies like the moon (it neither crashed into the earth nor skittered off into the solar system).

The second key element of the formal definition of "hypothesis" is **draw out and test.** It's only once an idea (a "tentative assumption") is articulated that data come into play: we use data to test if that idea holds up to quantifiable scrutiny. Extending our gravitational example, Newton went on to

---

[1] In business, we often are unable to "pick" the decisions that we must make; they are thrust upon us, linked to a ticking clock. We must make the best decisions we can with the information we have available at the time (this information can be quite limited). In science, we are generally more interested in things we can answer precisely and durably, rather than things we must answer immediately (some scientists may disagree with this in their own experiences, but it is a gross characterization of the profession). Hypothesis generation and testing is, in science, generally unconstrained by time and topic, at least not in the way it is in business.

conduct experiments with pendulums and to analyze observational data about the orbits of the moons around Jupiter and Saturn. The data are used to *validate* the hypothesis. It's not the *source* of the hypothesis.

The third element is **logical or empirical consequences.** In a world of finite resources—which is a characteristic of every business environment—validating hypotheses that yield results that are interesting but not actionable is...unproductive. Hypotheses need to be evaluated as to their *potential actionability* before any work begins to validate them. Our Newtonian example crumbles a bit[2] here, in that there is little evidence that Newton was considering the immediate, "quarterly" applications of his law of universal gravitation when he first published it in the late seventeenth century, but in business, the near-term applicability and actionability of hypotheses are critical.

Performance measurement and hypothesis validation are two sides of the same coin. They both focus on the comparison of an expectation to the data we observe. The difference is whether we want to be retrospective and observational, building on expectations we take for granted, or prospective and explanatory, generating creative new expectations and explanations for things we may have not seen before in the metaphorical library of received wisdom.

Performance measurement generates information alerting us to what is going right or wrong in the areas with which we are already familiar. Hypothesis validation generates information that helps us to explain *why* things are going the way that they are, or *how* things could be different if we were to tack in another direction.[3] Performance measurement, as we discussed in the previous chapter, produces helpful information, but it doesn't generate insight. Hypothesis validation generates *actionable information* in the form of insight.[4]

---

[2] The example "falls back to earth" at this point.

[3] Since we have a professor as an author, we would be remiss if we did not note that this portrayal of hypothesis validation is different from the portrayal we see in the scientific literature. In science we are often interested in "positive theory" that generates "falsifiable hypotheses." In other words, we want theories that posit things about the world, and we want hypotheses that can prove those theories wrong. A scientific hypothesis is an expectation of the world given a theory, and we don't set out to "validate" it; rather, we attempt to reject it. If we fail to reject the hypothesis, then we carry on accepting the default theory. We opt in this book to propose a portrayal of hypotheses that is more business relevant—one that better fits the everyday work technicians and executives do.

[4] To expand further on the previous footnote, in a scientific sense, you could have a hypothesis that is applied in the context of performance measurement. However, as we

WITHOUT HYPOTHESES, WE SEE A DROUGHT OF ACTIONABLE INSIGHTS

A common refrain among business leaders is that, while they are awash in reports and dashboards, they are in a drought when it comes to "actionable insights." This Lack of Actionable Insights Lament[5] is one of the key motivating forces that led us to write this book. Whether it is consciously recognized or not by business leaders, bemoaning a lack of "actionable insights" is ultimately an acknowledgment that data are not being put to productive use.

The process of hypothesis validation enables us to generate the actionable insights we need to remedy this dearth of actionable insights. But the methodology's application is often thwarted by the understandable directive to "find *more* insights." This response sounds to us a lot like when you tell a bored child to stop being bored.

The problem is not that we have a bunch of discrete insights hiding out in the data and they're just waiting for us to buck up and find them. The problem is that we, as professionals, have not learned the appropriate mental models for how to generate, test, and experience actionable insights (just as the child has not been given the appropriate tools to experience boredom appropriately). "Insights" are not created equally, they are not all interesting and informative, and we don't need more of them for the sake of discovery. Instead, we need to understand what a quality insight is and how to get to it.

Intuitively, we may feel like we are clear on what a quality insight is, but it's a concept that has sufficient intangibility, combined with a mental image of a metaphorical lightbulb—an "Aha!" moment—that nailing down a consensus is akin to driving a nail through a block of gelatin floating in the ocean. There is consensus, though, that the simple presence of previously unknown information or a quantified observation about something is *not* "an insight."

For instance, our chief revenue officer's report that "sales last quarter in Europe were down 15% year-over-year" may be worth knowing, and it's certainly interesting (and, possibly, even alarming!), but it's unlikely that this would clear the insight hurdle. The word itself—*insight*—is concise and connotes analytical

---

have formulated it, testing a hypothesis in the context of performance measurement does not generate an insight, because it is not actionable.

[5] The Lack of Actionable Insights Lament:
  I have data to my left.
  I have data to my right.
  I have data, really, everywhere,
  Alas! Nary an insight!

prestige, so it can get tossed around recklessly in the hopes that an observation in the data will surge power to a lightbulb in *someone's* head.

More often than not, though, it doesn't, and that prompts executives and technicians alike to sing another refrain of the Lack of Actionable Insights Lament. The Lament only leads to more observations-labeled-as-insights, which prompts directives to "find more insights," and then spirals into an endless cycle of "more" without reaching "value."

BREAKING THE LAMENTABLE CYCLE AND CREATING ACTIONABLE INSIGHT

Breaking out of this cycle of continuing to look at data without having it consistently yield insight boils down to two ideas that are not commonly understood.

First, **"performance measurement"** and **"insights"** are different **things.** Performance measurement does not deliver insights; it delivers information. Contrary to popular conception, a KPIs report is not chock-full of insights. In the previous chapter, we discussed how to use data to objectively, quantitatively, and productively measure performance with data. That measurement, definitionally, involves looking at previously unknown observations *of diligently established key metrics and how they compare to targets.* Performance measurements are not "insights," but they can be useful to quickly identify unexpected deviations from what we all expected to happen (both good and bad).

We need not judge any analytical deliverable based on whether it "yielded insights." Reports and dashboards often swim in a performance measurement lane, and the purpose of that lane is *only* to efficiently illustrate how we are delivering results relative to our expectations. But that doesn't mean they are useless. Indeed, they are incredibly valuable—they alert us to when things aren't going as expected.

Performance measurement tells us which things we need to dig into, but it does not provide us with the action we should take to change those things.

Insights, on the other hand, are actionable. They can inform us as to *why* something unexpected is happening. They can inform us as to *what would happen* if we were to change something.[6]

An **insight** tells us what could or should take place, and how we think we can achieve it.

We create insights to help us improve our situation by taking action.

Second, the actionability of insights comes from our ideas, not from the insights themselves. We can't sit back and wait for "insights" to wash over us so that we can select which ones seem ripe for supporting our

---

[6] We can search for insights that might help us improve our situation, even if everything is going as expected; things don't have to be going "unexpectedly" to necessitate an insight.

decision-making. We must start with what decisions we need to make (and are able to make) and then go in search of data that will help us make those decisions better.

In the last chapter, we introduced the two magic questions for performance measurement—two concise questions that, if answered well, drive alignment among stakeholders as to how a project or initiative will be meaningfully and objectively assessed. In this chapter, we'll explore how a "hypothesis validation" mindset puts actionable ideas first, to alleviate the Lack of Actionable Insights Lament.

ARTICULATING AND VALIDATING HYPOTHESES: A FRAMEWORK

One of our clients was a large healthcare system in the northeast. While the initial focus of our engagement had been the implementation of a business intelligence platform, the organization had long since had a preponderance of its data smoothly flowing into the platform, and all the users had been trained on how to use the tool. Yet, those same users continued to report that they weren't clear on what they were supposed to *do* with the data to which they now had direct access.

At this point, we had started training the marketing team on some of the concepts outlined in this book, including the importance of starting with hypotheses before diving into the data. We began attending a biweekly meeting which was attended by 80–100 people, including many of the marketers, as well as by representatives from the different marketing agencies they used. Each meeting included between two and four brief presentations about different marketing campaigns that were upcoming, in flight, or recently completed. Most of those presentations included a brief question-and-answer session.

Our presence at these meetings was purely in the role of observers. What we noticed was that the presentations followed a similar pattern: a few slides with a background about the campaign, then a few slides with charts showing some data from the business intelligence tool related to the campaign, and then a few more slides that included takeaways, next steps, or both. Our primary partners, who actually ran the meeting, agreed that, while these meetings were mildly informative, they lacked clarity as to whether the campaigns were meaningfully impactful (performance measurement), and they lacked evidence of data truly informing decision-making in the planning and execution of the campaigns.

At that point, we began simply listening to the presentations and the ensuing discussion in each meeting and capturing the ideas that we heard. On the fly, we converted those ideas into structured hypotheses and recorded them in a spreadsheet. Within a half-dozen meetings, we had captured more than 80 hypotheses in our spreadsheet. Most of those ideas—hypotheses—had not gone anywhere beyond some head nods and, "Oh, that's interesting" comments in the meeting itself. Some of the ideas received such an enthusiastic response that, despite never actually being validated as to their merit, cropped up again as having been applied to completely unrelated campaigns, *and this biweekly meeting was credited as the source of the idea.*

One example of this latter type of idea was the idea of "creative fatigue." A campaign that was promoting the availability of a particular type of procedure ran for multiple months, and the team thought that, since they had a limited set of visuals they were using for the campaign, that prospective patients were likely getting tired of seeing those same images over and over again and, by extension, the impact of the campaign was likely starting to deteriorate. The creative agency ran with this idea (for a fee!) and generated new images that could be swapped out in the advertisements mid-campaign. Now, there was *no evidence in any of the metrics that were shared* that this was happening. We are not saying whether creative fatigue was or was not in play. But not only did this mid-campaign creative swap happen for this campaign, it started to crop up as the standard operating procedure for many campaigns that ran for multiple months. None of the marketers running those campaigns had any supporting evidence, either, beyond the idea becoming a "best practice" in the organization. This best practice had a very real cost—the added expense of additional design work by one agency and the effort required to swap out the designs mid-campaign by another agency.

Eventually, we started using the last of the campaign presentation slots in this biweekly meeting to deliver bite-sized bits of training about how to put data to effective use—core concepts in this book boiled down to 10–15-minute presentations over successive meetings. When we got to the discussion of hypotheses, we pulled up our spreadsheet and showed the attendees that they already had loads of hypotheses that could be validated (*with data*) to give them more confidence in their decision-making. They just needed to recognize when they had a thought that could be translated to a hypothesis, capture that hypothesis, and then decide if it was important enough to follow through with to validate!

Articulating Hypotheses That Can Be Validated

There are numerous ways to validate a hypothesis, including theoretical, classical, and machine learning based approaches, which we will discuss in the next few chapters. But too often, folks pursue the validation of hypotheses that do not enable them to achieve useful outcomes or that were ideated simply because it's the received wisdom others gave them. We've seen far too many hypotheses articulated that, once validated at considerable expense using immense amounts of data and machine learning firepower, turned out to be useless because they didn't answer the right question. To effectively validate a hypothesis, we need to test it against information we gather from the world. But before we do that, we need to make sure we're evaluating hypotheses that matter.

The greatest service we can do for ourselves is to articulate a *well-formed hypothesis*, which ensures we make progress toward our goals if we validate it. A well-formed hypothesis states three things:

The Idea: The idea that we believe to be true—the "tentative assumption" discussed earlier in this chapter.[7] In the previous use case, the marketers assumed that creative fatigue decreased customer appetite for the healthcare system's service. But that was as far as they got, and stopping short prevented them from developing insights that could increase performance. There are two additional, uncommonly understood steps, required to make a well-formed hypothesis.

The Theory: The rationale or evidence that prompted us to believe the idea could be true. This evidence can come from a variety of sources, some of which give us more or less leverage on the "no-brainer-ness" of the idea. In the previous use case, we may believe creative fatigue is at hand because customers have increasingly clicked on advertisement feedback links to report that "I don't want to see this ad anymore."[8] Our evidence need not come just from the data at hand; it can also come from a thoughtful examination of the process at hand. For instance, we know that just by being human we can get tired of seeing the same thing over and over. Evidence can also come from secondhand sources. For example, we may read in a scientific advertising journal that creative fatigue has

---

[7] Technically, the answer to this first question is the actual hypothesis. But the next two components are critical when it comes to prioritizing which hypotheses are worth validating, so we should treat all three statements as part of "the hypothesis."

[8] In this example, we state one piece of evidence to support the formulation of the hypothesis. However, it can be useful to state multiple pieces of evidence because that creates more confidence that the hypothesis is worth exploring. The situation we explore cites advertisement feedback for "I don't want to see this ad anymore" as a reason to believe that creative fatigue is at hand. However, that same piece of evidence could be used to demonstrate that the content of the ad has become distasteful in light of current events. The context of the hypothesis must always be fully considered, and the more evidence we have to offer, the better the hypothesis will be received.

been scientifically identified after a certain number of exposures to the same ad within a certain period.

The Action: The action we will take if we're able to validate (or, technically, are "unable to reject") the idea. In the previous use case, the action would be to develop new creative assets to roll out mid-campaign for campaigns of a certain type or duration.[9]

Rather than simply answering these questions, we can use a fill-in-the-blank template to affirmatively (and concisely) articulate a hypothesis:

Articulating a Hypothesis: We believe [some idea] because [some evidence or rationale]. If we are right, we will [make some decision or take some action].

Another silly example serves to help us through the process of articulating a well-formed hypothesis. Extending the frivolous weight loss example from the last chapter, some hypotheses using this framework could be as follows:

- *We believe* that increasing our activity to walking or running at least 7,500 steps a day every day while not changing our current diet will lead to moderate weight loss *because* we read an article that referenced a study that indicated this would be the case. *If we are right*, we will commit to achieving this goal at least 6 days a week going forward.
- *We believe* that reducing the number of carbs in our diet will lead to moderate weight loss *because* a nutritionist who reviewed our current diet indicated that this would be the case. *If we are right*, we will be vigilant about our carb intake going forward.

These are run-of-the-mill tactics for weight loss, to be sure. But the point is that humans formulate hypotheses all the time, even if they don't realize it. In a business context, formulating and articulating hypotheses *clearly* is a

---

[9]Note that the action taken in this case comes at significant cost. The development of new creative assets represents an investment on which marketers and their teams would need to make a careful decision. If the action we will take is costless, and we are pretty sure it won't have any negative effect on the outcome, then the hypothesis may be well formed but less useful.

critical precursor to using data to *validate* those hypotheses.[10] And formulating hypotheses that can be proven wrong can prevent cognitive biases like *confirmation bias* from creeping in and seeding poor decisions.[11]

With that quick introduction, let's dig in a little deeper to each component of that hypothesis framing structure.

The Idea: We believe [some idea]

If a hypothesis is a "tentative assumption," then the core of articulating a hypothesis is affirmatively stating what that assumption is. We *could* simply say, "I *tentatively assume* [some idea]." That would be a mouthful (say "I tentatively assume that tentative assumptions are tentatively assumptive" quickly five times and see if your tongue doesn't cramp up!). More importantly, though, "tentatively assuming" connotes hesitancy, and hesitancy leads to inaction. When it comes to validating hypotheses, we want to be decisive!

"We believe" is something of a mental cheat code. It forces clarity of thought. As we've already discussed, no amount of data will deliver absolute truths, but it's helpful to articulate hypotheses in black-and-white terms. It's *okay* if we have some hesitation ("I'm not really sure. I kind-of think this might be the case, but I don't really 100% *believe* it!"). No anvils will fall on our head if we articulate a hypothesis as a "belief" that turns out to not hold up to validation with data. Clear expression of our idea is the key.

The ways to complete the "We believe..." statement are vast. Consider these examples:

- **"We believe** that our customers will prefer a seamless, 'out-of-the-box' setup experience, and that they will pay more to achieve it...."
- **"We believe** that employee dissatisfaction with our newly announced hybrid work policy is primarily driven by the element of the policy that requires them to be in the office on Mondays...."
- **"We believe** that, if we include the chance to win a prize for anyone who fills out our online lead form, we will see a much higher completion rate

---

[10] If you read these two weight loss hypotheses and thought, "What if someone is increasing their steps *and* cutting back carbs? How would they know which activity is having what effect?" then your instincts are good! This would be an example of "confounding," which is a topic we address later in the book!

[11] Confirmation bias is one of the many cognitive biases that arise out of our human need to process information more efficiently. It states that people tend to test hypotheses by searching for evidence that supports their current hypothesis rather than searching for relevant evidence that may disprove it.

for the form without substantially sacrificing the quality of the leads we get through the form...."

- **"We believe** that the advertising we do on Facebook does not actually deliver much in the way of value compared to the other channels in which we could be investing...."
- **"We believe** that investing in robotic automation processes will produce a higher quality product at a lower cost in the long run...."
- **"We believe** our rural oncology clinics are not serving the true level of need for the local populations...."

We will come back and build on these examples as we flesh out the rest of the hypothesis statement.

The Theory: ...because [some evidence or rationale]...

The next step in articulating a hypothesis is to pause and interrogate *why* we have the tentative assumption—the "belief"—that is the root of the hypothesis. Did we see a chart in a report for which the hypothesis would explain a spike in a metric? Did we see a competitor do something, which made us think they had figured something out about the customers for whom we're competing with them? Did we read an article or listen to a podcast that resonated with us to the point that we thought it might apply and be useful for our business? Was the idea simply...instinct? These are *all* valid "becauses!"

The "theory" part of the hypothesis statement serves two purposes:

- It forces us to slow down for a minute and *think*. Not for a day. Not for a month. Just for a *little bit* to mine our brain for context and rationale.
- It is key to the *prioritization* by which hypotheses get validated and when. Is there *overwhelming evidence* that the hypothesis is actually true? Then maybe no additional validation is warranted! Go take action! Is there little or no hard evidence that the hypothesis is true? That doesn't mean it gets thrown out, but it does mean that the upside of validating the hypothesis will likely need to clear a higher bar in order to invest in its validation. We'll cover this more in Chapter 7, in the table "Causal Evidence Ladder."

Let's go back to our previous examples and add potential "because" statements to them:

- "We believe that our customers will prefer a seamless, 'out-of-the-box' setup experience, and that they will pay more to achieve it **because our customer service team reports that 35% of the calls they handle are related to product setup, and we read through the reviews for our** product online, and there are a lot more complaints about setting the product up than there are about the cost of the product."

- "We believe that employee dissatisfaction with our newly announced hybrid work policy is primarily driven by the element of the policy that requires them to be in the office on Mondays **because we conducted an informal survey of our team and asked what they didn't like about the new policy, and the Monday-in-office requirement was overwhelmingly the most common response.**"
- "We believe that, if we include the chance to win a prize for anyone who fills out our online lead form, we will see a much higher completion rate for the form without substantially sacrificing the quality of the leads we get through the form **because we tried this at the last company we worked and were pleasantly surprised by the results—we quadrupled the number of leads, but the lead quality only declined by 15–20%.**"
- "We believe that the advertising we do on Facebook does not actually deliver much in the way of value **because we put a significant amount of investment into Facebook for years, and last quarter, when we shut it off completely, our sales revenue wasn't impacted at all. Plus, we, personally, have never paid any attention to Facebook ads.**"[12]
- "We believe that investing in robotic automation processes will produce a higher quality product at a lower cost in the long run **because our competitor who uses robotic automation on its assembly line consistently reports a lower rate of warranty claims in their quarterly earnings calls than we do.**"
- "We believe our rural oncology clinics are not serving the true level of need for the local populations **because, in a recent report from the State Department of Health, the government cited county-by-county cancer prevalence rates that are much higher than the number of patients we treat in our clinics.**"

Adding the "because" statements flesh out the hypothesis. *Someone*—us, a member of our team, a member of a separate research or analytics team in our company—may be tasked with validating the hypothesis, and the added

---

[12] We are agnostic as to the value of Facebook advertising in general and do not mean to suggest it should or shouldn't be used. The purpose of this bullet is only to present an example of how to build a well-formed hypothesis, using a case study from one of our clients in the past.

context of "because" can add a lot of value to their investigation. Often, it will reduce the costs associated with validation:

- Does the evidence look very strong on the surface, but it actually has serious flaws? Would simply addressing those flaws be sufficient to validate (or not validate) the hypothesis?
- Does the rationale point to a mechanism for validating the hypothesis more robustly? For instance, would a well-designed and *formal* survey of the entire company be a valid and cost-effective way to validate a hypothesis sparked by an informal survey of one team?
- When validating the hypothesis, what evidence should the validation also consider? For instance, the Facebook advertising hypothesis simply referred to "delivering value," but the "because" statement described a revenue comparison. Simply digging into the advertising data and reporting how many clicks the advertising received would be a miss, as the hypothesis was more about *incremental revenue* (and may require more effort to validate).

We admit that we're belaboring this structure a bit (we're two-thirds of the way through our belaboring, we promise!). While it may *feel* cumbersome, this structure lends itself to the articulation of well-formed hypotheses concisely, thoroughly, *and quickly.*

The real cost required by the process is human thought and creativity, which, all too often, is something that organizations wish could be replaced by "the data." It can't. Smart, motivated, thoughtful people are hard to come by, challenging to retain, and impossible to replace with data and technology. We've mounted this particular soapbox a few times over the course of this book, and we will mount it again from a few other directions, but it's a soapbox worth mounting![13] The best hypotheses come when we have the right people.

The Action: If we are right, we will...

The last piece of articulating a hypothesis is another "pause and think" step: *if* this idea turns out to be true (gets validated), *will we do something different than if it had turned out to not be true, or if we hadn't bothered to validate the hypothesis at all?*

---

[13] If you're finding yourself muttering "preach on!" under your breath, or even shouting it out loud, well, that's a little odd if you're *literally* doing that. If, though, you're reading this footnote and thinking, "Well, yeah, I kinda had that sort of thought," then an analytical angel just got its wings.

This, again, is a *thought* exercise, but it's the most valuable component of the formulation.

First, it provides a check as to whether the hypothesis is clearly and specifically articulated. For instance, if the first part of the hypothesis statement was, "We believe our website sucks because our customer satisfaction survey results for the website experience are very low," this action statement would be...what exactly? "If we are right, we will...make the website not suck?" That's not a particularly clear directive, so writing the action statement may send us back to update the hypothesis statement: "We believe our website's main navigation does not actually reflect what visitors are looking for..." or "We believe the 'Add to Cart' button on our product details pages is too far down the page, which means many users have trouble finding it...." In this example, writing the action statement may reveal that there are *multiple* hypotheses about the suckiness of the website. Breaking them out into separate hypotheses makes them much easier to prioritize, validate, and then act on!

Second, it provides a sanity check as to whether the action that would be taken is feasible and realistic. Consider another hypothesis regarding a website: "We believe that having a 'tracking consent' message pop up when someone comes to our site causes some visitors to leave the site prematurely...." If we're able to validate that hypothesis, will we simply stop tracking visitors? This seems unlikely. Will we remove the message and just track them anyway? In many places, this would be illegal (and would be unethical everywhere). The act of writing the action statement can reveal that the hypothesis, even if validated, would not be actionable! That should then either drastically lower it on the prioritization list *or* lead to an update of the hypothesis itself ("We believe that our 'tracking consent' message popup when someone comes to our site is unnecessarily off-putting and, with some design and copy changes, could be updated to reduce the number of visitors who leave the site prematurely...").

Let's return to our earlier examples and round them out by adding action statements:

- "We believe that our customers will prefer a seamless, 'out-of-the-box' setup experience, and that they will pay more to achieve it because our customer service team reports that 35% of the calls they handle are related to product setup, and we read through the reviews for our product online, and there are a lot more complaints about setting the product up than there are about the cost of the product. **If we are right, we will prioritize the development of features on our product roadmap that are tied to the setup experience.**"

- "We believe that employee dissatisfaction with our newly announced hybrid work policy is primarily driven by the element of the policy that requires them to be in the office on Mondays because we conducted an informal survey of our team and asked what, specifically, they didn't like about the new policy, and the Monday-in-office requirement was overwhelmingly the most common response. **If we are right, we will update the policy to require employees to be in the office on only two Mondays per month.**"

- "We believe that, if we include the chance to win a prize for anyone who fills out our online lead form, we will see a much higher completion rate for the form without substantially sacrificing the quality of the leads we get through the form because we tried this at the last company we worked and were pleasantly surprised by the results—we quadrupled the number of leads, but the lead quality only declined by 15–20%. **If we are right, we will consistently offer a prize for anyone who fills out our online lead forms, and we will experiment with different offers to identify which ones are the most impactful.**"

- "We believe that the advertising we do on Facebook does not actually deliver much in the way of value because we put a significant amount of investment into Facebook for years, and last quarter, when we shut it off completely, our sales revenue wasn't impacted at all. Plus, we, personally, have never paid any attention to Facebook ads. **If we are right, we will shut down our Facebook advertising for at least a year and will redeploy that budget to other advertising channels that we have not historically used and experiment to see if any of those provide an incremental lift in revenue.**"

- "We believe that investing in robotic automation processes will produce a higher quality product at a lower cost in the long run because our competitor who uses robotic automation on its assembly line consistently reports a lower rate of warranty claims in their quarterly earnings calls than we do. **If we are right, we will retrofit one of our factories, completely with assembly robots, and retrain our people to use them.**"

- "We believe our rural oncology clinics are not serving the true level of need for the local populations because in a recent report from the State Department of Health, the government cited county-by-county cancer prevalence rates that are much higher than the number of patients we treat in our clinics. **If we are right, we will conduct an investigation into the ways in which we can increase the level of service our clinics provide.**"

Notice that actions do not necessarily have to substantially change the nature of our business. For instance, in the rural oncology clinics, example, the executive says that if they are right, they will do more research. The action

component can simply be that we will further investigate something, thereby investing further resources. The key is that the action represents movement toward some nontrivial investment, or away from some nontrivial risk. Any real decision comes at some sort of cost, whether that be an investment that we make upfront to explore the idea, or some sort of harm that may come to our enterprise by doing the wrong thing.

In cases where the action is costless, and the action is guaranteed to be positively received, then just go ahead and do it. The same logic applies for why we don't experiment to find out whether parachutes help preserve people's lives when they jump out of airplanes.

Exercise: Formulate a Hypothesis

Take a minute to see if you can identify any hypotheses that are bouncing around in your brain right now. Can you fit them into this structure? Do they *immediately* flow into fully formed hypothesis statements, or do they require some additional thought? If it's the latter, then that's exactly the muscle we hope you and your team develop with some practice—adding one layer of thought clarity before diving into the data itself. That layer will pay substantial dividends when it comes to the focus, efficiency, and impact of the validation work itself. If, on the other hand, your ideas flowed smoothly into this hypothesis structure, then that's great! Were they written down somewhere already? They should be! That's where a hypothesis library comes into play.

CAPTURING HYPOTHESES IN A HYPOTHESIS LIBRARY

We've got some great hypotheses, and we have a great way to articulate them! So what should we *do* with them? Validate them, obviously! But it is impractical to think we can focus on validating any hypothesis that's worth validating at the instant it comes to us. For example, imagine we are generating hypotheses after noticing something aberrant in our most recent review of the marketing performance dashboard:

- One hypothesis came to us while having drinks with a customer after a long day of meetings. It's unclear if it's a good idea or bad one.
- Another several hypotheses came out of a Friday afternoon brainstorming session with our team, and many of them seem like they will take at least a quarter to validate.
- Two more hypotheses came up as we were reviewing the results of the latest marketing campaign, but we're due for a meeting with some external parties in 30 minutes.

The moment a hypothesis gets identified is rarely the ideal time to dig in and validate it. Moreover, some hypotheses aren't worth validating at all! This is where the *hypothesis library* comes into play.

A hypothesis library is exactly what it sounds like: a centralized, organized repository of all of the hypotheses we and our team have identified. This does not need to be an elaborate solution. As a matter of fact, we have often built the initial hypothesis libraries for clients simply using a spreadsheet: each row is a hypothesis. At its most basic, a hypothesis library can have just three columns—one for each of the elements in the hypothesis structure we just defined. See Table 6.1 for an example of a basic hypothesis library with the six examples we used earlier in this chapter.

In practice, hypothesis libraries wind up with additional columns (or additional *fields* if the hypothesis library is managed in a database—Jira, Basecamp, Sharepoint, Notion, AirTable, Smartsheets, or virtually any internal collaboration platform that has at least a modicum of customizability).[14] In most cases, it makes sense to record *who* came up with the hypothesis and *when* the hypothesis was captured. We often include some categorization of the hypotheses too—to which department or system or process the hypothesis is relevant, for instance.

TABLE 6.1   An Example of a Hypothesis Library

We believe...	Because...	If we are right, we will...
That our customers will prefer a seamless, "out-of-the-box" setup experience, and that they will pay more to achieve it.	Our customer service team reports that 35% of the calls they handle are related to product setup, and we read through the reviews for our product online, and there are a lot more complaints about setting the product up than there are about the cost of the product.	Prioritize the development of features on our product roadmap that are tied to the setup experience.

---

[14] You can also use the downloadable hypothesis library template at https://analyticstrw.com.

We believe...	Because...	If we are right, we will...
That employee dissatisfaction with our newly announced hybrid work policy is primarily driven by the element of the policy that requires them to be in the office on Mondays.	We conducted an informal survey of out team and asked what, specifically, they didn't like about the new policy, and the Monday-in-office requirement was overwhelmingly the most common response.	Update the policy to only require employees to be in the office on two Mondays per month.
That, if we include the chance to win a prize for anyone who fills out our online lead form, we will see a much higher completion rate for the form without substantially sacrificing the quality of the leads we get through the form.	We tried this at the last company we worked and were pleasantly surprised by the results—we quadrupled the number of leads, but the lead quality only declined by 15–20%.	Consistently offer a prize for anyone who fills out our online lead forms, and we will experiment with different offers to identify which ones are the most impactful.
That the advertising we do on Facebook does not actually deliver much in the way of value.	We put a significant amount of investment into Facebook for years, and last quarter, when we shut it off completely, our sales revenue wasn't impacted at all. Plus, we, personally, have never paid any attention to Facebook ads.	Shut down our Facebook advertising for at least a year and will redeploy that budget to other advertising channels that we have not historically used and experiment to see if any of those provide a meaningful incremental lift in revenue.
That investing in robotic automation processes will produce a higher quality product at a lower cost in the long run.	Our competitor who uses robotic automation on its assembly line consistently reports a lower rate of warranty claims in its quarterly earnings calls than we do.	Retrofit one of our factories, completely with assembly robots, and retrain our people to use them.

(continued)

TABLE 6.1 (*continued*)

We believe...	Because...	If we are right, we will...
That our rural oncology clinics are not serving the true level of need for the local populations.	A recent report from the State Department of Health, the government cited county-by-county cancer prevalence rates that are much higher than the number of patients we treat in our clinics.	Conduct an investigation into the ways in which we can increase the level of service our clinics provide.

Just Write It Down: Ideating a Hypothesis vs. Inventorying a Hypothesis

Some of the most promising hypotheses are often creative and original ideas. Intuitively, these flashes of brilliance, in the moment, seem unforgettable. And yet, we often forget them if we don't introduce a mechanism to help our brain remember them. This is because the idea occurs in short-term, or working, memory, which has a mind-bogglingly limited capacity.

This may seem elementary, but it bears noting. For us to be able to *remember* that idea later—even if only an hour or a day later—it has to be written it down. We write things down because our memories are fickle. Can you think of a time that you had a great thought or idea, assumed it was so powerful that you'd easily remember it, and then you couldn't for the life of you remember anything about it a few days or weeks later?[15] Inventorying our hypotheses is a great way to ensure that we do not lose track of the good ideas.

Writing our hypotheses down also kicks off the process of coordination and prioritization needed to validate them. It makes it possible to share our hypotheses with others, who can then give feedback as to the formulation of the hypothesis and the priority we believe it should have. It makes it possible for us to categorize our hypothesis into themes that might teach us something about the way our business runs. A hypothesis library enables us to efficiently share, assess, classify, and prioritize our hypotheses.

---

[15] If you cannot recall this ever happening to you, then we're pretty sure it did, but you...forgot about it!

An Abundance of Hypotheses

In a traditional library, it would be foolish to set an expectation that we would read every book. Similarly, with a *hypothesis* library, simply capturing and recording a hypothesis is not a commitment to *validate* it. That expectation needs to be set early and reinforced often.

In a hypothesis-oriented world, a scarcity of resources is an unalloyed positive. This seems counterintuitive: does *anyone* want to show up for work to find a to-do list that is outlandishly long and unachievable? Of course not! But that's the wrong way to think about a hypothesis library. Consider two scenarios:

> **Scenario 1:** Our team has the capacity to validate three hypotheses,[16] and our hypothesis library has three hypotheses in it.
> **Scenario 2:** Our team has the capacity to validate three hypotheses, and our hypothesis library has *20* hypotheses in it.

Which scenario would we prefer? Hopefully, you picked scenario 2. In scenario 1, one or two (or three) of the hypotheses may be absolute stinkers. But those are the only ones from which we have to work, so our resources will go toward validating *those three hypotheses.*

Now, consider scenario 2. Acknowledge the emotional reaction: "Oh, no! We have *20* hypotheses that we could try to validate, but we only have the bandwidth to validate *three*! We're overrun with hypotheses!" Now move past that emotional reaction and reframe it: "We have 20 hypotheses to *choose from*. Some of them look promising and impactful. Some of them are wild ideas that wouldn't even lead us to take any meaningful action even if they were validated. Oh. We get to choose *the most promising three* and focus on those! Yippee!"

In a hypothesis-driven organization, limited bandwidth relative to the number of hypotheses we have at hand can be a good thing. It means there is an abundance of ideas to choose from! And if those choices feel like potentially high-value hypotheses are getting left unvalidated, then a hypothesis library is an excellent place to look to identify how many and what kind of additional resources are needed.

---

[16] Different hypotheses will require varying levels of effort (time) to validate them. For the sake of making this point, though, we're going to pretend that all hypotheses require an equal amount of effort to validate. The point we're making holds up in the messiness of the real world.

You can use your hypothesis library card to check out up to five hypotheses at once!

Hypothesis Prioritization

With an abundance of hypotheses comes the need to prioritize. It is easy enough to get mired in endless cycles of prioritization, and it's equally easy to attempt to craft a complex, but perfect, formula for objectively prioritizing.

Neither approach is productive.

We cannot know the value of the insight any individual hypothesis will deliver before we conduct the analysis. Think about it: to *know* what value the validation of a hypothesis would deliver means we would have to *know* the results of the validation work itself. If that was knowable, then we wouldn't need to do the work to do the validation in the first place!

But we can do our best to try to "t-shirt" size it. Hypothesis prioritization is a human exercise. It requires a level of comfort with uncertainty, good judgment, and a recognition that there is no perfect answer.

This is where we build out the hypothesis library a bit further by adding some heuristics to aid with prioritization. The specifics of what criteria get included can vary based on the specifics of your organization, but a typical set of criteria would include the following:

Level of Effort—how much effort (time, cost) will be needed to validate the hypothesis?[17]

Strength of Theory—how strong is the "because" statement in the hypothesis definition?

Alignment to Business Goals—how closely can the hypothesis be linked to a business priority?

These are not criteria that need to be scored with a high degree of fidelity: a simple "high," "medium," or "low" is fine. The goal is to be able to get through them *quickly*. Combine the three scores (if high = 3, medium = 2, and low = 1 then simply sum up the scores; reverse this for Level of Effort: high = 1, medium = 2, and low = 3) to get an overall score, and then sort the library by score.

This is an intentionally and necessarily blunt instrument. The goal is *not* to get a perfectly ranked list of hypotheses. Rather, the goal is to get the clearly *most* promising hypotheses to the top of the list and the clear stinkers to the bottom of the list.

Alignment to Business Goals

Even if we had unlimited bandwidth, it would be nearly impossible to act on everything that's important, all at once. Assume for a second that we generate quality insights from all of our well-formed hypotheses—thousands of hypotheses and insights. We are awash in sensational insights that have enabled us to see the world through new eyes, as if we are seeing the Matrix. Even then, we reach a natural limit on the number of decisions we have the focus or ability to make.

Each decision requires specific information; we must know what we need to decide on and what information would enable us to make the best decision possible—or at least avoid a poor choice. If we search for insights on concepts that bear no relationship to the decision at hand, then we've produced more insights, but not any greater ability to decide.

Consider the problem of hiring a sales workforce: we only want to hire as many salespeople as we need to meet the demand that we can fill. If we over-hire, we may spend more than is required to capture the demand and

---

[17] This will be dependent, in part, on *how* the hypothesis will be validated. The following chapters outline the main categories of hypothesis validation techniques.

burn more cash than we bring in. If we under-hire, we may not have the capacity to capture the demand. We need insight on the level of demand available to weigh our cash flow needs against the workforce investment. If we search for insights on demand for products by our competitors that we don't plan on selling, then we've produced more insights on demand, but we've failed to generate information that will enable us to calibrate the number of salespeople we should hire.[18]

The Ongoing Process of Hypothesis Validation

Once you've separated the wheat from the chaff, the discussion can transition to *which* resources are available to test the hypotheses. For instance, the top two hypotheses may require running an experiment, but the resources equipped to design and execute an experiment are already fully booked; the third highest hypothesis, though, may be validated with some market research, and the research team has some capacity, so that hypothesis gets prioritized for execution. Alternatively, there may not be enough money to run an experiment, but there may be enough to run a quick survey of our top five customers.

The prioritization of the hypothesis library should be an ongoing process—hypotheses in the library get validated and closed, and new hypotheses get added, so establishing a regular cadence of reviewing the current list of proposed hypotheses keeps resources focused on validation work that is most likely to lead to meaningful business impact.

The fidelity with which we assess these criteria, however, should be commensurate with the size of impact and risk mitigation entailed in the action proposed. If we're considering closing down a struggling business unit, then a score of "high" is not nearly powerful enough. But the same logic applies: perhaps the criteria in this case falls into a "mega" category that demands the hypothesis must be tested with the most care and attentiveness.

---

[18] You could argue that the information on other products is useful to "identify latent demand" or "discover new products we should sell." Perhaps that is useful, but it doesn't enable us to make the decision at hand. It instead introduces new questions to answer that may not be top priority. In fact, the tendency for insights to create more problems than they solve can serve to slow decision-making down by introducing questions that seem more urgent than they are. We fail to appreciate the analyst's ability to set the agenda—on nearly any topic they may desire—by introducing off-topic insights. We also fail to appreciate our own ability as leaders to ask the right questions, especially when they didn't "come from an exploratory analysis of the data."

Tracking Hypotheses Through Their Life Cycle

Identifying, capturing, and prioritizing hypotheses just gets us to the starting line. To *realize* value from hypotheses, we have to do the actual work of validation. That's the subject of the next three chapters. But as that validation work progresses, the hypothesis library can continue to be a useful tool for tracking the progress of that validation work. Ideally, multiple hypotheses are in the process of being validated at any given time.

Consider some additional fields to include in the hypothesis library:

Status—Options can include Proposed, Accepted, In Work, Completed, Canceled.

Validation Approach—Selection of the high-level techniques available to the organization for validation: anecdotal, descriptive, scientific (see Chapters 7 through 9).

Link to Details—once a hypothesis is being validated, there will be a range of documents (or "artifacts"); this is where we can provide a link to where those documents are housed.

Validation Result—Whether the hypothesis was successfully validated: Yes, No.

Validation Completion Date—When the validation work was done, in date format (i.e., YYYY-MM-DD).

Action Planned—What the action suggested by the hypothesis validation exercise is (e.g., offer coupons for $10 to customers).

Action Owner—Name (and contact information) for the person who is accountable for making sure the action happens.

Action Date—When the action was completed (or scheduled to be completed), in date format (i.e., YYYY-MM-DD).

Action Results—If an action was planned, were there measurable results from the action?[19]

Wow! That's a lot of additional fields in the hypothesis library! This makes sense, as the process of validating a hypothesis can be thought of as a mini project. Show this list to any project manager, and they will vigorously

---

[19] This may seem obvious, but the results of actions are not always directly measurable. Depending on the scale and import of the action, conducting a performance measurement exercise—Chapter 5—is the best way to identify if the results delivered are what was expected.

nod their heads (and, likely, propose adding *additional* fields based on the specifics of your organization).

SUMMARY

Hypothesis validation is a decision support tool. Its goal is to reduce uncertainty around decisions that are being made now and in the future. Before validating any hypotheses, though, we need to do two things:

Clearly articulate each hypothesis. A hypothesis starts with an *idea* (*not* with data, although seeing some data on a report or in an analysis might have sparked the idea) and should have the potential to lead to an action. A helpful way to ensure this is to restructure (through careful thought) any question or idea into a simple and consistent structure: "We believe *[some idea]* because *[some evidence or observation]*. If we are right, we will *[take some action]*."

Catalog and prioritize hypotheses on an ongoing basis. As much as we like to think that our brains are thoroughly reliable vessels for retaining our ideas, in practice they are embarrassingly leaky sieves. Plus, hypotheses stored only in the memory of one person cannot be easily combined with the hypotheses of others. A *hypothesis library* is simply a list of identified hypotheses to which multiple team members can contribute. The core structure is that of the hypothesis framing described earlier, but it can then be used to quickly assess hypotheses on different criteria, such as the strength of supporting evidence for the hypothesis, the alignment of the hypothesis with business goals, and the expected level of effort to validate the hypothesis. This, in turn, provides a jumping off point for identifying which hypotheses are most worth validating in the near term.

These two aspects of hypothesis validation—clearly articulating them and then cataloging and prioritizing them—are the foundation of shifting an organization to the effective and efficient validation of hypotheses, but they're not the validation work itself. That is the topic of the next three chapters.

MEASURE THIS CHAPTER

And now, it's once again time to contribute to the performance measurement of this book by visiting https://analyticstrw.com and answering the two-question survey for this chapter.

We believe that most readers will take a couple of minutes to do this at the end of each chapter because anyone who is reading this book is definitionally a high quality and detail-oriented human being. If we are right, we will use the existence of the results as evidence with as many audiences as we can that performance measurement can be well and meaningfully done even on something as seemingly tricky as measuring the performance of a book.

Hypothesis Validation with New Evidence

In the last chapter, we focused on how to articulate, organize, and prioritize hypotheses. In this chapter and the next two chapters, we'll dig into the techniques we can use to validate them and the various considerations around those techniques.

The first step is determining if *new evidence* is actually *needed* to validate the hypothesis. This is determined by answering three questions:

- What evidence do we already have?
- How strongly does that evidence alone already validate the hypothesis?
- How high are the stakes regarding the decision that the validation of the hypothesis is intended to inform?

By way of a silly (if deadly!) example, consider parachutes. We've never scientifically tested whether parachutes reduce the probability of death for skydivers,[1] but we're pretty darn sure they work:

> *I believe wearing a parachute will reduce the probability I expire after my first skydive because parachutes decrease the speed at which I may crash into the earth, they've been used by almost everyone intentionally jumping out of an airplane ever since people started jumping out of airplanes, and because almost no one who hasn't worn one has lived to tell their story the next day. If I'm right, I will wear a parachute when I jump out of an airplane.*

Knowing whether parachutes are effective is a mission-critical piece of information for anyone who plans to jump out of an airplane in flight. Do we need to validate this hypothesis? Testing whether they are effective wouldn't take much effort, either. We could simply randomly assign some skydivers to receive parachutes and some to *not* receive parachutes during an already-booked skydiving trip. We would then relieve the assigned skydivers of their parachutes, proceed with the trip, and take the pulse of everyone who completes the trip from the airplane to the ground—tallying up the results based on whether or not the individual was wearing a parachute. Easy-peasy! But also...untenable.

---

[1] Smith, G.C.S. and Pell, J.P. (2003). Parachute use to prevent death and major trauma related to gravitational challenge: Systematic review of randomised controlled trials. *BMJ* 327(7429), pp. 1459–1461.

Obviously, no one in their right mind would ever seek to scientifically validate this hypothesis. But *why* wouldn't they? The answer gets to the core of hypothesis validation: we need information to make the best decisions, but our *ability* to gather information is constrained by the time, investment, and, in this case, ethical considerations under which we can gather it. In economics, we call this a *constrained optimization* problem. If we could, we would take all the time we need, spend all the money we need, *and* ignore any and all ethical considerations if all we cared about was getting as "right" an answer as possible. In reality, we don't have unlimited time or money, and we *do* have a conscience! So, we have to make decisions within a set of pragmatic constraints.

HYPOTHESES ALREADY HAVE VALIDATING INFORMATION IN THEM

Hypotheses themselves are informative. In our skydiving example, we already have information that 99.999% of people would consider more than sufficient to support validation. In fact, we can show directly where this information is coming from in our well-articulated hypothesis. Recall that three things compose a well-articulated hypothesis: the assumption, the theory, and the action. The skydiving hypothesis already contains information in each of its three components:

- **Tentative Assumption:** We know this is an important hypothesis because the implication is that the user won't survive without it.
- **Theory:** We know intuitively that if we fall to the earth from a thousand feet up, without any protection, we will decelerate from terminal velocity when we reach the ground at a rate that would be, well, terminal. This information is baked into our DNA. The other anecdotes are just icing on the cake.
- **Action:** There's no world in which we wouldn't wear a parachute when skydiving.

The *strength of the theory* (which, if you recall, is a dimension on which we suggest scoring hypotheses in our hypothesis library) is, in this case, what drives the certainty. For the sake of argument, let's say this information gets us 99% of the way to deciding we will wear a parachute (we're 99% certain, in other words). That suggests we only need 1 more percentage point of information to get to 100%. To give us 1%, we need only a small amount of evidence.[2] Alternatively, we could invert the hypothesis:

> *I **believe** wearing a parachute will increase the probability I expire after my first skydive **because** parachutes are difficult to use, they may not deploy, and there's always a chance a flying superhero rockets to my rescue. **If I'm right**, I will not wear a parachute.*

The information in this inverted hypothesis gets us, let's say, about 1% of the way to deciding we *will not* wear a parachute. We would need the most extensive and conclusive evidence possible to get us the rest of the way. We're not even sure we would ever believe it if ever a "convincing" study were published.[3]

The ideal method of hypothesis validation we choose should produce a level of evidence that is commensurate with:

- the level of support we already have for the tentative assumption we've made, and
- the significance of the action to be taken.

If we have little information, and the action is significant, our hypothesis validation method must generate high-quality, precise evidence regarding its veracity; if we have a lot of information already, or if the action is insignificant, we need less evidence and can use a lighter-weight validation method.

100% CERTAINTY IS NEVER ACHIEVABLE

As human beings, we crave certainty. As non-omnipotent beings, we cannot have it. We can get *close*, but even in the absolutely-most-close-to-a-guarantee-as-possible situation, there is no guarantee. Our skydiving example is

---

[2] Many people confuse this idea of 99% certainty or "99% confidence" with the concept of confidence levels in statistics, saying that the statistics say we are "99% confident," or "95% confident." This is an inappropriate malapropism. When we use a 95% confidence interval, we are actually saying something else: we are saying that based on previous data, we believe 95% of the outcomes we could observe will occur within that range. Same for 95%, 80%, and so on. We're doing our best to avoid digging too deeply into the subtle, but important, semantics that exist throughout statistics in this book, but this one warranted at least a footnote.

[3] We would also immediately file an ethics complaint with The Hague.

illustrative: while we can be *nearly* certain that, if we jumped from an airplane without a parachute, we would perish, there are documented cases of parachutes failing to open and, for one reason or another, the jumper living to tell the tale.

In business, it's rare to even get close to the 99% + certainty that we had with our parachute example. Even worse, in general, there are diminishing returns when it comes to the incremental cost for each step we take closer to (but never reaching) absolute certainty. Beyond the fact that it's not *possible* to achieve 100% certainty, there are many cases where it's not really *necessary* to dramatically reduce the uncertainty in a decision: less important hypotheses are less risky, which implies the downside risk of making the wrong decision is limited.

Recall two of the dimensions on which we scored our well-articulated hypotheses in Chapter 6. One was **Alignment to Business Goals.** If a hypothesis *is not* aligned to business goals, then it *is not* an urgent hypothesis for which a decision must be rendered right now. If a hypothesis *is* aligned to business goals, it *is* one that is worth validating with some level of urgency. Some hypotheses may be more urgent to validate than others because of the impending risks of delaying the decision. The more urgent the hypothesis, the fewer options (techniques) we have to reduce our uncertainty: some techniques require time that is simply not possible or feasible.

For instance, when hurricane Katrina hit New Orleans in August 2005, FEMA and the federal government were required to leap into action immediately to mitigate the risk of death and further destruction. (Many viewed their response as too slow and insufficient to solve the problems that New Orleanians were suffering.) Decision-making and actionability were of the utmost urgency, and therefore, the methodologies the leaders could use to collect and validate hypotheses for interventions were limited to those that could produce answers—or, at least, reduce uncertainty as much as possible—in a very short period; the leaders could not bring in a bunch of scientists to run a randomized control trial as to how to most efficiently allocate resources to rehouse people whose homes have been destroyed. This prompted debate among policymaker circles on how resources should be spent by the federal government to address the problem, without full information.

The other dimension for scoring a proposed hypothesis in Chapter 6 was **Level of Effort:** How much effort (time, cost) is needed to validate the hypothesis? Sometimes, we're just too constrained to be able to invest in the development of new evidence to reduce our uncertainty as much as we would like to in a perfect world. In *many* cases it is prohibitively expensive to conduct a controlled experiment—the "gold standard" of evidence collection that enables us to make strong causal inferences and validate hypotheses powerfully (we'll explore controlled experimentation later in this chapter and then much more thoroughly in Chapter 9). For example, running a controlled experiment to validate the impact of advertising could require the deployment of a minimum television spend of $75,000 per experiment due to minimum vendor spend requirements, and that may consume the entire media budget for the campaign.

The general point is that we must select a validation methodology that enables us to produce enough evidence to meaningfully inform the decision at hand while staying within several different constraints. With that in mind, we'll dive into three general classes of information that can be produced by hypothesis validation methodologies in our pursuit of good decisions.

METHODOLOGIES FOR VALIDATING HYPOTHESES

To validate a hypothesis, we need new information, and that new information can be categorized into three forms: anecdotal evidence, descriptive evidence, and scientific evidence. We then add that new information to the information we already articulated during the formation of our hypothesis.[4] If the new information gives us enough confidence to take the action the hypothesis implies, we do so. If it doesn't, we don't.

There are many ways to gather the new information required to validate a hypothesis. Or in other words, there are many ways to elicit evidence that our tentative assumption has merit. But not all of these ways produce evidence powerful enough to justify the investment we might make—or a risk we might take—in changing something.

For "little" questions—low stakes, small impact, easily reversible ones—we may not need very strong evidence. But for existential questions, we want to be as confident as possible that we've got the right answer. We call this concept the *ladder of evidence*: What information would we need to see to convince us that we should take the action we articulated in our well-formed hypothesis? The ladder of evidence has three main categories: anecdotal, descriptive, and scientific. In that order, each category provides increasingly powerful evidence.

---

[4] The operating term here is "new" information. The information we gather must enable us to learn something new related to the tentative assumption we've made.

Anecdotal Evidence

The first category of evidence is **anecdotal evidence**, and it is collected casually or, at least, nonsystematically:

- Informal conversations with several of our customers asking them what their experience was and how our product could be better.
- Asking coworkers who we consider experts in the topic area of the hypothesis what they think.
- Studies or surveys that are summarized in magazines, newspapers, and other published materials in which ideas or statistics are quoted that support the hypothesis at hand.

We know what anecdotes are, but we don't necessarily stop and think what they represent in an analytics context, which is *evidence*, albeit *weak* evidence, that supports or refutes an idea (hypothesis). Anecdotal evidence is a primary means through which we, in business and life, implicitly provide "proof." For example, when we include testimonials or quotes in our PowerPoint decks to "prove" that the work we do is useful and trusted, we are providing our audience with anecdotal evidence. In its early stages, user experience and qualitative research often produces results in the form of anecdotal evidence—six to eight users who participate in a usability study for a new website design, for instance. When our teenager quotes a report that shows how lucrative being a professional online gamer can be, she is providing anecdotal evidence in the hopes that we will use it to a validate a hypothesis we likely did not have: "I believe that my daughter should spend more time doing online gaming instead of her schoolwork because this could be a lucrative full-time profession for her, but only if she plays enough to become a top-tier player. If I am right, I will encourage her to drop out of school to pursue gaming as her vocation."

At a high level, anecdotal evidence tends to fall in one of two categories:

- **Personal observation**—evidence we personally collected through observation (listened in on a handful of calls in our call center, asked a neighbor their opinion on a product prototype, personally went through the registration process on our own website and noted steps that seemed confusing, etc.).
- **Secondary research**—data that others have collected, analyzed, and summarized (in an article or a blog post or an academic paper), but which is relevant evidence for the hypothesis that we are validating.[5]

We collect and employ anecdotal evidence constantly, and we're certainly not going to make a case that we should stop doing so! But it's worth understanding both the strengths and the weaknesses of this evidence that resides on the lowest rung of our evidence ladder.

Strengths of Anecdotal Evidence

Anecdotal evidence is often inexpensive to collect, and it can provide a quick read on the validity of the hypothesis at hand. As such, it can be fantastic for the consideration of a less risky hypothesis because we may already have strong intuition as to why we should take the action, or because we have nothing to lose in trying it out.

Anecdotal evidence can also provide rich intuition about the lived experiences of the individuals our decision will affect. We hear too often of CEOs who have fallen out of touch with their customers because they are hidden

---

[5]This type of formal research is still considered "anecdotal" because it is "summarized" *by someone else*. It is rare for someone else's research to have addressed the *exact* scenario that is the focus of our hypothesis, and aside from thoroughly written and vetted academic or scientific papers, many relevant assumptions and decisions made during the conducting of that research are unknowable. While it feels rigorous to point to a statistic ("Less than half of data and analytics (D&A) leaders (44%) reported that their team is effective in providing value to their organization, according to a new Gartner, Inc. survey."), the results are an anecdote—one bit of research, conducted with unknown motivations, with limited information available as to the match for the hypothesis at hand.

behind layers of management and dashboards and who make bad business decisions that their customers reject accordingly; we also hear too often of the analyst who conducts a flawless statistical analysis—with the latest machine learning firepower—only to realize that the metrics on which they based that analysis were fundamentally flawed. Anecdotal evidence can help to steel decision-making processing against these gaps.

One of our clients shared a story from when he had been recently minted as an analytics vice president. He had spent the better part of a quarter working on an analysis of customer ratings given to the company's sales representatives as part of his first big report. The client had never examined the underlying data linked to the ratings, which contained narrative accounts of customer experiences, and he trusted the rating scores to accurately represent the customer experiences. Just before the client walked into a presentation with the CEO, he was in the antechamber discussing the results of the study with the sales vice president, who told him he had seen the customer ratings linked to the customer reviews during his performance reviews: the customers frequently accidentally reversed their responses on the rating scale, sometimes selecting "1/5" for excellent service instead of "5/5." This essentially undermined the entire analysis, resulting in the client cutting the metric from the deck on short notice. But the CEO still got the pre-read and was looking forward to discussing the results. Yikes!

Because anecdotal evidence is often both low cost and quick to collect, it can also be a useful "sanity check" on evidence gathered elsewhere—the statistical analysis of customer calls to the call center that suggests that customers are increasingly satisfied with their experience with the brand when they have to call back at least three times to get their issue resolved doesn't square at all with what the call center supervisors report (anecdotal evidence) is the case. This anecdotal evidence could trigger a review of the methodology and approach that was used in the statistical analysis, likely uncovering an error. Saved by the anecdote!

Weaknesses of Anecdotal Evidence

Relying *only* on anecdotal information, though, can be risky. Remember, it is the form of evidence that is on the lowest rung of our evidence latter and, as such, provides the weakest form of evidence when validating a hypothesis. When we decide to pursue the action associated with a hypothesis based on anecdotal evidence, we tacitly assume that the anecdote(s) we reviewed are representative generally of the things—the customers, coworkers, products, etc.—that would be influenced by our action, which may...or may *not*...be the case!

In particular, the assumption that data are representative of the broader group when they are not can be problematic if we decide to take significant—high stakes or expensive or risky—action based on just a few anecdotes. For example, if one day, we are walking down the hall and our coworkers Michael and Catherine are complaining about the new HR software that was released, we may discover new information that helps us to validate our hypothesis that the HR software has changed employee satisfaction (in this case, employee satisfaction has decreased since the new software was deployed). But it is also possible that Michael and Catherine are historically disgruntled employees who would have likely never been satisfied with *any* change that we might have made. In this case, we have selected a biased sample of the individuals to be influenced by the action we would take upon validating the hypothesis.

It is also possible that Michael and Catherine are simply grumpy *today* because they discovered earlier this morning that the snack room was no longer going to stock their favorite brand of granola bars. Michael and Catherine may historically be very pleased employees, perfectly representative of the employee pool, but due to the vagaries of day-to-day discomfort, may provide us with biased anecdotes in that moment.

Anecdotal evidence can also be biased by our own interpretations of the data we collect. For instance, if we were the grumpy ones on that day that we passed Michael and Catherine and heard them discussing the new HR software, they may have simply been discussing the facts of the change in a neutral way, and it was our own disposition at the time that interpreted their overheard remarks—anecdotal evidence—as being negative.

In short, anecdotal evidence can be biased and misrepresentative. If the evidence is biased, then it is possible the hypothesis will be inappropriately validated—or invalidated—leading to poor judgments (especially in the case of highly impactful hypotheses). Even with the greatest care, gaffs will occur. When they're identified, proceed with extreme caution. It's painful, but sometimes the best course of action is to toss out that aspect of the research. Or if not, at least recognize the degree to which it has introduced additional uncertainty in the validation of the hypothesis. That may be an uncomfortably high degree!

Descriptive Evidence

The second category of evidence is **descriptive evidence**, which is data that have been collected methodically and quantitatively. In many ways, it is just anecdotal evidence, but systemically organized and at a greater scale. This type of evidence is one rung higher on our evidence ladder than anecdotal evidence, which means it generally provides strong*er* evidence for the validation (or invalidation) of a hypothesis. But it's the middle rung. The evidence it provides is still weaker than *scientific* evidence.

One form of descriptive evidence is *primary research*, which, in many ways, is what happens if anecdotal evidence is rigorously extended to the point that the "anecdotal" qualifier no longer applies—rather than casually asking a handful of individuals for their thoughts on a topic, ask several hundred or several thousand people who are a representative sample of the "population of interest" a carefully worded and structured set of questions through a survey or through one-on-one interviews.

Another form of descriptive evidence is data that we have collected at some reasonable scale within systems that we own or to which we have direct access—digital analytics data that capture the behavior of users of our website and mobile app, profile and activity history of customers and prospects that is captured in our customer relationship management (CRM) system, call details and disposition information from our call center management system, product and inventory details from our enterprise resource planning (ERP) system, and so on.

The breadth and depth of descriptive evidence sources is, well, very broad and very deep!

Strengths of Descriptive Evidence

You will notice that, as the ladder of evidence increments, the number of units available for our analysis usually increases.[6] Anecdotal analysis includes one, or a handful, of observations, whereas descriptive evidence includes a larger number of observations.

When we move to descriptive evidence, we have collected a greater number of anecdotes that we hope are more representative of the individuals who would be influenced by our action. We also assume that our interpretation of the anecdote is not biased for any individual anecdote. For instance, we assume that when we read an anecdote from Meredith, who was quite displeased with the service we provided to her, we do not discount Meredith's feedback because we personally know that she is grumpy about all service that she receives. When we pursue an action based on descriptive evidence, we have committed to equally applying judgment across any anecdote that has been received in a systematic way. This reduces the level of bias that may be introduced on any individual observation if we are fair in the application of our scoring process.

In fact, the key pitfalls present in the creation of evidence can be placed under an umbrella of "reducing bias." Research inherently involves

---

[6]This is not, however, always the case. An analysis producing scientific evidence, which we discuss in the next section, may rely on fewer units than a comparable analysis producing descriptive evidence. The scientific analysis will still likely provide more powerful information for decision-making owing to its ability to systematically reduce bias in the results.

evaluating some subset of a population and then trying to make inferences (draw accurate conclusions) *about* that population. There will almost always be some sort of bias in that process, so it's key to be aware of the different sources of bias and then strive to reduce them. With descriptive evidence, we generally see less bias than we do in anecdotal evidence simply because we have more units available to represent the population for which we are trying to make inferences.[7]

Weaknesses of Descriptive Evidence

We have a tendency—with *all* forms of data—to think that there is a clear and singular path to analyze, interpret, and summarize the results. This is rarely the case.

Bias Induced by Analysis Decisions

One public example—not validating a hypothesis (presumably), but using research to make an advertising claim—comes from a poster campaign promoting Colgate toothpaste back in 2007. The poster included the statement: "More than 80% of Dentists recommend Colgate" and "Colgate, used and recommended by most dentists." Does this seem like dentists have a strong preference for Colgate? The sneaky part here is that, in the research, the question about toothpaste recommendations was a *multi-select* question. Dentists could select *multiple* toothpastes. So, the statements were true, but they were also misleading.[8]

Outliers and Missing Data

Another common decision point when analyzing historical data has to do with how to handle outliers and missing data:

- **Outliers.** For example, a survey asked 1,000 people to estimate how much additional they would pay for a given product feature. Of the respondents,

---

[7] It is worth noting here that descriptive evidence can be induced to contain greater bias than anecdotal evidence when the researcher makes analysis decisions that mask the truth. This is because at smaller scale, anecdotal evidence can be examined on a case-by-case basis, and the raw data can be objectively interpreted by any number of other researchers. In descriptive analysis, it is nearly always infeasible to examine every record, and the researcher may decide to showcase certain subsets of records that support their argument. This bias is not intrinsic in the process *per se*; rather, it is introduced by the researcher.

[8] See: https://marketinglaw.osborneclarke.com/retailing/colgates-80-of-dentists-reco mmend-claim-under-fire/.

995 provided an answer between $0 and $50. The other five answered: $250, $500, $1,000, $1,500, and $10,000. Should those five higher answers be included in a summary of how much respondents would pay? The average without them was $12.70. The average *with* them was $25.88! There is no "right" answer here.[9] A combination of a deeper exploration of those five respondents, combined with a judgment call, will dictate the "right" way to handle these outliers.

- **Missing data.** For example, a survey asked 1,000 people about their experiences with a brand. As a "screener question," the survey asks for the respondent's household income. One quarter of the respondents left that question blank. Should those respondents be included in the overall analysis of the survey? The answer is: it depends. It's possible that the respondents who left that question blank skew higher or lower than those who answered the question. Omitting those respondents may bias the conclusions of the research! It may be appropriate to include these respondents in some aspects of the analysis and exclude them in others. A combination of judgment calls and application of statistical techniques is called for. Alas!

Analysis Paralysis

"Analysis paralysis" is a real thing: it is easy to get caught up with the curse of knowledge when it comes to research and begin second-guessing the validity of any results that use it. That is the wrong response! Two healthier—and less despair inducing—reactions are simply this:

- Recognize that all analysis brings a level of uncertainty along with it.
- That uncertainty can't be eliminated, but an informed eye can identify the biggest sources of that uncertainty and, in some cases, reduce it with a bit of extra care.

We hear a lot about Type I and Type II errors in analytics circles. Type I errors are when we choose to do something that we shouldn't have (a false positive). Type II errors are when we choose *not* to do something that we should have (a false negative). Both types of errors can result in false insights that are harmful to the business.

---

[9] To prevent our Statisticians Guild cards from being revoked, we will point out that this is one of the reasons that statisticians often prefer the median over the mean. In this example, the median without the five outliers was $12. The median *with* the five outliers was...also $12. This pedantry is beside the point of our example, though.

Ironically, the more analysis you do, the more likely it is that you will commit a statistical error *just* by fact that you have done more analysis.

Type I errors are committed far more often than most realize. It turns out that, even if there is no true relationship between the "Xs" and "Ys" we're studying, the probability that at least one of the relationships proves statistically significant rises as the number of tests increases.

Suppose a business analyst assesses whether each of 20 variables available in the company data lake are related to customer satisfaction. So the analyst may look at whether the quality of the product is related to customer satisfaction, whether customer tenure is related to customer satisfaction, and 18 other variables. For the sake of illustration, suppose that all of these factors are entirely uncorrelated with one another and that the relationship between them and customer satisfaction is exactly 0 for everyone. Believe it or not, the probability that the analyst will find that at least one of those variables has a statistically significant relationship to customer satisfaction is 64.2%![10]

This may seem like it's starting to get into advanced statistics. And, well, it is, but we can try to shortcut our way around that by honing in on two key ideas:

- The *intuition* here is something that we absolutely can and should work to develop: the more digging into the data we do looking for relationships between variables, the more likely we will be to find a relationship that is not "real." This is something of a paradox because we also *need* to dig into the data—often quite a bit—to find relationships that *are* real (and useful).
- Statisticians (or data scientists, or analysts with some grounding in statistics, or economists, or psychologists) have developed both the intuition *and* the mathematical techniques that we have relegated to a footnote here and periodically throughout this book. If we can meet them with our shared intuition, we will get along swimmingly and productively!

---

[10] Assuming each hypothesis test is run at an "alpha threshold" (i.e., target p-value, statistical notion of surprise often labeled contentiously as the "significance threshold") of 0.05, which is the default value for most statistical tests, the math is $1 - (1 - 0.05)^{20} = 0.642$. An easy way to adjust for this is an accounting trick called the Bonferroni correction. The Bonferroni correction simply divides the alpha threshold by the number of tests you've run. In this case, the corrected computation is $1 - (1 - 0.05 / 20)^{20} = 0.05$. Cool, right? No? We assure you, in certain circles it is, and that's not even because "Bonferroni" is a fun word to say!

Let's take one more swing at the "intuition" piece. Pretend that you have a top-of-the-line analytics machine. This machine is the *best* piece of equipment on the market when it comes to finding relationships between two variables. It's not perfect (remember: uncertainty will always exist; analytics and statistics fundamentally recognizes this reality). It's "only" 99% perfect. The machine does one specific task: when given any two variables, X and Y, it tells you if they are meaningfully related ("correlated" in stats-speak).

This is exciting!

We try it out by feeding the machine two variables as a test where we know the correct answer: the height of each of our employees by day and the maximum temperature that day. The Analytics Machine tells us that there is no meaningful relationship. Correct!

We then try another test where we also know the answer. We feed the machine the maximum temperature and the minimum temperature every day for the past year. This time, it responds that these two variables *are* meaningfully related. Again. It's correct!

To be thorough, we come up with 98 more tests for the machine where we *know* the correct answer, and we feed each one to it. The machine *almost* gets all of the tests right, but it gets *one* of the tests wrong. This is actually *expected*.[11]

We feel pretty good about the machine at this point, as it's given us 99 correct answers out of 100—that's A+ work! And this gives us an idea. We actually have 100 variables, and we want to look at every *pair* of variables within the data set and flag if there is or is not a meaningful relationship between any of those pairs. This is 4,950 comparisons (you can check the math if you'd like, or just trust us)! The machine doesn't care, though. That's the beauty of machines! You feed it these 4,950 comparisons and get back a mix of responses—some of the pairs are reported as having a meaningful relationship with each other, while others are not.

We do some quick math and realize that 49–50 of these responses are... wrong. We don't know which ones, though! If we homed in on any *specific* pair, there is a 99% chance that *it* has been correctly reported. If we simply try to brute force our way to insights by having the machine "analyze all the data," then we *know* there will be some "wrong" results returned.

---

[11] We're dropping back into a "note for the statistician" here to acknowledge that we are taking some shortcuts. We're working with an overall "accuracy" metric—not worrying about Type I vs. Type II errors—and we're treating the 99% as being something that would work out to exactly one error in every 100 observations. We're working on the *intuition* here without getting bogged down in the nuances. Yes. We agree. The nuances are important. Just not. Right. Now!

Even with all of the time in the world, and with all of the data in the world, the results we get are ultimately useless without structured thinking and discipline. This sort of thinking gives us the structure and discipline we need to get the most informative and useful results, and in Chapter 8, we will dive further into the structure and discipline needed when developing descriptive evidence.

Scientific Evidence

The third category of evidence is **scientific evidence,** which is produced by drawing strong conclusions from research designed or data collected *specifically* to test a hypothesis:

- We often make *broad inferences* about the entire population of our customers based on a smaller analysis of a sample of them because it is cost-prohibitive or infeasible to analyze the population. If we assume that the sample we analyze is a random sample of the population, then statistical principles enable us to draw definitive conclusions about the population from the sample. Using scientific methods, we can introduce design considerations that ensure the sample we analyze is a random sample of the entire population, but we often must do so at the outset of the design process rather than after the data have been collected.

- We often want to make definitive statements in the form of "X caused Y." We call these *causal* claims. These statements are useful to us because they help us to better understand what we can do to intervene in business situations to achieve the outcomes we desire. For example, if our sales numbers are decreasing, and we know our pricing is *causing* the sales numbers to decrease, then we can take definitive action to change our sales numbers by changing our price.

Scientific evidence is a special type of descriptive evidence. It is *like* descriptive evidence because it usually takes the same "consistent" tabular format, and the analysis required to produce it is conducted similarly. Scientific evidence is *different* from most descriptive evidence, however, because the researcher or analyst adds special assumptions during the analysis process that make the conclusions drawn from the descriptive evidence more powerful. These additional assumptions enable us to make generalized inferences from descriptive analyses.

Scientific analysis produces information that can generalize through *inferences* about the broader world. Scientific statistical analysis produces *inferential statistics* rather than *descriptive* statistics. That is to say, the statistics scientific analyses create apply beyond the scope of the specific data analyzed and may be used to make broad claims about what was, is, and will be. Results produced by descriptive analysis are constrained to the data analyzed and the procedure through which the researcher analyzed them.

This is not to say that scientific analysis produces a perfect and reliable result in every case. Rather, by following scientific procedures and making scientific assumptions, we get evidence that is of higher quality, therefore getting us closer to (but *never* fully achieving!) 100% certainty in our hypothesis validation process than descriptive evidence will.

Strengths of Scientific Evidence

Scientific evidence gives us a definitive, precise answer that generalizes to the situation about which we are hypothesizing. This increases the certainty with which we can act. In situations where we need as much certainty as possible, scientific evidence is our friend. The drawback, as we will discuss, is that scientific evidence can be expensive and time-consuming to produce. It can also require expertise that our team may not have, but fear not: in the following few chapters, we discuss some of the science-grade tweaks we can make in our descriptive analyses to upgrade the quality of the information we get from them.

Scientific analysis produces such strong evidence because it excludes *sources of bias* that can cause descriptive analysis to produce skewed results. Results can be *biased* upwardly or downwardly. When we have an upwardly biased estimate for a treatment intervention, it looks like the intervention is more effective than it actually is. For example, consider a business situation in which we might spend $2 million distributing mosquito nets to our workforce in a swampy area where it is very likely they will contract malaria from mosquito bites. If our analysis shows that workers who use mosquito nets are 10 times less likely to contract malaria, we will feel perfectly fine spending that $2 million. But if our analysis shows that people who use mosquito nets are just 1.1 times less likely to contract malaria, then we will probably feel less certain that spending $2 million on mosquito nets is the right choice, and we may choose to spend it on another intervention that is more effective, like anti-malaria medications.[12] Both effects are positive, but one effect is much larger than the other.

The situation gets even trickier when the effects we estimate are upwardly biased to the point that they look positive, when, in reality, they are negative. For example, imagine we have developed a drug that our analysis suggests slightly improves the probability a patient survives a particular form of cancer, when the drug actually decreases the probability that the patient survives, but bias in our methodology masked this reality. Because of a biased result, we would end up giving people a drug that we thought was helping them, when it was actually harmful.

Scientific analysis can remove major sources of bias, including selection bias and confounding bias, when done right.

Selection Bias

Selection bias is when the data we use in our validation are not representative of the overall population of interest. For instance, if we stood at the entry gate to a major league baseball stadium on game day and asked 500 people if they enjoyed watching baseball, we would get an overwhelming number of "Yes" responses. If we then used that data to make statements about the overall American population and their enjoyment of the sport, we would grossly miss the mark. That's because there was *bias* in who we *selected* for our data collection.

---

[12] Bias that positively affects the magnitude of our estimated impact will influence us to choose an inferior option. Bias that negatively affects the magnitude of our estimated impact will influence us to avoid a potentially superior option. Bias in the magnitude of an estimated effect, specified incorrectly, is why most Type I and Type II errors are committed.

While the baseball stadium survey is an obvious and extreme example, selection bias can sneak in more subtly and still be just as damning. For instance, consider a marketer who wants to validate a hypothesis about whether some new messaging would be appealing to their prospective customers. They add a survey to their website to ask some questions about the proposed new messaging, but that limits their research to people who are already aware of the brand (they're on the brand's website already) *and* who are willing to pause their browsing to respond to a survey (which may skew toward individuals who are already more loyal customers). There is a very real risk that selection bias will cause them to draw inaccurate conclusions.

Selection bias in business often also comes from a source called *survivorship bias*, in which the units we analyze today are only able to be analyzed because they lasted long enough to make it into our data set, whereas many units relevant for the true analysis we want to conduct didn't make it into a data set because of some attrition factor in the past. A common example in stock market analysis is the analysis of historical returns of companies in the S&P 500 today, which all have done well enough not to go bankrupt and which all have not yet been acquired by another company. If we are investigating what factors improve the operation of a company, we will not include any companies that went bankrupt due to poor factors in our analysis because none of the companies that are available for an analysis went bankrupt (they all "survived").[13]

The main way we get around selection bias when using scientific evidence is through random sampling from the population for which we want to make inferences. The beauty of random sampling is that a random variable is uncorrelated with any other variable that could influence the selection criteria of making it into the sample that we analyze. Therefore, when we have random sampling, we have

---

[13] An even more literal example of survivorship bias is an example from World War II that is likely at least somewhat apocryphal, but it does illustrate the point. Allied planes were getting shot down by the German military, so the Allied forces initiated a project to add reinforcement to the planes. The instincts of the military leadership, so the story goes (again, this is likely at least partly apocryphal), was to study the patterns of bullet holes on the returning planes and add reinforcing steel plates to the areas that tended to have the most holes. The mathematician Abraham Wald was part of the task force assigned to figure out the details, and he pointed out that the planes being studied were the ones that successfully *returned*. Presumably, the distribution of bullet holes across all planes would be fairly even, so the planes that were hit in places that caused them to fall from the sky were not part of the data they had to study. Therefore, the steel reinforcing plates should be added to the areas of the planes for which the returning planes did *not* have any bullet holes: the planes that were hit in those locations did not return. They did not "survive," and the initial analysis was, therefore, biased by not including them.

the mathematical ability to make inferences about the broader population from which the data were sampled, only by analyzing the sample. There are some pretty cool, but esoteric, mathematical theorems invoked here; if you would like to learn more about them, we encourage you to reach out to an expert.

If you were to analyze what factors drive companies to profitability in the first 20 years of the new century, you would probably see that things like smaller EBITDAs (earnings before interest, taxes, depreciation, and amortization) are counterintuitively related to outsized returns. In truth, it was the injection of cheap and large technology investments that drove the growth of the most successful companies during that time, and the companies that did not invest or did not have access to cheap capital folded or were acquired. Survivorship biases the insights we would draw without a true scientific analysis.

The same problem is endemic in customer analysis because often the customers who stuck with the company are the only ones who end up in the data being analyzed. And what's more, the data are usually being analyzed to better understand what causes customers distress so that executives can correct the problems. The distressed customers are no longer in the data set because they stopped buying the products due to that distress.

Random sampling is not a guaranteed mechanism for correcting this issue. The correction is, instead, to take a disciplined approach to defining the unit of analysis and the criteria for inclusion in the data set. We always want to make sure that all of the relevant units are included in our data set before analyzing it because the implicit conditional probabilities generated can be misleading.[14]

A good scientific analysis will correct for this by treating units that did not survive as comparable units for analysis, but with missing outcomes when observed. Therefore, a great many more companies who used to be in the S&P 500, or could have been in the S&P 500 today, will be included in the previous stocks analysis.

The question of how to analyze missing data, of course, is not the subject of this book. But the point stands: scientific evidence corrects for common oversights involved in analysis like selection and survivorship bias.

---

[14] A good example: it is more likely for a person to be killed by a cow than to be killed by a coyote. This would seem to suggest that humans should avoid cows more than coyotes. But the only reason this statistic is the case is because humans herd cattle and don't herd coyotes, bringing them into closer contact with potentially errant cows more often. The units that need to be included for a good analysis—cases in which humans were commonly in contact with herded coyotes—are not included. If we do not adjust for this in our analysis, we will draw the wrong conclusion. This is not an issue of random sampling; this is an issue of structured scientific thinking.

Confounding Bias

The principal source of bias that scientific analysis removes is *confounding bias*. In a nutshell, confounding can cause us to misattribute an explanation for why something happens. One of the classic examples here is an economist's investigation of the relationship between sales of ice cream and the rate of crime in a certain area. She finds a clear relationship between ice cream sales and crime rates, and as such, she draws the conclusion that there is some relationship between the two of them. Perhaps people become sad after being robbed, and then decide to buy ice cream to quell their sorrows. Perhaps criminals become hungry after committing a crime and decide to buy ice cream in order to satiate their appetites.

In reality, a common, unobserved variable confounds the relationship the economist studies: summertime. When it is hot outside and kids are out of school, they are more likely to buy ice cream, increasing ice cream sales. And when it is hotter outside and kids are out of school, they have more free time with which to commit petty crimes. This is a "spurious correlation"—a situation when two variables (ice cream sales and crime) *are* statistically relatable to each other (correlated) but can be presented in way that egregiously oversteps (spuriously so!).

We will discuss one of the most common sources of confounding bias— time and how to adjust for it—in the next chapter on descriptive analysis techniques. Yes, you heard that right: *time*. We are willing to bet 80% of the analyses you've seen, proving that two things are related to each other by plotting two lines increasing and decreasing together over time were fundamentally flawed. Stay tuned for Chapter 8!

But in many cases, it is impossible to control for confounding variables because it is often impossible to observe all the variables that could be related to the outcome we are analyzing, let alone perfectly articulate all of the relationships between them. Ronald Fisher, a venerated statistician, used to call this problem his "demon." Whenever he would conduct an analysis, no matter how he did it, the demon of confounding bias would creep into his results in the form of "unobserved heterogeneity."[15] In other words, things he could not control for, or did not measure, were inducing relationships between the interventions and outcomes in which he was interested.

It was for this exact concern that Fisher began systematically investigating the role of randomization in assignment to interventions. The field of randomized controlled trials (RCTs) today emerged largely because of this concern. RCTs are a group of techniques that go by many different names (A/B testing, matched market testing, clinical trials, field experiments, and more!), and short of splitting the world into multiple universes or developing time travel, they are the closest we can get to finding causal truths to inform our decisions. For the remainder of this book we will refer to RCTs as "controlled experiments." We're doing this because it's plain English, and if you're having a discussion with a colleague, regardless of their depth of statistical knowledge, they should have at least a basic idea of what you're talking about when you say, "controlled experimentation."

Controlled experimentation is known as the "gold standard" in scientific literature because it (usually) eliminates all other possible causes of a relationship, leaving just the relationship in question to which the researcher can attribute the effect. It does this by employing "random assignment." Random

---

[15] "Unobserved heterogeneity" is another one of those $10 phrases. Beyond being fun to say, though, and being a phrase that will give you instant cred with any statistician or econometrician, it's a relatively straightforward concept. Consider an analysis of a randomly selected pool of students from across the United States that assessed their race and their score on the SAT. Using just these two variables, there appears to be a clear relationship: black students score lower than white students. Confounding factors here are both the household income of the students and the quality of the education that each student received. These are *differences* in the underlying data ("heterogeneous factors") that were not "observed" (or, in this example, captured and considered). This *unobserved heterogeneity* contributed to a flawed interpretation of the data.

assignment is a shortcut that enables us to definitively exclude all other potential unobserved causes of the outcome, relative to the intervention of interest, because random variables are, by definition, uncorrelated with any other variable in the analysis. And if we assign units to the intervention when the random variable says to do so, then the intervention is also uncorrelated with any other variable in the analysis. Voila! We can now analyze the data without the need to worry about confounding bias.

If you're thinking, "Wait a minute. I intuitively understand why a controlled experiment works. Why did you have to go and introduce a bunch of fancy language—random assignment, intervention of interest, uncorrelated variables—into this? Now, I'm not so sure!" That's okay! Your intuition is correct, but it's useful to deepen that intuition. We consider these types of studies further in Chapter 9, on the production of scientific evidence through controlled experimentation, and it will be fun!

Causal Claims

Hypothesis validation often hinges on causation. Hypotheses can be ideas about a causal relationship between a controllable phenomenon and a desired outcome. Briefly, through this lens, following are the six hypothesis examples we used in Chapter 6:

- An easier out-of-the-box setup process for our product will *cause* an increase in customer satisfaction.
- Our hybrid work policy *causes* employee dissatisfaction.
- Offering a prize drawing for completing a website lead form will *cause* an increase in quality leads from the website.
- Redeploying our spend on Facebook advertising to another channel will *cause* an incremental lift in revenue.
- Robotic process automation will *cause* higher quality outcomes.
- Rural oncology clinics *are not causing* the best possible health outcomes.

Now that these examples are all framed as causal claims...don't you want the answers to them? Causal claims are the 400-pound gorillas of analytics because if you can answer them convincingly, you will have produced a truly insightful iota of knowledge that has expanded the boundaries of the organization's collective knowledge. Establishing and quantifying causal links is tricky and includes trade-offs. But you can do so through scientific analysis.

Weaknesses of Scientific Evidence

So why don't we just produce scientific evidence every time, if it corrects for all of these common issues that undermine hypothesis validation?

Well, scientific analysis can be quite expensive. Hiring analysts who are experienced in scientific analysis as full-time employees can sink a P&L, especially when there is a disconnect between the analyst's ability to explain why they need what they need and the manager's ability to provide it. One thing we see a lot is students who have been trained at the Master's and PhD level to conduct scientific analysis, who then enter industry under the supposition that everything will be just as easily packaged as it was during their coursework. This mismatch between expectations and reality can, when not corrected, result in a lot of interpersonal strife and lack of impactful results. We also see many students who graduate with experience in the latest and greatest machine learning techniques who struggled to explain them and their utility, justify their cost, or even apply them correctly to the problem at hand. In fact, most analyses do not require the latest and greatest machine learning and artificial intelligence tools, and what clients value is not a hammer looking for a nail, but the right instrument to achieve the right result.

Scientific analysis can also be expensive simply because the minimum spends required to conduct analysis at the appropriate level of statistical power can be high.[16] Television media testing at the media market level can require minimum spends of $75,000 or more per market, and this amount may consume the entire media budget before the test is even run.

Scientific analysis can be quite time-consuming. The point of a scientific analysis is usually to answer a precise question very well, in a way that can extrapolate to a number of general situations. The less precise the question gets, the more analysis and structured thinking it will require. In fact, scientific analysis is often entirely unequipped to answer very broad and unspecific questions generally. Consider the "theory of everything" in physics: it's been worked on for decades, and scientists still disagree as to when it is useful and how to apply it. In business, we do not have a timescale on the level of decades with which to make decisions. We usually have to make decisions urgently, in a few days or weeks.

Running controlled experiments can take weeks because it can take weeks for the design to acquire enough subjects to produce a statistically relevant result. For a large pharmaceutical client, for example, we observed that it took months to acquire the number of subjects we needed to test the advertising

---

[16] Statistical power is governed by the amount of information that can be gleaned from the number of units in an analysis. When units do not vary much on the outcome of study, then we need a larger sample size to claim that our hypothesis is statistically validated.

campaign for a specialty drug on a small group of physicians. In that case, the client had a few quarters of time to gather the data before making a larger media spend commitment. But sometimes, we just don't have that luxury of time.

MATCHING THE METHOD TO THE COSTS AND IMPORTANCE OF THE HYPOTHESIS

There are two sides to the equation of hypothesis validation. The first side is what costs and risks are associated with the action. In Chapter 6, we gave you a framework with which you can establish the high-level costs and risks associated with the hypothesis. The second side is the strength of the evidence that we can produce. In this chapter, we discussed the methods with which we can produce increasingly powerful evidence. The goal is to be able to match the hypothesis validation method we use to the rigor that is required for us to confidently be able to take the action articulated in the hypothesis.

Evidence   **Risk**

If our hypothesis suggests the action is that we should change the color of a button on our website, the investment required to make the change is a quick line of code that may cost us $10, and the risk is disrupting our one hundred monthly users who don't even buy anything, we do not need strong evidence to justify the change. On the other hand, if we're considering closing a business unit because it is not profitable, doing so would require an investment of $30 million, and it would risk the degradation of our brand (in addition to a public relations disaster), we would want to have powerful evidence that was the right decision.

Not all hypotheses need scientific evidence to be validated. In many cases, anecdotal or descriptive evidence will do just fine (of course, with a few of the conceptual tweaks that we point out in the following few chapters). But our hope is that, after reading this book, you will notice that you start to exert *scientific thinking* about your anecdotal and descriptive evidence more often. You can employee a critical eye in your use of anecdotal and descriptive evidence now that you are aware of some of the biases that creep into them.

As we covered in Chapter 3, the one way to eliminate uncertainty entirely is to develop the power of omniscience and play out multiple scenarios in parallel universes and compare the results. Since that's not practical, Table 7.1 outlines a useful "ladder" of causal evidence—three macro-level techniques, each with less ability to establish causality than the technique immediately above it.

TABLE 7.1 The Causal Evidence Ladder and When It's Needed

Technique	Strength of Evidence	Example
Scientific	High	Random assignment of different "treatments" to different "groups" and then measuring the difference in the results between the different groups for some metric of interest.
Descriptive	Medium	Using available data to estimate characteristics of a population *or* identifying relationships between variables that will continue to hold in data that has not yet been collected or generated.
Anecdotal	Low	A straw poll of our customers to figure out how often they use the user manual we include with our most popular product.

We mentioned causal questions in our section on scientific analysis. If we are asking a causal question, we need to have a scientific analysis. This is because it is only through the scientific techniques that we can achieve either the elimination of unobserved heterogeneity, or what we in science call "selection on observables," the conceptual ability to make causal inferences based only on the observed data that we have in the database. But if a descriptive analysis will suffice for our decision-making purposes, we should simply rephrase our question so that it doesn't imply causality.

SUMMARY

Hypothesis validation—a phrase that we, hopefully, have thoroughly burned into your psyche at this point—is how we use data to reduce uncertainty in our decision-making. Our decisions are based on causality—we have a desired outcome (effect) that we're hoping to achieve, and we want to make decisions to take actions that will lead to (cause) that effect. This is why we say that causality is at the root of effective hypothesis validation, although we also acknowledged that getting *strong evidence* of causality can be prohibitively expensive or not possible. In those cases, we fall back to *weaker evidence*, but even weak evidence can reduce uncertainty!

While it is as true as it is alliterative to note that "correlation is not causation," we've found this to be such a surface-level statement that many organizations know the phrase but fail to apply it. The ladder of evidence framework provides a broader intuition about the utility of analysis in any hypothesis validation exercise.

In the next two chapters, we will do a deeper exploration of descriptive evidence (Chapter 8) and scientific evidence (Chapter 9). We are not devoting a chapter to anecdotal evidence because there isn't a whole lot more that can be said beyond what we covered in this chapter: we use it all the time, and that's okay, but it's critical that we recognize it for what it is, including that, while it *is* "evidence," it is *weak evidence.*

MEASURE THIS CHAPTER

And now, it's once again time to contribute to the performance measurement of this book by visiting https://analyticstrw.com and answering the two-question survey for this chapter. We've worked hard to ensure that we've minimized the bias in our approach for collecting this data. (There might be a little survivorship bias at play...but hey, *you're* still reading!)

CHAPTER 8

Descriptive Evidence:
Pitfalls and Solutions

Descriptive evidence typically comes from the analysis of historical data. We find data sets ripe for analysis in our enterprise data lakes, in our CRM and point-of-sale and ERP and HR systems, in the Excel spreadsheets that we have created by organizing the information we gather, and in publicly accessible data sets that we can download from the government and other sources online. We use a subset of this data for performance measurement, as we discussed in Chapter 5, but the totality of collected and managed data is both broader and deeper than the aggregated rollups that we use for tracking KPIs against their targets, which means this data can be a mechanism for validating hypotheses on short notice.

In fact, the descriptive analysis of already-collected data is the workhorse of most analytics teams, which are under pressure to produce insights for urgent priorities and without much resourcing. In a business context, the main benefits of historical data analysis are twofold:

The data have already been collected—by definition, there is no need to *plan* or *instrument* any additional data collection because the data already exists!

The hypothesis validation work can be done immediately—since the data already exist, they can be analyzed at any point; there is no "wait for the experiment to run and then analyze the resulting data" as is the case with a controlled experiment.

For these reasons, many organizations devote all—or virtually all—of their hypothesis validation efforts to analysis of historical data. While this will continue to be the reality (and we are by no means saying that this shouldn't happen), it's important to recognize the trade-offs inherent in this sort of analysis. Simply "charting the data and eyeballing an interpretation" without considering the biases and limitations of descriptive analysis is like subsisting on a diet of Snickers bars—quick and enjoyable in the moment, perhaps, but not effective (and downright counterproductive) over time!

HISTORICAL DATA ANALYSIS GONE WRONG

To illustrate, let's take an example based loosely on a real-world scenario that the authors encountered with a client. The marketing team was active with their posting on various social media channels, and they thought that their social media activity was probably driving orders of their products, although they could not directly link that activity to orders.

They plotted both metrics over time as shown in Figure 8.1.

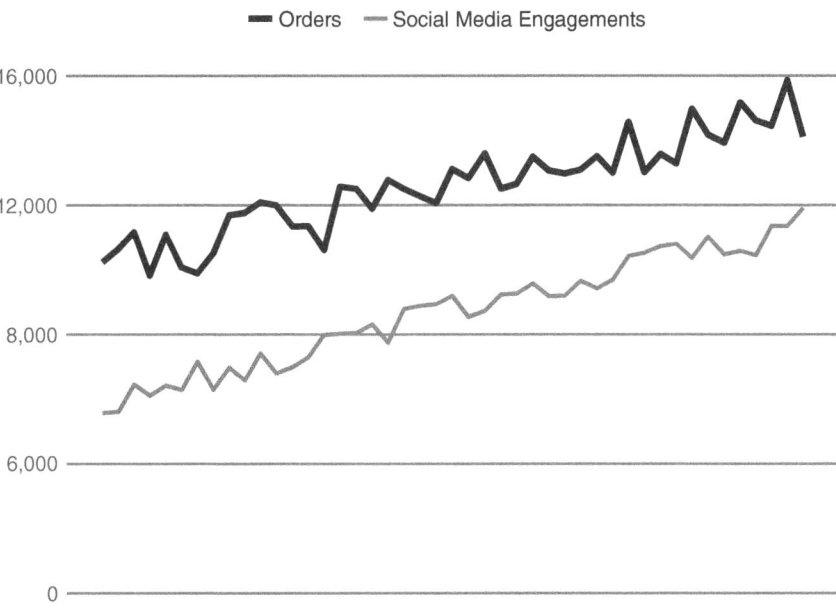

FIGURE 8.1   Social media engagements and orders over time

What is your initial reaction to this data? It might be like theirs: "Wow! It certainly looks like social media engagements are driving orders!" But before jumping to that conclusion, the team decided to take the exact same data and look at it as a scatterplot instead—each day would use the **Social Media Engagements** value for *x* and the **Orders** for the day as *y*. They then drew a line-of-best-fit for the data to the chart to model the relationship between the two variables. The resulting plot is shown in Figure 8.2.

The resulting plot is not surprising. But since scatterplots are a good way to look at the correlation between two metrics, they also included the *coefficient of determination*, which you've likely encountered here and there by its more commonly used name: R^2. Without going into too much detail, R^2 varies from 0—*no* relationship between the two metrics—to 1—a *perfect* relationship between the two metrics (the dots would line up on a perfectly straight line). An R^2 of 0.79 is considered *high* in a business analytics context.[1]

---

[1]We've oversimplified R-squared here. Technically, the coefficient of determination must be computed given a regression model, which may have *more* than two variables involved. But for the purposes of this book and the points we're making, we'll let it slide.

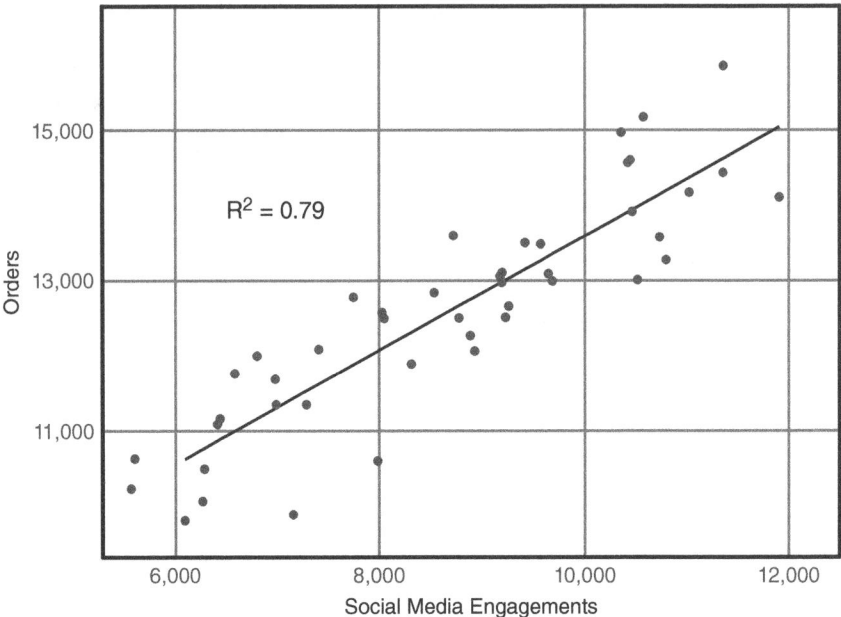

FIGURE 8.2 A scatterplot of social media engagements and orders

So, was the team's theory correct?

Well...no!

There were two fundamental flaws with their conclusion:

Correlation is not causation—we suspect you spotted this one. It's a biggie! Just because two metrics move in the same direction doesn't mean that one is causing the other.

The metrics aren't actually correlated with each other once you account for the effect of time—this is the trickier one, but it requires the application of a simple statistical technique to reveal the lack of correlation.

Because the first issue is fairly obvious, let's dig into the second one. In the analysis of "time-series data" (data that occurs *over time*—a common type of data in many business contexts), there are a lot of caveats and considerations. We're not going to go deeply into those, but we'll explain one of them. Consider that *if* these two metrics are correlated, then it's not so much that "when one is high, the other is high" and "when one is low, the other is low," which is what we've just demonstrated. Rather, if they're *truly* correlated with each other, then a slightly different framing is in order: when one metric *increases*, the other metric should *increase proportionally*, and when one metric *decreases*, the other metric should *decrease proportionally* as well. To check if this is the case, we can use an econometric technique called "first differences," which simply looks at the *change* in each metric from day to day compared to the *change* in the other metric from day to day. (Feel free to read those last two sentences again—it's a simple and intuitive idea, but you will be forgiven if it takes a beat to process it.)

If we derive that data and create a scatterplot of those *changes* (the "first differences"), the resulting chart is quite different, as shown in Figure 8.3.

The R^2 for the relationship between these two easily derived metrics is 0.00!

The interpretation of the result is simply this: while both metrics are generally trending upward *over time*, they do not actually appear to be changing *with each other*. On days when social media engagement increases, it turns out that orders do not increase, and vice versa. We don't even have to go to the

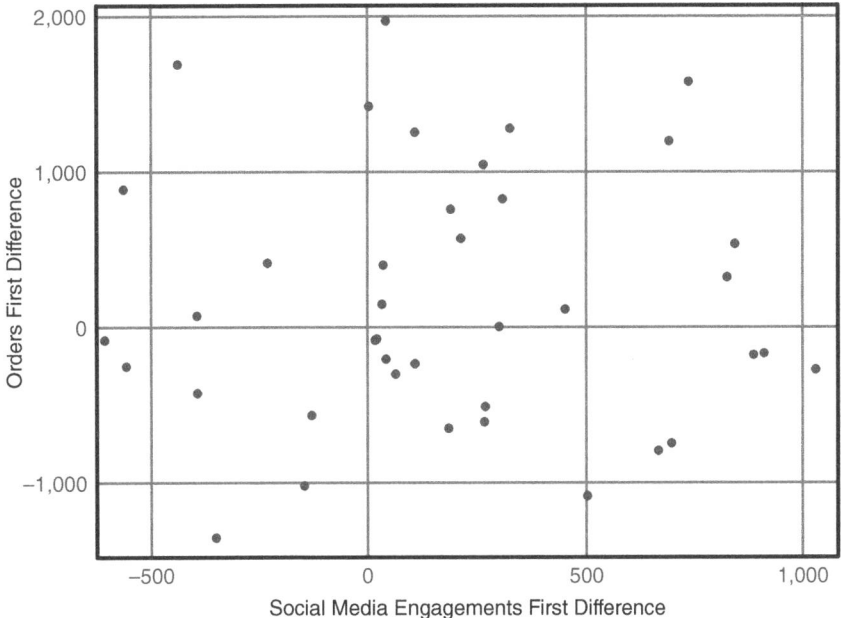

FIGURE 8.3 Scatterplot of the Day-to-day Change in Social Media Engagements and the Day-to-day Change in Orders

"correlation is not causation" handwringing because we don't even have correlation![2] And there is our first technique: first differences.

When conducting analysis on time-series data, you must be wary of confounding "due to time." We mentioned this in Chapter 7. Our point here is to introduce a specific technique you can now use, but it is also to illustrate a critical concept: descriptive data that appear to tell a clear and compelling story may simply be descriptive data that are being misinterpreted.

DESCRIPTIVE ANALYSES DONE RIGHT

We want you to leave this book with some healthily critical perspectives when either conducting analysis of historical data yourself or consuming such an analysis that has been conducted by others. It is beyond the scope of this book to provide a complete survey of the wide range of statistical techniques that can be applied to minimize stumbles into pitfalls of overly simplistic interpretation of analysis results. However, you can use the key ideas we describe now as lenses through which to view any analysis.

Unit of Analysis

The unit of analysis is the fundamental level at which we wish to aggregate the information we have to draw conclusions about our hypotheses. For example, in the previous chapter, we discussed anecdotal evidence that we collected on a person-by-person basis from Michael and Catherine to evaluate whether people liked the software we had introduced. The unit of analysis in that case was the *person*, because each unit of information corresponded to a unique person. The unit of analysis was not the *department*, which would be considered an aggregate of several people within a department.

The unit of analysis is important for three reasons. First, it tells us specifically the level at which we want to validate our hypothesis. If our hypothesis concerns the effect of the new software on people at our company, then we would be interested in gathering data at the person unit of analysis. If our hypothesis concerns the effect of the new software on the productivity of

---

[2] Now, you could also say that perhaps the orders are taking place a number of days after a social media engagement happens, and that's why we do not see the changes happen on the same day. However, it's just as easy to do that analysis by looking at the relationship between first differences for social media engagements and the aggregated differences for orders over the next week. You would still get a correlation coefficient of zero after adjusting for the time trend, in this case.

departments at our company, then we would be interested in gathering data at the departmental level instead of the person level. Knowing this upfront can help us collect the right level of data before we have to conduct the analysis we care about. Too often we've seen clients who collect data at the wrong unit of analysis, for long periods and at great expense, only to find that it was the wrong unit required to answer the question that they had.

Second, articulating the unit of analysis immediately reveals who should and who should *not* be included in the data collection process. If we are trying to validate a hypothesis with a tentative assumption like, "I believe more people shop at our stores on the weekends," then the unit of analysis is the day, and we must include all the days of the week in the analysis. We once had a client who wanted us to answer this question and gave us only data from the weekends! We couldn't conduct an analysis because there were not enough units in the comparison set (in fact, there were no units!).

Another example here comes from the manufacturing industry. Executives often want to know not only how many defects there were in a given day, but the types of defects that there were, by product or production line—questions emerging from a wide range of hypotheses regarding improving top-line or bottom-line results. These sorts of questions require us to group the data we collect by product or production line, meaning that we must observe all production lines to produce a meaningful analysis that compares them. It also requires us to score the outputs on the basis of defect type, which ultimately is also included in the groups for analysis. If we want to produce a meaningful analysis that compares them, we must collect them all (or, at least, the relevant ones). Too many business leaders and analysts alike ignore these dimensions when conducting their analyses, and it either results in questionable conclusions or requires significant urgent investment to go back and collect the data at the eleventh hour. Mapping it out up-front is always worth it.

Third, it tells us the relative weight that any individual anecdote contributes to our overall ability to validate a hypothesis (remember: descriptive evidence comes from lots of anecdotes written into a spreadsheet or a database). For instance, if our unit of analysis is the person, but we have one summary interview that we gathered from an entire department that is not broken out by person, we would perhaps consider that department interview to be more informative than any individual's interview. As such, we wouldn't want to treat the departmental interview as equal to an individual's interview in the analysis. If we were working in a spreadsheet, we may replicate the row contributed by the department proportionally to the number of people in the department (effectively "weighting" it at a higher rate).

It is often to our advantage to collect information at the most granular unit level, even if we intend to aggregate it back up to a higher unit of analysis to relate it to our hypothesis. In fact, the more granular units are ultimately the only ones at which we can put our actionable hypotheses to work. For instance, consider analyzing data at the time-series level for sales. Such an analysis over time is useful for identifying problems, but we can't just go to our sales numbers and tell them to do better. Instead, we have to go to our sales representatives individually and make recommendations on how they can improve or provide them with enhanced incentives. Collecting data at the right unit of analysis helps us to act on our hypotheses.

It can be tempting to think that the solution here is to always collect data at the most granular level possible. As we just noted, granular data can be aggregated and, in the process, be transformed into different units of analysis, and the reverse is not true. But like so many aspects of business and life, there are trade-offs. In this case, there is a very real cost to data collection, storage, and management. There is also a cost to perform aggregation work. Consider a website that has its home page viewed 1 million times each month. If "daily page views" is the unit of analysis, and we collect the data at that level, then this is 28–31 rows of data for each month included in the analysis.[3] An entire year's worth of this data could easily be managed in Excel. If, instead, the team decided to also collect some form of *unique ID* for each visitor who generated each page view, then that data would suddenly explode to be a million rows of data for each month—roughly 12 million rows for the year. While this data *could* be aggregated into a summarized data set that has 28–31 rows per month, there is a wrinkle: Excel can only handle just over one million rows of data in a spreadsheet (and it tends to get sluggish when it tries to do that), so this aggregation step would require manipulation of the data with an entirely different tool just to do the aggregation needed to start the analysis!

In short, understanding and thinking about the unit of analysis is a worthwhile habit to develop. If you find yourself having to think harder than you expected, then you're likely saving yourself a lot of grief as you or your team gets deeper into the analysis. This thought work *will* help you orient your analysis for the purposes of either describing the data at hand or making inferences about a broader population of units based on the data, which is a distinction we'll dig into in Chapter 9.

---

[3] It's unlikely that you are only collecting data for the home page of your website. And as in the examples we just went through, you likely will need this same data for other pages on your website. The math here is pretty easy, though: just multiple that 28–31 by the number of pages on your site. 1,000 pages? 28,000–31,000 rows of data. Keep that math in mind with this next part!

Independent and Dependent Variables

One of the first steps in the application of many statistical methods is to identify the independent variables and the dependent variable of interest. This turns out to be a useful lens through which to consider any analysis:

- **Dependent variable**—this is the variable (metric) of primary interest for the analysis. It's the *output* or *outcome* of interest. In any given analysis, there can only be *one* dependent variable.[4]
- **Independent variables**—these are the variables that we think *have affected*, or might have affected, the dependent variable. There can be multiple independent variables at play as part of an analysis.

Regardless of how deeply we will be diving into an analysis, we can start by asking ourselves, "What is my dependent variable? What are my independent variables?" Once those questions are answered, we can then identify which independent variables we can directly impact and which independent variables we cannot. If *all* of our independent variables are ones that we cannot impact, then we need to stop and ask ourselves what the results are going to do for us in practical terms. Is the analysis worth continuing? Check back in on our hypothesis—the "If I am right, we will..." statement *should* point toward one or more independent variables that we *can* impact!

To illustrate, consider one of the hypotheses we used in Chapter 6:

We believe that the advertising we do on Facebook does not actually deliver much in the way of value because we put a significant amount of investment into Facebook for years, and last quarter, when we shut it off completely, our sales revenue wasn't impacted at all. Plus, we, personally, have never paid any attention to Facebook ads. If we are right, we will shut down our Facebook advertising for at least a year and will redeploy that budget to other advertising channels that we have not historically used and experiment to see if any of those provide a meaningful incremental lift in revenue.

---

[4]This is not strictly and absolutely true. However, complexity skyrockets when factoring in multiple dependent variables into a single statistical model. In practice, there are often multiple variables of interest, but it is generally more effective to consider these to be separate analyses—only incorporating a single dependent variable within each analysis. Of course, we're heading down a slippery slope as to what the scope of "an analysis" is. There can certainly be "one analytics project" that brings together multiple single-dependent-variable analyses.

The *dependent variable* in this case is "sales," since this was what was called out in the "because" statement as evidence for the hypothesis.

The primary *independent variable* of interest is "Facebook advertising." If an analysis of the data shows that Facebook advertising is not delivering enough value, then the budget will be removed or reduced from that marketing channel, so this is an independent variable that *can* be impacted.

There are likely other independent variables, though. What else might influence sales? A list of these additional independent variables may include the following:

- **Paid advertising through other channels:** Paid search advertising, display advertising (banner ads), radio advertising, TV advertising. These are all independent variables that we *can* change.
- **Product features and pricing:** Does the underlying nature of the product(s) or services that we're selling and their pricing impact sales? If so, then these may be additional independent variables, albeit ones that may be outside *our* ability to impact. And if they have not *changed* in a meaningful way over the period leading up to and during the Facebook advertising, they may be ones that we can exclude from the analysis.
- **The economy:** If consumer spending increases or decreases, is it likely that that is a macroeconomic factor that will impact our sales? If so, then it's an independent variable that should be *considered*, although this would be one that we *cannot* impact.
- **Competitor behavior:** Does the rollout of new or updated products, changes in marketing, or changes in pricing by our competitors potentially impact our sales? If it's reasonable to assume so, then these are additional independent variables, albeit also ones that we cannot impact.
- **Time of year:** Are our products/services something that have *seasonality* in them? Has there *always* been a drop in sales during the summer months, for instance? If so, this is another independent variable that can be considered. Alas! It's another one that we cannot impact!

These lists can get long quickly![5] The goal is *not* to then factor *every* identified independent variable into the analysis. Apply your (good!) judgment as

---

[5] As it turns out, this example, which started with a hypothesis about Facebook advertising is a common starting point for marketing (or media) mix modeling (MMM). MMM uses historical data—with a mix of controllable and uncontrollable independent variables—to estimate the incremental impact of each advertising channel. An MMM would provide potentially actionable information beyond the Facebook advertising hypothesis. A more precise—less uncertainty—way to determine the impact of

to which ones are most likely to have a meaningful impact on the dependent variable to pare the list down.

We consistently see this step get skipped, both by business leaders and by the analysts supporting them, and that's unfortunate. Simply going through the exercise can be eye-opening when it comes to identifying which aspects of a business problem are within our control.

This exercise also drastically reduces the chance that we will introduce bias into the results. In particular, including a broad set of relevant independent variables in our analysis decreases the risk of what is called *omitted variables bias*.

Omitted Variables Bias

We're taking another brief dip into statistical language here. It will be brief, and if you're confused, we hope to remedy that shortly!

Consider a classic example: customer purchases of boutique clothes and customer education levels. Imagine a new data analyst working at a high-end retailer who has been tasked with validating a hypothesis that the retailer's best customers have higher levels of education. She is given some data that her predecessor had already compiled, which consists of three columns of data:

- The customer's email address
- The customer's total purchases of clothes
- The customer's reported level of education (high school, college, graduate school)

"This is perfect!" the analyst thinks. "My dependent variable is the purchases of nice clothes, and my independent variable is the level of education!" She then conducts a quick analysis and the result is clear: customers who are more highly educated buy nicer clothes! The analyst concocts a theory: when a customer is more highly educated, they value a sense of aesthetic and style that is more refined; they more deeply research the company's commitments to social responsibility and sustainability, and they prefer to purchase high-end clothing as a result. The recommended action is clear: *get more customers who go to graduate school!*[6]

---

just Facebook advertising would be to run a controlled experiment, as we will dig into further in Chapter 9. One hypothesis, and we've now identified two completely different approaches to validating it! Neat, right?

[6] Or read another way, the results would suggest the action to "take all of your high school and college educated customers and send them to graduate school." That would be an expensive strategy!

Even if you are not familiar with this example, you can likely spot the problem: highly educated people tend to come from higher income brackets, and people from higher income brackets tend to buy nicer clothes. Income is a variable correlated with both education and high-end clothing purchases; income is a *confounding* variable, in that it affects *both* the dependent variable *and* the independent variable of interest.

If income is correlated with both purchases and education, but we don't include it in our analysis, it will appear as if education by itself is highly related to purchases. Without including the income variable, we bias our estimate of the strength of the relationship between education and purchases. But if we *do* include income in our analysis, it will tend to explain a lot more of the purchase behavior, relegating education to a much lower level of correlation with the purchases. In fact, it is often the case that if we include both education and income in our analysis simultaneously, then the originally discovered "significant" relationship between education and purchases will attenuate to an insignificant, or even nonexistent, one.

This is *omitted variables bias*. If we exclude an important variable from the analysis, it can lead us to draw the wrong conclusions from the analysis. In this case, the analyst originally drew the conclusion that the company should focus on customers who go to graduate school. But by including the income variable in the analysis, that recommendation becomes much more questionable.

Omitted variables bias happens because of the presence of unaccounted-for *confounding variables*. We discussed confounded relationships in Chapter 7. Omitted variables bias is one result of failing to account for them, whereby we may find a strong relationship between two variables that, once corrected for, ends up being much weaker, or perhaps even a relationship in the opposite direction. Omitted variables bias happens frequently, especially in cases in which there *is* an actual relationship between the independent and dependent variables, *and* that relationship is causal, but it just is not as strong as it appears to be. The other result, of course, is a failure to ascribe the outcome we are studying to its true causes.

Confounding variables bring with them a mix of good news and bad news:

- It's **good news** that simply thinking about and identifying them at the outset of an analysis can give us a broader perspective about the key factors within the hypothesis we're validating. Additional **good news** is that, when they're identified *and* measurable, they can sometimes be accounted for ("controlled for" in stats-speak) to improve the validity of our analysis.[7] In fact, it is possible to entirely remove confounding and make causal statements when all of the relevant variables are observed (measured) and included in the analysis (this, however, is nearly always impossible to do).

- The **bad news** is that accounting for confounding factors requires the introduction of "control variables," and that requires the application of some statistical methodology.[8] The other **bad news** is that there very well may be confounding variables that we fail to identify (aka, "unknown confounders"). This particular bit of bad news is one of the central reasons that controlled experiments are more causally valid than historical data analysis—a well-designed and well-executed experiment actually *accounts* for confounders automatically; it's a key benefit of the "random assignment" aspect of experiments that we briefly touched on in Chapter 7 and will dig into further in Chapter 9.

When validating a hypothesis using historical data, see if you can identify any confounding variables. They can drastically impact the conclusions you draw if you don't account for them!

Time Is Uniquely Complicating

We touched on time-series data in the social media engagement vs. sales example earlier in this chapter, but it's worth calling out on its own. Time-series data are any data that we find plotted on a line chart or a bar chart where the x-axis is some representation of time: day, week, month, quarter, or year.[9]

---

[7] We say they can only sometimes be controlled for, because without scientific analysis, which we discuss in the next chapter, we have no definitive way to know the direction of the effect, or whether the counterfactual is well-defined enough in the analysis to draw a causal inference.

[8] The authors have a Pavlovian reaction when they hear the bell ring of confounding variables in need of the application of statistical techniques, but we realize that we're not normal. In most cases, including control variables is one of the more straightforward tasks in statistics, but it definitely helps to have someone on your team with the knowledge and skills to do that.

[9] In case you are thinking, "Oh, so I can simply plot time on the y-axis and I'm all good?" then you can take your smart mouth right to the principal's office for a good talking to. Time is *occasionally* appropriately plotted on the y-axis of a chart, but that is rarely recommended. And to answer your question: no.

The fundamental challenge with time is that, not only do our independent variables and our dependent variable change over time, but an abundance of potential confounding variables get introduced along the way:

- Our customers and prospects *change over time* (their age, the age of their children, their income, their family structure, where they live, where they work, etc.).
- The macro economy *changes over time.*
- The weather *changes over time* (both on an annual basis—colder temperatures in the winter and warmer temperatures in the summer—and on a day-to-day basis—rainy to sunny to cloudy to all the variations in between).
- Intraweek behavior tends to *change over time*—we tend to live in a different world on weekends as opposed to weekdays.
- Major events *occur over time*—a competitor's introduction of an industry-disrupting product, a once-every-four-years sporting event (the World Cup, the Olympics), a geopolitical disruption that upends supply chains, a pandemic that suddenly changes...everything.

You get the idea. Many—maybe even *most*—of these factors may not affect the hypothesis we're validating, but it's a near certainty that some of them (and others not captured in the previous list) will. Proceed with caution when working with time-series data! It may be all we have, but it introduces complicating factors.

Describing Data vs. Making Inferences

Whenever we collect data, we have something useful to analyze in support of our hypothesis validation process. Sometimes we simply want to *describe* the data at hand with descriptive statistics. For instance, we may wonder, "in this database, how many people are named Paul?" There is no issue with describing the data at hand by summarizing it up into any number of statistics that may help us validate our hypothesis. As a matter of fact, performance measurement, as discussed in Chapter 5, primarily uses descriptive statistics (for outcome-oriented measures with targets set for them): total revenue, total qualified leads, customer churn, employee satisfaction, etc.

When it comes to descriptive statistics and hypothesis validation, though, we are often attempting to make an *inference* about the broader world. For instance, we could have a hypotheses, "We believe there are enough people named Paul in the world who would be good candidates for our services that we should launch a campaign specifically targeting people with that name." There is an issue with describing the data at hand in this case. If we want to make an unbiased inference—that is, an inference that gives us a reliable answer—about the number of people in the world named Paul, then we must prove that our data are representative of the population.

It seems like a silly distinction, but it is an important one because it helps us to communicate the level of certainty that we have in the information produced by our descriptive analysis.

There are two distinct types of uncertainty that come into play in a purely descriptive analysis. The first source of uncertainty comes from bias: how close to the "right answer" do we think we actually are? We discussed selection bias in Chapter 7, and this is one major problem that prohibits the ability of the analyst to make inferences about the population from a sample of data. When conducting a descriptive analysis, we have to distinguish whether we are trying to describe the greater population that the descriptive data are supposed to represent, or if we are simply trying to say something about the data at hand. This is a little bit of a catch-22 because most of the time we are really trying to describe the population from the data at hand; it almost seems like a trick to qualify our results as "nonrepresentative" if we are trying to validate hypotheses about the greater population!

The second source of uncertainty comes from what we call *sampling variability*. We discussed random sampling in Chapter 7 as the solution to getting rid of selection bias when we want to make inferences. But one of the problems with sampling variability is that it can *create* a level of uncertainty in the results we produce, *even* if they are representative of the broader population. When we take a random sample, that random sample may give us—because of randomness—a different answer from the answer we would have gotten if we had taken a random sample on a different day.

We just can't get around uncertainty by employing random sampling unless we move to observe the entire population about which we are trying to make inferences; even then, there can be random error introduced through the measurement instrumentation we used to produce the data, or variability owing to the time at which we observe the data, and so on.

The good news is that uncertainty owing to random sampling is predictable and quantifiable. We can create confidence intervals[10] around the inferences

---

[10] We know. Statistical jargon alert! Alas! We're about to get a *little* deeper into this jargon. Confidence intervals are something that crop up (or should crop up) as part of the output of many statistical techniques. Once we're clear that we *never* know "the perfect truth," confidence intervals are how we can quantify how close to the truth we expect we are—the smaller the confidence interval, the less uncertainty we are operating with. Unfortunately, shrinking a confidence interval typically comes with a cost. Trade-offs!

we make, communicating that even if we are not exactly right about, for example, the number of people named Paul in the world, that we believe that the "true" answer is within a certain range. Depending on the rigor and depth of our analysis, that "certain" range may be narrow or broad.

In fact, it is best practice to include ranges of uncertainty owing to sampling variability in any statistics that we report. If we are trying to predict how much money is going to come in next quarter, it's much better to have a high scenario, an expected scenario, and a low scenario, rather than a single expected scenario, because it helps us better understand both our downside risk and our upside potential. Our colleagues will, contrary to popular belief, usually be quick to accept that we may not have the exact answer, and in fact, we will be less subject to criticism if our "expected" prediction is wrong. The simple fact of including a range communicates that there are any number of random things that can happen in the world to throw off what we think is going to happen, but we should still move forward with the expectation of our best prediction.

Quantifying Uncertainty

As much as we think of data as being the source of objective truths, when it comes to the application of data to validate hypotheses, it rarely is. Even in the context of analyzing historical data, the "truth" in the data is limited to *what* factually happened and never absolute truths about *why* it happened (much less definitively what *will* happen). Since our interest in validating hypotheses is generally about inferring causes and effects, we need to acknowledge that we're constantly operating in the realm of uncertainty.

When it comes to effective analysis, a range of tools and techniques for *quantifying* the level of uncertainty are part of the result. The following is an incomplete list of terms that do just that—varying techniques and resulting terms depending on the specific type of analysis:

- Margin of error
- Confidence interval
- Prediction interval
- Statistical significance (at a given confidence level)
- p-value
- R^2
- Standard deviation
- Standard error

While it is beyond the scope of this book to dive deeply into any of these, we hope that, after reading this book, you see the presence of this sort of terminology in the results of analyses as positive (albeit linguistically cumbersome) elements to be factored in when considering the interpretation of an analysis. Uncertainty is not a binary concept—it *always* exists, and the proper application of inferential statistics techniques quantifies the *degree* of uncertainty.

In general, increasing the amount of data in an analysis will decrease the level of uncertainty. This is not always the case, though, as it really depends on the hypothesis being validated and what data are being applied. The main takeaway is that the only "truths" available from data are factual statements about the past or present. All other data-driven statements have inherent uncertainty within them.

Linear Regression: A Case Study in "Uncertainty" as the Defining Difference Between Math and Statistics

While we have done our best throughout this book to stay away from deep dives on statistical methods, we are taking a shallow dive here by giving the most basic of explanations regarding one of the most common and most powerful techniques: linear regression. Several key underlying principles are illustrated in this basic explanation, which should give you some useful additional intuition about key aspects of analyzing historical data: the dependent variable, independent variables, and quantifying uncertainty.

As our example to illustrate this, consider a case where we are looking for ways to improve employee satisfaction. Our company has an unlimited paid time off (PTO) policy, but we've read various reports about how such a policy can be counterproductive, as many employees are hesitant to take advantage of it. We have a hypothesis that employees' satisfaction with their work is affected by how many days they have taken off in the last 3 months, and we're going to dig into the data to find out.

We have a clear set of components:

- Our *dependent variable* is the employee satisfaction score, which we gather directly from employees through a periodic survey that asks them a number of questions and then calculates their satisfaction as a number between 0 and 100, with 100 being the "most satisfied with my job" result.
- We have only one *independent variable* for the sake of this analysis, and it's the number of paid vacation days that the employee has taken in the 90 days immediately preceding the assessment of their satisfaction.

Linear Regression Digression (cont'd.)

Linear Regression Digression (cont'd.)

- We have identified one potential *confounding variable*, in that it may be that employees' general inclination for happiness may be a driver of their satisfaction score, and it may also be *correlated* with the amount of vacation they take. We don't have data that measures this, but we've tucked it into the back of our minds as a potentially relevant factor.

We're now set to do our analysis.

Remember the Formula for a Line: y = mx + b?

The formula for a line, $y = mx + b$, is something that every child learns in middle school. Importantly, this formula is a *mathematical* equation rather than a *statistical* one. The difference is that math is *deterministic*—it's cut and dried and perfectly formulaic—while statistics are *probabilistic*—they acknowledge and account for uncertainty.

If our hypothesis holds, then we can think about the relationship between vacation days and satisfaction as the formula for a line. Perhaps, even, we briefly don our Omniscience Cap and the formula for that line comes to us:

$$y = 0.65x + 40$$

where y is the number of vacation days the employee took in the last 90 days, and x is the employee's satisfaction score.

We can visualize this relationship on a chart as shown in Figure 8.4. There are three components of this equation:

- y (employee satisfaction) is our *dependent variable.*
- x (the number of vacation days taken) is our only *independent variable.*
- 40 is the *y-intercept.*

According to this chart (and to the underlying equation), we know *exactly* what the employee's satisfaction score will be based on how much vacation they've taken in the last 3 months. With just two beats of thought, we know this is not realistic[11]—other factors are at play, and there is no

---

[11] We now regret having purchased the Omniscient Cap from that shady looking fellow on the path into town. Clearly, we should have bought the magic beans he was offering instead!

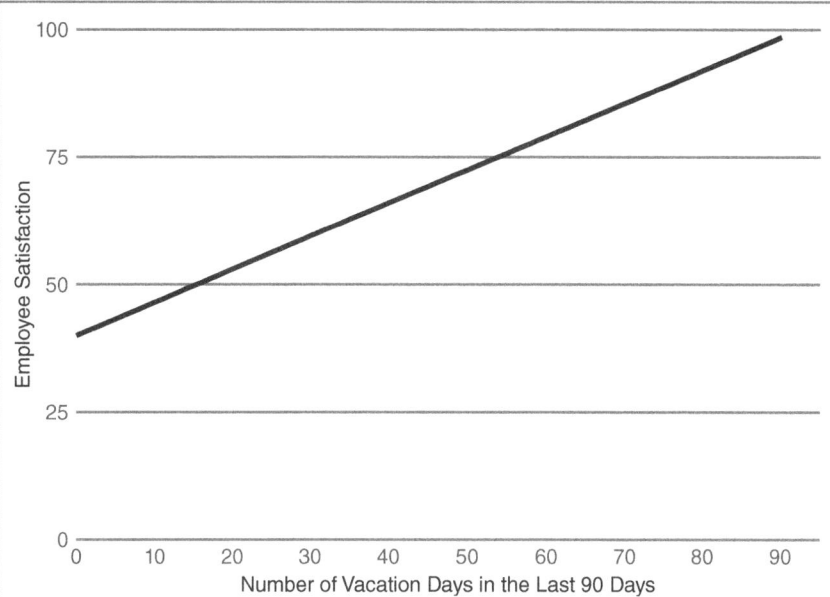

FIGURE 8.4 Employee satisfaction based on how many vacation days have been taken

way that the relationship will be this clean and definitive! *Every* business scenario that assesses the relationship between multiple variables—is a *statistical* exercise rather than a *mathematical* one.

This is where *linear regression* comes in as a more appropriate technique than simply the *formula for a line*.

Noise and Uncertainty: A Business Reality

In practice, how would this relationship have been determined? We would have taken the data from our employee satisfaction tracker and smashed it together with data from our vacation tracking platform. We would have quickly realized that, of the 117 resulting data points that we have, *no one* had taken more than 17 days of vacation in the 90 days prior to having their satisfaction assessed. And if we plot each of those 117 points, we see that things are quite a bit messier than a simple line, as shown in Figure 8.5.

For starters, in a *mathematical* world, someone could have taken 90 days of vacation in the last 90 days. In the practical world, this would only apply to someone who has been on an extended leave...and then was

Linear Regression Digression (cont'd.)

Linear Regression Digression (cont'd.)

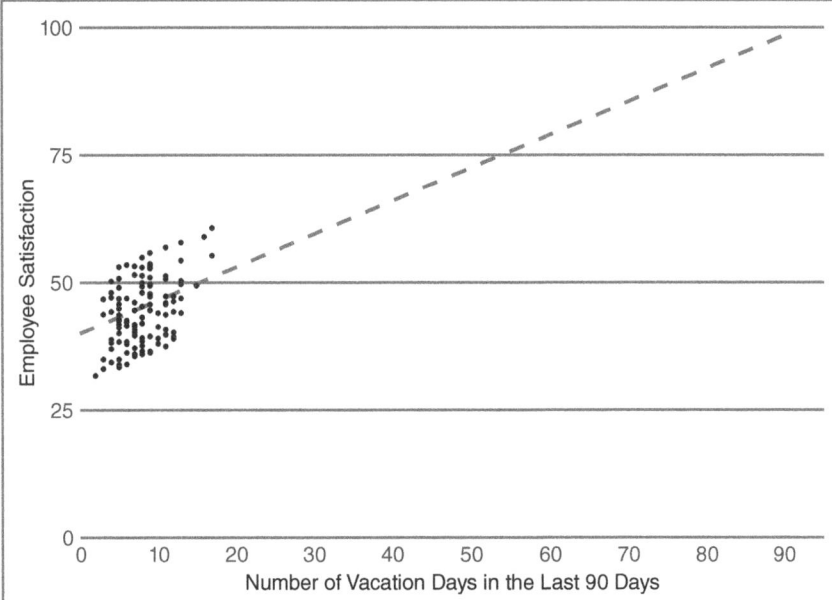

FIGURE 8.5   The actual data used to generate the line

surveyed as to their satisfaction on the very day they returned to the office. The data we have has no one who has taken more than 17 days of leave in the last 90 days. This concept is known as *statistical support*, which is to say that we should only make inferences within the range that is allowed by the observed data. Even though the formula for the line could extend all the way to 1,000 days, it is hard to imagine that a company would still employ someone after the employee invoked the unlimited PTO policy continuously for 1,000 days (not to mention that it would require breaking the space-time continuum for someone to take 1,000 days of PTO in a 90-day period!)

We can zoom in and plot the data with the maximum number of days of vacation being 30 days, and we'll go ahead and remove the line for now. The result is shown in Figure 8.6.

Now the data looks a lot less like the clean line we started out with: instead of being ordered in a tight line, back to back, the points are scattered.

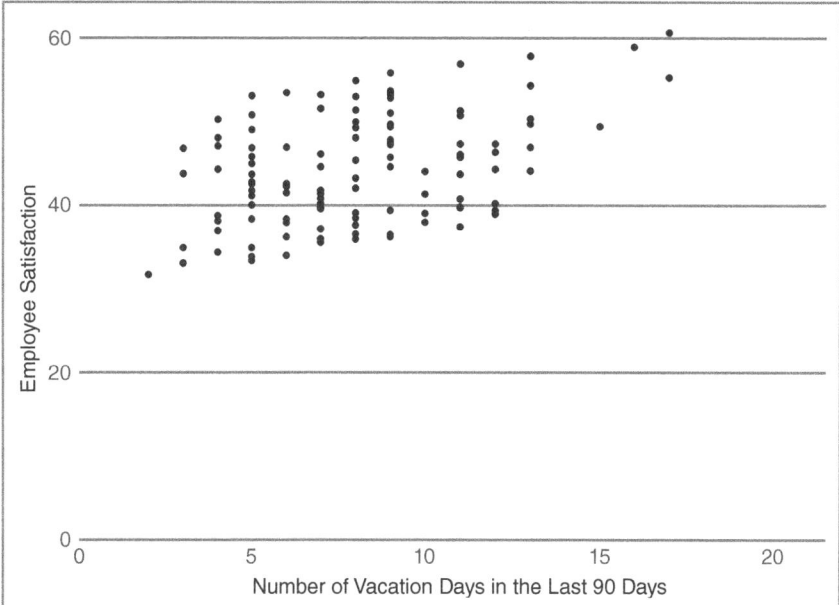

FIGURE 8.6 Vacation days and employee satisfaction, zoomed in

It turns out that a *regression* line uses a formula that is similar to the formula for a line, but it comes along with a few bonuses. The most basic formula[12] for a linear regression is:

$$y = \alpha + \beta x + \varepsilon.$$

This should look pretty similar to our formula for a line:

- α ("alpha") is the y-intercept, so it replaces the b in the formula for a line

Linear Regression Digression (cont'd.)

---

[12] A properly robust version of the formula is $Y_i = \beta_0 + \beta_1 X_{1i} + \ldots \beta_n X_{ni} + \varepsilon_i$. This is a generalized form that handles an unlimited number of independent variables and, just to reduce the number of Greek characters in play, subs out β_0 for α, which has some elegance to it that we will acknowledge here but not explain. Are you getting annoyed with our lack of "digging in," or are you rejoicing that we've glossed over these details?

Linear Regression Digression (cont'd.)

- β ("beta") is the slope, so it replaces the m in the formula for a line
- ε ("epsilon") is the *error term*, which did not exist in the formula for a line. This is the key!

It's the error term, ε, that gets us from *math* (the formula for a line) to *statistics* (linear regression), and it's a representation of the *uncertainty* that exists in our data. Using the data shown in Figure 8.6, if we run a linear regression, the results are:

$$y = 40 + 0.65x + \varepsilon.$$

While the terms are reordered a bit, and we've got that pesky "ε" added in, this formula is quite similar to our original equation. That pesky "ε" just acknowledges that, for any given number of days of vacation (x), if we plug that into our equation, it's not going to come up with *exactly* what y (employee satisfaction) is. The difference between what the equation returns and the actual employee satisfaction is the "error" for the model in that *specific employee's case*.

That error will vary from employee to employee as well as from survey to survey. The model may generate a result that is too high, or it may generate a result that is too low. "ε" is a single Greek letter that acknowledges that: "Whatever the model returns, it will generally be different from reality by some amount." The uncertainty that we discussed in the previous section is described by this epsilon term.

How "Good" Is the Model?

The range and variability of ε is an indication of how "good" a model is—how much uncertainty rides along with the model as a hypothesis validation tool. We're oversimplifying things a bit, but that uncertainty gets quantified by some additional information that gets calculated along with the base equation for a linear regression (or *any* statistical model).

This additional information comes out as some specific summary terms for the model. We're going to describe just two of them here—both the summary term and the value that was returned for that summary term in this specific example:

- $R^2 = 0.18$: This tells us that the "model" (the equation) explains *18%* of the variation in employee satisfaction scores. This makes sense: *lots* of

---

factors go into employee satisfaction, and if we thought we could fully explain it simply based on an employee's recent history of taking time off, we would be delusional. This tells us that some combination of *unaccounted for independent variables* and *noise* explain the remaining variations in employee satisfaction. Eighteen percent is not nothing, though!

- *p-value* < **0.01:** This starts to get into tricky territory,[13] but essentially, the p-value is a value between 0 and 1 that can be thought of as a percentage between 0% and 100%. It is the probability that, if there were no *actual* relationship between the independent variables and the dependent variable, that the values seen in the data would have been observed. Essentially, the lower the p-value, the more likely the model is detecting a "real" relationship. In this case, the p-value is less than 0.01 (less than 1%), which makes us fairly certain that there is a "real" relationship being detected.

Given that there are entire college-level courses devoted to the ins and outs of regression modeling, we've obviously cut some corners with this explanation. What we hope you take from it, though, is some intuition about independent variables, the dependent variable, confounders, and the nature and quantification of *uncertainty* that is inherent in any use of historical data to validate hypotheses.

SUMMARY

In this chapter, we shared some pitfalls and solutions for common issues in the production of descriptive evidence that we have observed during our careers. This chapter is by no means a complete treatment of the descriptive analysis of data. But our hope is that you walk away from it with a more nuanced understanding and appreciation for validating hypotheses with the many types of analyses that fall into this category.

---

[13] Shockingly tricky territory, actually. Any statistician reading this book has already been triggered, and at least 3 in 10 of them will read the simplified statement that follows this footnote and be inspired to dash off a lengthy email to the authors about how this is a dangerous oversimplification. We don't think it is given our intentions with this whole example.

Descriptive evidence is not as informative as scientific evidence, and that is why we have distinguished between the two. We often can *only* produce descriptive evidence because scientific evidence can be too time- and capital-intensive to create. **The important thing is that we understand the limitations of descriptive data.** It is better to frame the results in terms of "limited applicability" or "potentially biased," rather than to sweep under the rug its inability to compel broad conclusions. We introduced scientific evidence in Chapter 7, and we will discuss techniques for producing it in the next chapter!

MEASURE THIS CHAPTER

And now, it's once again time to contribute to the performance measurement of this very book by visiting https://analyticstrw.com and answering the two-question survey for this chapter. We're sure the evaluator responses are scattered widely at this point!

CHAPTER 9

Pitfalls and Solutions for Scientific Evidence

There aren't many things more disappointing than being *sure* that something is going to work out, and then realizing...it won't. When evidence is presented as "scientific," it carries with it an air of certainty. Cue the bold declaration: "Of course my hypothesis is validated, and we should pursue its implications immediately...I used science!" Ultimately, when that scientific evidence generates conclusions that are proven wrong—but which were trotted out by someone as if they were dogmatic certainties—the faith others have in the analyses produced by that person can be seriously degraded. We may get a few points docked for our analysis being wrong, but we lose the farm when we're just plain foolish with the way we went about it.

The point of this chapter is to arm you with an understanding of *how scientific evidence should be generated* (and where people go wrong), so that you know when to put your stock in an analysis. Scientific evidence is not a silver bullet, and as we've stressed throughout this book, it is impossible to achieve 100% certainty about really anything. The problem really sets in when we develop unfounded certainty in something because we have produced faulty evidence, which we accordingly overweight in our consideration of a decision. It's like charging headlong off a cliff for a bungee jump and then realizing we connected the wrong band to our belt.

The production of scientific evidence is, at its core, about making generalized inferences that can broaden the scope of the insights we generate. The two major types of inferences to consider for the purpose of business analytics are as follows:

- **Statistical Inferences:** "What is the *general nature* of X?"
- **Causal Inferences:** "If I do X, will it *cause* Y to happen?"

Any question that takes one of these forms will produce, if answered appropriately, scientific evidence. But as we discussed in Chapters 7 and 8, the evidence must overcome the two biggest pitfalls associated with inferential data analysis: *selection bias* and *confounding*. In this chapter, we will explore how to know if the design of an analysis accounts for these pitfalls, and we promise it won't be too technical!

MAKING STATISTICAL INFERENCES

Broad *inferences* are necessary in business. We may wish to infer general characteristics about our population of potential customers, or the reliability of our manufacturing process, or how effective our marketing and sales teams are at generating sales. Inferences like these are important in order to make decisions about which new products to create, where to invest in factory refurbishment, and how to allocate the coveted bonus pool to our staff.

But without accounting for selection bias, we will consistently get wrong answers. The *most common pitfall* we see in analyses that purport to be scientific—and in descriptive analyses that analysts over-extend—is that they fail to think about, check for, and correct selection bias. One common use case in which analysts fail to account for selection bias is in the analysis of customer feedback surveys. Customer feedback is often collected through a pop-up form on a company's website or through reviews that can be submitted via a ratings website or app store. Our clients will look at this customer feedback and infer that it represents their customer base more broadly. In truth, the majority of people who click on these feedback forms already have a vested interest in expressing either vehemently positive or negative viewpoints towards the company's products and services. The people who *select into* giving feedback provide data that, once analyzed, represents skewed and extreme views about the customer base. And when no attempt to account for the selection bias is made, the analyst in charge ends up making broad claims about the customer base that make the customers look like an awfully melodramatic group! This is damaging, because it can cause the business to make decisions to overly cater to the most extreme customers, which often make up a smaller chunk of the business.

Recently, businesses that value reviews—like hotel chains and companies that have mobile apps—have begun to create user experiences that promote selection bias in the reviews process. If you use apps on a smartphone (and if you're reading this book, it's likely that you do), have you noticed that an app will issue a pop-up asking if you're having a good time using the app. The pop-up asks you to answer **Yes** or **No**. If you answer **Yes**, the app will ask you to leave a review on the mobile app store platform. If you answer **No**, however, the app will ask you to privately submit feedback to the company (rather than leaving a review on the app store). In doing so, the companies select customers who have positive experiences into leaving reviews, generating "5-star" review averages that are reported publicly. This is potentially deceptive because if app store users realized this was happening (and we're not sure if they do), they would lose trust in the review averages the app stores report.[1]

Questions asking for broad generalizations require broad, representative *support*. Not evidentiary support, but rather, *statistical support*. The concept of

---

[1] Can you believe that? Analytics being used improperly, on purpose. Who'da thunk. The irony of companies doing this is that it eliminates their ability to make informed decisions about the quality of their product based on the customer review data they've already collected. Companies have to go out and gather entirely new, representative data from their customers to get good customer feedback that can be integrated into the user experience.

statistical support is intuitive: if we want to say anything with analytics about a general population of people, we have to have representation from all the different types of people in the population.

Detecting and Solving Problems with Selection Bias

We can't detect selection bias just by looking at the sample of data that we have already. Detecting selection bias requires careful thought and planning, which we can think about as a three-step process:

1. Define the population.
2. Compare the population to the sample.
3. Determine what differences are unexpectedly different.

Define the Population

The first step is carefully defining the rules that would qualify an individual person (or "unit" in the case of inanimate objects), as a member of the population about which we are generally trying to say something.

Defining the population is a conceptual exercise. For example, if we want to say something about our existing customer base—and therefore need to be able to make general inferences about our customer base as a population—we first need to know their characteristics.

High-level characteristics exist in transactional data, and they can be reviewed and summarized to give us a relatively detailed picture of our customer base: shipping addresses can reveal location and state; the amount spent can reveal cost sensitivity; the products bought can reveal affinity; email address can reveal age (yes, "aol.com" emails are associated with people who came online in the 1990s).

Compare the Population to the Sample

Once we apply the same summarization that we used to define the population to the sample of data and question, we will have a comparable set of characteristics. We can then compare the distributions[2] of these characteristics between the population and the sample.

---

[2] "Distributions" is a broad and deep—and often bell-shaped!—concept in statistics. It's a powerful way to compare "groups" of different sizes along different dimensions. Visually, distributions are represented as histograms or density plots that provide a much richer understanding of "the nature" of a group with regard to a single characteristic than a single number—be it the median or the mean—can provide.

In our example from the first step, we defined four population character-istics: location, average order size, product affinity, and age. That means that we now have the ability to make five comparisons between the population and the sample. For example, we can see if the percentage of customers in the sample from California is the same as the percentage of customers from California in the population. We can see if the average amount spent by the customers in the sample is the same as the average amount spent by the cus-tomers in the population. And so on.

Determine What Differences Are Unexpectedly Different

Each comparison we make between the sample and the population *will* gener-ate some difference. Sometimes the difference will be small (or even zero!); other times, the difference will be large.

"Small" and "large" are relative concepts. We need to determine what we would have *expected* the range of potential differences to have been owing to sampling variability (which we discussed in Chapter 8) and test whether the differences we observe in our comparisons exceed the expected range.[3]

With our differences in hand, we can now demonstrate whether the sam-ple looks like the population on the basis of the characteristics we have defined. This technique, sometimes referred to as "balance checking" can be a powerful tool to detect selection bias.

There are well-established techniques for performing these comparisons, and enlisting the aid of an analyst or statistician who is familiar with these techniques is ideal. However, we don't want to gloss over the broader point: avoiding selection bias requires checking that the sample—the data at hand—is reasonably similar across relevant characteristics as the broader population about which we are trying to draw conclusions.

Random and Nonrandom Selection Bias

It is possible, to a certain extent, to correct for selection bias when the distri-butions of the data in the population and the sample are available.

When the sample is misrepresentative, but we believe that misrepresenta-tion happened simply due to random chance, we can use a technique called *post-stratification* to correct for selection bias. We won't get into the technical

---

[3] We have to be careful not to fall prey to the issues of *multiple comparisons* here. Multiple comparisons problems emerge when we test multiple statistical hypotheses without adjusting for the fact that at least 1 in 20 is bound to come up as significant by chance.

details of post-stratification here, but put simply, post-stratification adjusts the results we get in the sample to reflect what they likely would have been had a more representative sample been drawn from the population. There are some very real caveats to how far post-stratification can take us—principal among them being the fact that when we have *non*random selection bias, there's really not a lot we can do! But it is a technique that should be considered, as its use or lack of use can have a very real impact on the resulting power of the analysis.

A bigger problem emerges when we have *nonrandom* selection bias. In other words, when there is some specific process by which the customers or units that we are analyzing made their way into the sample, then we can be in real trouble. In the interest of introducing some drama into our exploration of this topic, let's imagine a nefarious executive who wants to juice the numbers to make a case that the changes he demanded be made to the company's mobile app have improved the users' experience. He does this by putting his finger on the scale as to who makes their way into the sample of customer reviews of the app. The executive was very forward-looking, and one of the changes he had demanded be made was how the in-app prompt about whether the user was enjoying the app gets delivered, and the conditional logic employed depending on their answer: only users who indicate they are enjoying the app are prompted to post a public rating and review.

By only prompting customers with good experiences to create a public customer review (the data in the sample!), the executive is introducing nonrandom selection bias. The only way to correct the data would be to reconstruct the exact process by which the executive decided to include certain customers into the sample and then go back to the population to recollect information from the people and units that were *excluded*. In this example, it likely would not even be possible to go back and recollect that data, getting ratings and reviews from the customers who indicated they were *not* enjoying the app experience.

The Scientist's Mind: It's the Thought That Counts!

In closing this section, we reflect on a key point: it's *thinking about the structure of the problem* that helps us conduct a scientific analysis to produce strong evidence. The methodologies we have introduced can include the analysis of numbers, but the substance of the evidence comes from the *thought process*.

We often are limited to the data at hand, and that data may have very real limitations, including random or nonrandom selection bias. So, what are we to do? There are a range of options:

Ignore the limitations. This, of course, is a terrible idea.

Collect new data that doesn't include these limitations. This is ideal, but it may not be feasible due to time or resource constraints.

Employ relevant statistical techniques to the original data to mitigate the limitations to the extent possible. This may not be feasible, either, as resources with the training and skills to do this work may not be available.

Proceed with caution and acknowledge the limitations. Identify and articulate the limitations of the data, but then go ahead and use it by giving it an *appropriate* level of weight in oour decision-making process.

We hope this book is giving you the confidence and knowledge to *never* exercise the first option, to identify and capitalize on opportunities to exercise the second and third options, and to be equipped to fall back on the last option as needed!

MAKING CAUSAL INFERENCES

The day-to-day in business and life is replete with *causal questions*. We mentioned a few causal questions of the form, "does X cause Y?" in Chapter 7. Here are a few more for consideration during this section:

- Does advertising via email *cause* sales of our products to increase?
- Does canceling the office's free Friday lunches *cause* employee satisfaction to decrease?

Whenever we have a causal question, we need to make a *causal inference* to answer it. Causal inferences result from analyses that account for *confounding bias*. Confounding bias is the **most common pitfall** we observe in the production of scientific evidence. We defined and discussed confounding bias in greater detail in Chapter 7. Moreover, the potential outcomes framework we discussed in Chapter 3 provided a deeper and broader intuition about causation.[4]

---

[4]To refresh your memory, the potential outcomes framework simply notes that, any time we do something (or something happens), there is the *actual* outcome, which we can observe and measure, and then there are one or more *potential* outcomes—what we *would* have observed if we had done something else (or done nothing, which still counts as "something else" in this context).

One analytics exercise in which we see confounding bias rampantly is a marketing technique called *attribution*. Attribution assigns credit for customer conversions to the different types of marketing activities that promoted the company's products and services to the customer (e.g., email, direct mail, display advertising, billboard advertising, television advertising). If the customer opened and clicked on an email promoting the product that they later converted on (purchased), the email campaign is given all or some "credit" for the conversion. The marketing team compares the amount of credit given to each marketing channel to determine which channels are most effective at generating revenue in return for investment. The channel with the highest marks gets the highest investment.

But attribution is often subject to confounding bias because it assumes that the customer purchased the product *because* of the advertisement (the "causal arrow" flows from the ad to the purchase: Ad → Purchase). In many cases, customers have already resolved to buy the product, when—surprise!—they're shown an ad for the same thing they're about to buy. The fact that the ad is shown, and that the customer is resolved to purchase, happens simply because they are a customer of the company's. In fact, if the company were to send an email to every one of their customers advertising the product, then every customer who buys the product (especially brand loyalists who were going to buy it anyway) would have their purchases attributed—at least in part—to the email.

Personalization and targeting algorithms can make this problem even worse when they are not built to prevent it from happening. If the algorithm detects, based on web browsing data, that a customer has put the product in their cart to check out, and that signal is incorporated into the decision to show that customer an advertisement, the causal arrow is reversed (it flows in the opposite direction: Purchase → Ad). The imminent purchase causes the ad to be shown! Attribution approaches usually don't account for causality, and as such, the business may believe their ad did a good job on their most loyal customers, who were going to buy anyway.

The result? A lot of money spent doing something that didn't move the needle.

Detecting and Solving Problems with Confounding Bias

Confounding bias can be difficult to detect if we haven't thought critically about the sources from which it can come. The first step to detecting confounding bias is to carefully consider what we call the *data generating process*:

the way in which the world operated to produce the outcomes and data sources we're using to test our hypotheses:

1. Create a list of things that could affect the concept we're analyzing.
2. Draw causal arrows.
3. Look for confounding "triangles" between the circles and the box.

Create a List of Things That Could Affect the Concept We're Analyzing

Take out a blank piece of paper and a pen. In the middle, write down the name of the concept you're studying (for instance, "conversion" on a purchase), and draw a box around it. Then, write down the names of other things that you imagine can affect that concept (for instance, "seeing an ad," or "shopping online"), and draw a circle around each one.

This first step helps us to start thinking about all the things that could be related to the concept we're studying, just by writing all of them down. There's no requirement for what's on the sheet and what's not. It is just an exercise meant to get us thinking about the factors that might cause the thing that we care about (ideally, including ones that we hadn't thought about before).

Figure 9.1 demonstrates how we may think about enumerating in a graph the items that could be related to the purchase conversion example in the previous section.

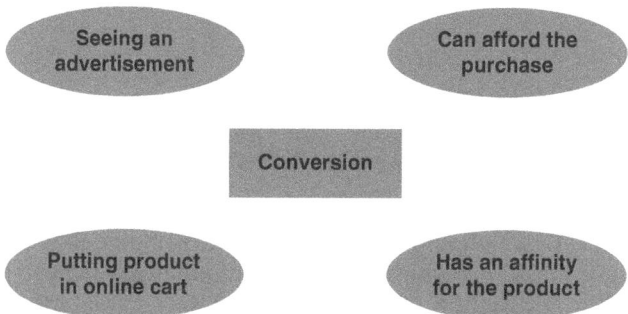

FIGURE 9.1   Graph of items related to purchase conversion

Draw Causal Arrows

Then, connect the boxes by drawing arrows between them. If we think one circle "causes" the main box *or* any other circle (if we think box A causes box B, then draw an arrow from A → B). Not every circle needs to be connected to another (or even to the box in the middle). Just connect the ones we think have causal relationships. What starts to emerge is a web of relationships mapping all of the concepts together. Each of these concepts is associated, ideally, with a data field (but if it's not, that's okay—that will just reveal some data gaps that we will need to consider). The final step is then to look for confounding.

Figure 9.2 demonstrates what the graph looks like after connecting the boxes. You can see that many relationships have been added, but you can see that we've drawn a two-sided arrow between "Putting Product in Online Cart" and "Seeing an Advertisement" to reflect the idea in the previous section that it's possible that the causal flow goes either way.

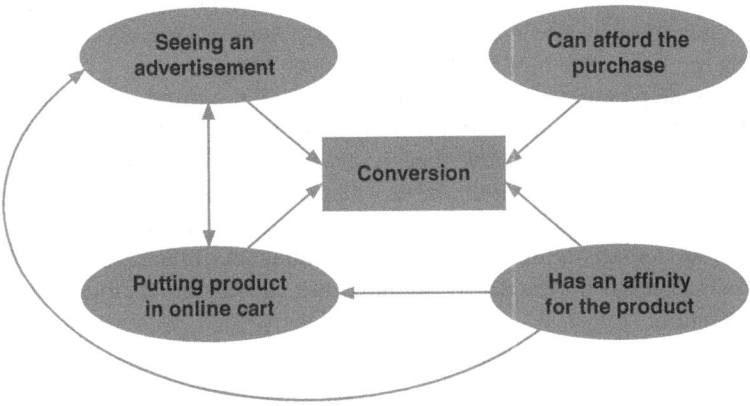

FIGURE 9.2 Adding arrows to our graph

Look for Confounding "Triangles" Between the Circles and the Box

A triangle occurs when there is a circle A that "causes" both the main box B and another circle C, which in turn also causes the main box B. If we find a triangle, we have found a confounded relationship that has the potential to introduce bias into our analysis. This highly conceptual analysis does not give us statistical proof of confounding. But it does give us the theoretical grounding to claim whether confounding bias might exist. As an added benefit, it will also often introduce other variables into the mix, the relationships between which we may wish to bookmark for further hypothesis validation.

Figure 9.3 shows the potentially confounded triangle detected between "Putting Product in Online Cart," "Seeing an Advertisement," and "Conversion." This alerts us to the fact that we need to carefully parse through the causal implications of the relationship between our advertising and conversion.

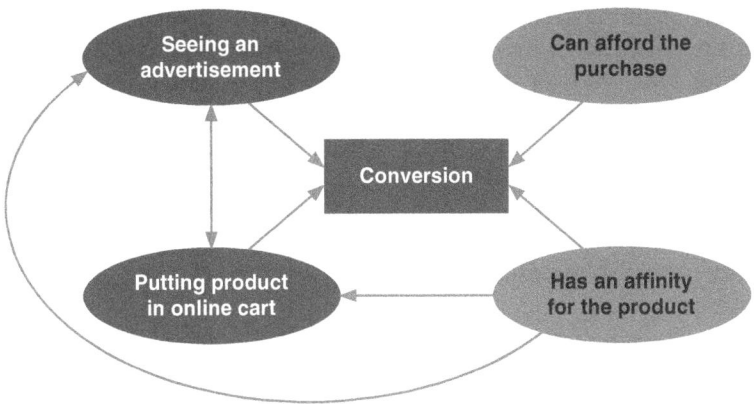

FIGURE 9.3 The potentially confounded relationship

Solving for Confounding in the Past and the Future

What to do once we've detected the *possibility* of confounding bias is a whole other problem. If we are conducting a **historical analysis** of data from the past, confounding bias can be impossible to remove; it's "baked in" to the history of the world.

For example, suppose our office manager canceled free Friday lunches, and we were interested in seeing if the cancellation of those lunches was making employees upset. We could use employee satisfaction survey results before and after the cancellation of the lunches to see if there was a difference, but our analysis would be subject to the same "time confounding" that we discussed in Chapter 8. If we find employees got more upset, it's possible that their attitudes were degraded by the same reason free Friday lunches were cancelled: the company has been running out of money over time.

Moreover, we can't go back in time to observe the counterfactual timeline, in which free Friday lunches were never canceled, to draw a conclusion about the effect of the cancellation. (We discussed the idea of counterfactuals and potential outcomes in Chapter 3.)

There are some techniques that can analyze historical data in a way that lets us approximate what the counterfactual potential outcome would have been. We call these analyses *natural experiments* and *quasi-experiments*, and there are a variety of techniques—instrumental variables, regression discontinuity, difference-in-differences—that experienced analysts with scientific training can use to complete them. But these approaches require specific data sources and technical expertise that may not always be available.

If we are planning to conduct an **analysis in the future**, but haven't yet collected the data, then we're in luck, because we can *proactively* solve for confounding bias. We can do this by performing *controlled experiments*. Controlled experiments (when done well) avoid the problem of confounding entirely by creating a miniature "parallel universe": a counterfactual to which we can easily compare "what happens to B when we do A" to "what would have happened had we never done A to begin with."[5] Controlled experimentation, properly done, is the most intuitive way to make causal inferences (or, in other words, establish causation).

Controlled Experimentation

Controlled experiments are the closest we can get to measuring the results of two different courses of action at the same time without achieving omniscience. But when we talk about experimentation in this way, we mean something very specific. We want to be very careful here to not confuse "trying something" with "experimenting." In some contexts, these are synonymous, but in the context of validating hypotheses, this definition is loose and unhelpful. The "controlled" modifier in "controlled experimentation" is key!

Consider a meeting convened to consider whether our company should lower its prices to increase demand and, ultimately, overall revenue.[6] It's not hard to imagine the team sitting in a meeting and wringing their hands over the premium that their customers pay relative to their competitors when the idea of an across-the-board price cut gets floated.[7] But will it work? No one really knows. Then the most senior person in the room says, "I haven't heard any better ideas. We might as well try it and see what happens!" Heads nod. A decision has been made. The meeting adjourns, and everyone *feels* like they're doing right by the data. They'll drop the prices as an "experiment" and see what happens!

Some version of this happens regularly in many organizations with which we've worked. What the team has in their collective mind's eye is that the "experiment" will result in a sharp and visibly unambiguous change. In reality,

---

[5] Read more about these cool "parallel universes" in Chapter 3, in which we discussed counterfactuals and the potential outcomes framework.

[6] This was the example we walked through in more detail—with charts!—in Chapter 3. We're briefly revisiting it here because that was six chapters ago, but if it doesn't ring a bell, you *might* want to quickly flip back to Chapter 3 and review the potential outcomes framework section and examples. It's the one with a series of line charts!

[7] "Floating an idea" is another way of saying...anyone? Anyone? That's right! "Hypothesizing!" You're getting this!

the results are often messier and more subtle (*even* when there is a real effect from the change) than the sort of abrupt and dramatic jump that was hoped for. In short, ad hoc "experiments" don't really tell us much at all in our pursuit of scientific evidence.

The Gold Standard of Causation: Controlled Experimentation

The specific type of experimentation that is the gold standard for determining causality is *controlled experimentation* (or even more formally, a *randomized controlled trial*—an "RCT" as a more linguistically manageable acronym; we're generally sticking with "controlled experimentation" throughout this book). In a controlled experiment, one group gets "treated" one way, and another group gets "treated" a different way.

For the purposes of validating hypotheses, we often must treat one group with the thing that we hypothesize will make a difference and treat the other group with nothing (or if some treatment *has* to happen, then with "whatever they've historically been treated with"). If done properly, this isn't quite pulling off a multi-verse, but it does divide the universe into two (or more) groups *at random* and then compares the results between them. For lots of either deeply technical or plainly obvious reasons, this is a statistically robust way to get pretty close to *observing* counterfactuals! And observing the counterfactual eliminates confounding bias.

Controlled experiments go by a lot of different names depending on the industry:

- In the pharmaceutical industry, *clinical trials* are controlled experiments.
- In the social sciences (anthropology, economics, political science, psychology, and sociology), controlled experiments are often referred to as *field experiments*.
- In digital experience design, *A/B tests* are controlled experiments.
- In digital advertising, *matched market tests* are controlled experiments.

The same underlying principles apply across all of these, even if the motivations for using them and the "unit of analysis" (more on this in a bit) differs.

One popular origin story for this form of controlled experimentation goes back to 1747 in what is often considered the "first clinical trial."[8] One of the many perils of long-duration sea voyages at the time was scurvy.

---

[8] https://www.bbvaopenmind.com/en/science/leading-figures/james-lind-and-scurvy-the-first-clinical-trial-in-history/.

Deprive humans of vitamin C entirely for a while, and the body starts to struggle—swollen and bloody gums, teeth falling out, skin hemorrhages, open sores—ultimately leading to death. In 1747, Scotsman James Lind was the surgeon aboard the *HMS Salisbury*, which was patrolling the English Channel during the War of Austrian Succession. Eight weeks into the voyage, a number of the sailors had fallen seriously ill with scurvy. Lind divided 12 of the sick sailors into six pairs, and then he treated them each with a different dietary supplement: diluted sulfuric acid (!), vinegar (!), cider, two oranges and a lemon, sea water (!), and a "purgative mixture" (!). Even without having the benefits of the citrus/scurvy connection that we have from our twenty-first-century vantage point, the two sailors who were given the oranges and lemons, presumably, felt like they'd gotten the best end of this deal! As we might expect, these were also the only two sailors whose condition improved.

While this is often considered the first clinical trial, it is not necessarily a *well-designed* clinical trial:

- The number of subjects was small (only two per "treatment"), which makes the study severely "underpowered."

- There was no "control" group—no pair of sailors was given *no* treatment.
- Whether the assignment of each sailor to a particular treatment regimen was truly random is unknown.

On top of those problems with the study design (from our high-and-mighty twenty-first-century vantage point), some historians have started to think that the tale is apocryphal: it makes for a nice story, but Lind may have done some embellishing of the tale after the fact.

Nonetheless, the idea of a "fair trial" is useful, and the general idea can be carried forward a few centuries to the present day and applied in a business context.

The Fundamental Requirements for a Controlled Experiment

For controlled experiments to work well in a business context, they need to meet *three* specific requirements. These requirements are relatively straightforward to understand, and if they are *fully* met, then the analysis of an experiment's results is also pretty straightforward. Before we get to those two requirements, though, we have to address two nontrivial caveats:

- There are still some statistical calculations and knowledge required to analyze and properly interpret the results of a controlled experiment, even when they are perfectly executed.
- Deviating from any of these requirements, even if it seems like a minor deviation, almost certainly will add significant complexity to the analysis of the results and will reduce the quality of the conclusions that can be drawn from the results.

Providing all of the details of the ins and outs of designing, executing, and analyzing experiments is beyond the scope of this book, but we are going to describe those three fundamental requirements to at least provide you with a solid intuitional foundation.

Controlled Experimentation Requirement 1: Random Assignment

Earlier, we discussed the role of random *sampling* in generating a representative sample. Random *assignment* is different because it involves actively assigning individuals, one-by-one or in blocks, to receive a treatment. But it invokes the same mathematical logic that ensures that a randomly drawn sample can be compared closely to a population: when we randomly assign people to groups, we're going to get two groups that look just about the same. Moreover, the groups are expected to look the same on every possible dimension, *even the ones for which we haven't even thought to collect data!*[9] These perfectly balanced groups enable us to ignore confounding bias because there's no characteristic a person could have that makes them more likely to get the treatment than another (i.e., nothing that could *confound* the treatment). Formally put:

Random assignment means that each subject has an equal likelihood of receiving any of the treatments in the experiment.

One of the *potential* problems with the scurvy treatment "medical trial" from the middle of the eighteenth century that we called out earlier was that we don't know whether the selection of which sailors received which treatment was truly chosen at random. We *do* have strong evidence that the power of *true* randomization was not fully recognized and adopted in the social sciences and medical trials until the middle of the twentieth century! As Gerber and Green note in *Field Experiments: Design, Analysis, and Interpretation*, before the 1950s, "Randomization was more akin to crude oil, something that periodically bubbled to the surface but remained untapped for centuries until its extraordinary practical value came to be appreciated."[10]

A real-world example that the authors encountered was with a consumer brand based in Europe that was looking to make a push into selling in the United States. A central component of this push was to do heavy digital advertising. The company wanted to know how effective that advertising was, so it decided that it would run the ads as a geographic test, running the ads in some areas and not running it in others, and then comparing the resulting revenue.

This sort of advertising test is often referred to as a "matched market test," and a common way is to split the different geographic regions in the United States by Designated Market Areas (DMAs), which are a standard set of just over 200 "media markets" that are a common mechanism for

---

[9] This is the "unobserved heterogeneity" that we referred to back in Chapter 7. Since you are still reading the footnotes this far into the book, we felt you would appreciate us making that connection for you.

[10] Gerber, A.S. and Green, D. P. (2012). *Field experiments: Design, analysis, and interpretation.* New York: W.W. Norton & Company, p. 6.

advertisers to specify *where* they want their ads to run. DMAs do *not* overlap, and, together, they encompass the totality of the United States. The standardized and widely used definition of DMAs is generally a great basis for controlled experimentation.

In the case of this company, the experiment was going to have half of the DMAs receiving the advertising and half of them not. With a simple spreadsheet that listed all of the DMAs, the organization used a random number generator to randomly assign which DMAs would get the advertising (the "treatment group") and which would not (the "control group").

If they had stopped there and executed the experiment, they would have been fine. But they got a little fancier with their planning, as one of the marketing directors noticed that the San Francisco (and Oakland and San Jose) DMA had wound up in the control group—the group that would not get the advertising. This seemed like a big miss, as high tech workers were one of their key target audiences. So, they swapped out that DMA with another one. The slippery slope was under way!

Several other team members started reviewing the list and identifying other markets that were slated to not get any advertising that they really expected to be substantial markets for them. So, they swapped out a few more. Sure, they wanted the rigor of data behind their decisions, but it would be lunacy to have that mean they weren't going to advertise for a while in some of their key markets!

These adjustments to the test design, while well intended, would have seriously undermined the integrity of the test itself; the marketers were starting to put their fingers on the scale to ensure that the markets that were most likely to buy their products (with or without advertising) were going to receive the advertising. Conversely, as part of this reshuffling, markets that were *least* likely to buy their products (with or without advertising) became also *less* likely to receive advertising. Good thing we caught it before it went out.

Random assignment eliminates the risk of confounding. And randomization works wonders when it is true randomization. "Mostly random," or "we just made a few tweaks" is *not* random, which is the fastest way to reverse alchemy a "gold standard" into "fool's gold."

Controlled Experimentation Requirement 2: No Sharing Treatments

The second requirement for a good experiment is that the units randomly assigned to the treatment cannot accidentally (or intentionally) share their treatment with units assigned to the control. If that happens, we end up having units that we thought were not treated being treated, and that can cause the treatment effect we estimate to look a lot smaller than it actually is.

For example, consider two roommates who enroll in a weight loss study for a new energy drink. One of the roommates gets assigned to the treatment and, upon drinking it, is energized and starts getting into a wicked exercise routine. The other roommate is not assigned to the treatment and is told to continue living their life as usual. The roommates are good friends, though, and do a lot of things together. That means, as the first roommate increases the frequency with which they work out, they regularly invite the second roommate to come with them, and the second roommate often does. When it comes time for the data to be analyzed, the second roommate ends up skewing the control group because they lost weight due to the effect of the energy drink, even though they never drank it.

Another classic example of interfering treatment assignment is known as the *hotspot effect*.[11] In the canonical study, police officers were assigned to patrol city precincts at random, to see if having an officer in the precinct decreased crime. When officers would go into certain precincts that had higher levels of crime, it would force the criminals to disperse to other precincts where there weren't any officers assigned. As such, when the analysis was done, it looked like the police officers were much more effective than they really were because control areas without patrolling officers had much higher levels of crime, but those much higher levels of crime were caused by the treatment itself. This is sort of like sharing the treatment, but in reverse: due to the treatment, control units were "anti-treated."

In marketing research, this happens all too often. The solution for this is to make sure that the units at which we assign the treatment are "household" or "blocked" together and that the risk that one group's reaction to the treatment leaks into another's is minimized or eliminated. Otherwise, the results will look wildly different (and be interpreted differently) than they should be.[12]

Controlled Experimentation Requirement 3: Treatment and Results Must Be Available at the Same Unit of Analysis

The third requirement for a controlled experiment is simply that the different treatment groups have to be measurable at the same level of analysis. This is a straightforward requirement, even if it initially sounds complicated:

---

[11] For a good example of this type of study, see: Sherman, L.W. and Weisburd, D. L. (1995). General deterrent effects of police patrol in crime "hot spots": A randomized, controlled trial. *Justice Quarterly*, 12(4), pp. 625–648.

[12] This area is remarkably deep and complex as a topic of scientific research. If you're interested in reading more, explore the topic of "spillovers" in Gerber and Green's *Field Experiments: Design, Analysis, and Interpretation*.

- When a clinical trial is run for a new medication, the patient outcomes are compared for the group of patients who received the new medication compared to the patients who received a placebo.
- When an "A/B test" is run on the landing page for a website, the downstream behavior (online orders, revenue, etc.) for the group of visitors who saw the "A" design on the landing page are compared to the group of visitors who saw the "B" design for the same page.
- In a "matched market" test based on DMAs (as we described in the previous section), the revenue for the DMAs that received the advertising is compared to the revenue for the DMAs that did *not* receive the advertising.

This may seem obvious, but we are surprised how often we run into confusion on the subject. It's not enough to simply *randomly assign treatment* (although this *is* a requirement!). Being able to identify the *results* broken out by that assignment is critical.

For instance, it would *not* be useful to have a digital billboard randomly swap between two different messages throughout the course of the day as a test to see which one resulted in more revenue for the store it was advertising. It would be essentially impossible to identify which message had been exposed to which in-store customers (and it would be likely that some customers received *both* messages depending when and how often they drove past the billboard).

Note this does *not* mean that, for a controlled experiment to be valid, that the treatment and the results have to be measured at the level of each individual person. This is often infeasible and, in many cases, unnecessarily intrusive. In the DMA-based geographic matched market test we described earlier, for instance, while individual people ultimately were advertised to (or not) and individual people ultimately made purchases (or not), the alignment of the "treatment" and "outcomes" was at the *DMA* level.

This requirement cuts two ways:

- The treatment and the result *must* both be identifiable at the same "unit of analysis" (person, group of website visitors, DMA, etc.). If not, then the test will not be able to be analyzed effectively.
- The treatment and the results *only* need to be identifiable at the same unit of analysis—perfectly valid tests can often be run without person-level fidelity in the assignment and measurement!

If all three of these requirements are fully met, then the key ingredients for a valid controlled experiment are in place!

Some Cautionary Notes About Controlled Experimentation

While controlled experiments are the gold standard for identifying causation and, in a perfect world, every decision would be backed up by a well-executed experiment, there are a number of challenges and cautionary considerations with this hypothesis validation technique. We don't want to scare you away from experimentation, but it would be irresponsible to not briefly outline some of the main ones:

Experiments require careful planning, execution, and analysis. By their very nature, when considering using an experiment to validate a hypothesis, we are considering data that has *not yet been collected*. This means that, while the hypothesis will be validated (or not) using the gold standard of causality, it requires getting the experiment designed, implementing it, waiting while it is running, and then analyzing the results. This takes time. And while experiments are conceptually elegant and straightforward, the best way to avoid pitfalls is to include someone with an appropriate level of statistical expertise to assist with the design of the experiment on the front end and then the analysis of the results once the experiment has been completed.

Experiments require a sufficient volume of test subjects. One of the ways that an experiment can wind up being unhelpful in the validation of a hypothesis is if it is "underpowered." This simply means that there was not enough data collected to sufficiently reduce the uncertainty inherent in the results of the test to make them useful. Depending on the hypothesis being validated and the experiment that has been proposed, if there is not going to be enough volume in the test, it may not be worth conducting. This, again, is where a statistician or data scientist can be of enormous use—assessing the situation and determining if a valid experiment design is available.

Results can only be extrapolated so far. The results of an experiment provide very clear and specific information about the causal relationship between what was being tested (the treatment) and the result of interest (the effect). They do not provide a "model" that can be broadly extended or applied. For instance, in our DMA-based advertising example, while a well-designed experiment will give us very good information about the incremental revenue impact of advertising at whatever level we ran the advertising, it will *not* give us reliable information as to the revenue impact should the advertising level be doubled (or halved). As such, it's important to be very clear on what relationship we are looking to assess with the experiment to ensure it is validating the hypothesis being examined.

In short, while experiments are the gold standard of causality, they're not the be-all-end-all that is the most appropriate tool for every hypothesis that warrants validation. And while we have given a general introduction to these tools to overcome confounding bias and make causal inferences, we encourage the reader to seek expert assistance when designing and implementing controlled experiments.

SUMMARY

Scientific evidence—evidence produced to make generalized and causal inferences—produces high-quality evidence we can use as part of our hypothesis validation exercises. But as we have hopefully shown in this chapter, the quality of scientific evidence does not necessarily come from the specific analytical methodologies we employ. Rather, scientific evidence gets its weight from carefully thinking through the problem and then applying powerful assumptions that bolster the quality of the insights generated.

The material we covered in this chapter might seem intimidating, but hopefully, you now have a deeper intuition when it comes to validating hypotheses—what can and cannot be expected from the data under different conditions and what to watch out for as you work with your teams to put data to productive use.

MEASURE THIS CHAPTER

And now, it's once again time to contribute to the performance measurement of this book by visiting https://analyticstrw.com and answering the two-question survey for this chapter. Note that we're not asking you to complete the survey only if you are enjoying the book: we're expecting that to reduce the bias in our sample at least a little bit!

10

Operational Enablement
Using Data

If you've gotten this far, you've read in Chapter 6 how to generate great ideas through the actionable hypothesis framework. You've used the techniques in Chapters 7–9 to convince yourself and your peers that they are great ideas. Now, it's time to put them into action. But taking action on a great idea is much harder than generating the idea in the first place.

Insight does not beget action. Actions are costly, and they involve trade-offs. Data and analytics—including machine learning and artificial intelligence (AI)—can make the implementation of our ideas more effective, more efficient, and more fulfilling to our team members who use them. And if we can make the implementation of our ideas better, we can provide more value to our organization and our customers without sacrificing our bottom line.

Operational enablement is the practice of making actionable ideas *work*, by providing the technological and people-skill capabilities that are necessary to achieve our desired outcomes. The practice of operational enablement makes it more efficient to execute an idea, or a portfolio of ideas, by providing shared resources that reduce implementation costs.

Data are integral to operational enablement. When there are ongoing business processes that *must run* if the business is to operate, there are often data that are defined inputs to those processes. These data track the ebb and flow of financial transactions, auditable logs, cloud server interactions, and enterprise resourcing decisions, rendering a single source of truth for what happened and when. That source of truth is required to enable the business to efficiently execute on its ideas because without it, it would be nearly impossible to coordinate activities toward a common goal. Data are particularly well-suited for operational enablement because they are inexpensive and reliable, reducing coordination costs without the need for a great deal of ongoing investment.[1]

These data sources operating as the organizational lifeblood are intricately related to performance measurement. Metrics used in performance measurement often rely on data being used for operational enablement.

These data are also related to the practice of hypothesis generation, validation, and implementation. In the hypothesis generation phase, we often use

---

[1] Although operational enablement investments using data can be expensive up-front, they can also be robust and long-lived. As of this book's writing, Southwest Airlines still operated a version of Microsoft Windows from 1992 for its flight scheduling processes, sending flights to and from distant locations without the need for the latest data platform capabilities. That version protected it from the global IT outage that resulted from the CrowdStrike security patch failure in July 2024, prompting its social media team to poke fun at other airlines with a "who's laughing now" social media post.

the data available to notice irregularities and form theories. In the validation phase, we often use the data available for anecdotal, descriptive, and scientific analysis (although we warn the reader not to rely too much on the data available because it risks producing smaller thinking than is necessary to succeed).

In the implementation phase, when we wish to act on an insight we have generated, we must engender different behaviors in our business. That means that we must create a new business process, or adapt an existing process, for our organization's employees and systems to adapt to the new behavioral requirement. Operational enablement of insights is the art of updating the flows of data the business already has—and sometimes introducing some new ones—to reflect our insight's associated action.

In this chapter, we discuss operational enablement from the organizational perspective: how should leaders think about adapting and scaling the implications of their insights generated by the actionable hypothesis framework?

THE BALANCING ACT: VALUE AND EFFICIENCY

Putting our full weight behind a big decision that could be revolutionary in its value for our organization or our customer can end up coming with a big price tag. Even if it's not expensive in terms of the dollars-and-cents we need to spend to make it happen, it can be quite expensive in the number of man-hours—or in the social and political capital required—to accomplish it.

Suppose, for instance, that we find through the hypothesis testing framework that our call center employees performed much better in resolving customer complaints when using customized scripts in their conversations with customers. We then investigate whether it would be possible to bake this new "custom scripts" process into the call center's standard procedures. We would need to not only train the employees on how to use the scripts in their conversations; we would also need to create a scalable process that can *affordably* provide those scripts based on customer data.

To solve the scale problem, we could hire people who focus on nothing but writing scripts in real time for the call center representatives. But this comes at significant cost and overhead. We would need to train those people. We would need to pay them. And we would need to keep them happy to reduce attrition rates, as routine script writing is a rather boring and thankless job. We are hard-pressed to imagine an entire staff of people paid just to write scripts on the fly for call center representatives; they would have to secretly listen in on the calls, violating the customer's sense of trust, or at least creating an awkward situation in which there are three people on the call, but only two who speak. It is almost a certainty that the representatives relying on the scripts they write would grow frustrated with the delivery: a slow, teleprompter-esque interface riddled with typos.

Alternatively, we could use a technology platform to provide the scripts to our call center resources. The technology platform could use a large language model (LLM)[2] that would ingest data about the customer at hand, the situation the customer has raised in the present conversation, and how the call center representative speaking to the customer behaves. Then, the LLM would output a highly effective script, focused on resolving the customer's problem, and feed it to the call center representative, who can implement it with a more human touch. The platform would be able to do this at a lower cost than the cost we would incur by hiring several script writers, which would potentially solve our affordability problem.

But to achieve this vision of an AI-powered, knock-out call center, we would still incur costs in terms of effort and capital: How would we get access to such a platform? Would we build it by hiring data scientists? Would we buy it from a technology vendor? Would our employees need training to trust the platform and adopt it? These costs can add up.

Moreover, how would we integrate its outputs into our call center process? Would it be entirely systematized, producing outputs that the call center representative simply reads from a computer screen? Do we need a new application framework to transcribe and process the conversation in real time? Should it interface with a customer relationship management (CRM) system that contains information about the customer calling and is retrieved using their caller ID? These business process questions must be answered, too, including what startup and ongoing costs they would add to the process.

Let's say we go through the exercise of implementing such a system. As expected, customer complaints are now globally resolved at a greater rate than they were before. The important question becomes: does resolving customer complaints increase the amount of revenue coming in from those customers? And, if so, is that increase sufficiently large to justify the investment when combined with the costs of the process change in an ROI calculation?

If it doesn't, even though the new process and technology were able to improve the quality of our service, the exercise did not result in an ROI that would make it "worth it." Indeed, there is some research to suggest that

---

[2] A large language model, or LLM, is a machine learning technology known as generative artificial intelligence (generative AI). It is very good at producing outputs that reflect natural language used by humans. LLMs are increasingly popular because their text outputs are sometimes imperceptibly different from the text a human would generate if asked to perform the same task.

companies are more profitable when they provide poor customer service via their call centers and interactive voice response (IVR) systems because the customers who are most expensive to satisfy end up leaving anyway, and the customers that have issues that are trivial but require lots of time to resolve do not have the anger or patience to make it through the arduous "hassle costs" required to actually resolve the problem (these hassle costs actually protect the company from having to take action, like refunding an order).[3]

When these costs get too high, even a great insight can look rather deflated, because it can become clear that the cost of implementing it exceeds the value it is anticipated to generate, and hence, the value the company can capture back through the pricing of its services and products. This is the tension of operational enablement. Whatever we do in business, and whatever value we create for our customers, we must ultimately be remunerated for providing that value, such that we are able to deliver it at a lower cost than the remuneration received. We can sell incredibly valuable products at high prices, but if we don't have a way of delivering those high value products at a lower cost that what we bring in, we won't be in business for very long.

With the right framework for thinking about data-driven operational enablement, we can deal with the problems associated with the implementation of our ideas more confidently, knowing that there really *is* a way to deliver the value we've discovered…without breaking the bank.

THE FACTORY: HOW TO THINK ABOUT DATA FOR OPERATIONAL ENABLEMENT

A simple way of thinking about any business, or business process, is to imagine it as a small factory. Raw materials make their way into the factory. A mechanism inside of the factory operates on those materials to produce some output. Then, that output makes its way out of the factory. It's easy to imagine the processes of a manufacturing business, or a steel refinery, in the context of the factory mental model, because these processes take place in, well, factories.

It's similarly easy to think of pure operational data pipelines as if they were in a factory. If we're moving customer and order data around from point A to point B to enable a computer-driven process like shipping fulfillment, for

---

[3] Dukes, A. and Zhu, Y. (2019). Why is customer service so bad? Because it's profitable. *Harvard Business Review*. https://hbr.org/2019/02/why-is-customer-service-so-bad-because-its-profitable.

example, then it sure looks like a factory: in an extract-transform-load operation ("ETL" operation), data are *extracted* from one place (the inputs), *transformed* or transported (the mechanism), and then *loaded* into another location (the output).

It's harder, though, to imagine how the mechanism underlying transformations in "knowledge work" fits into the factory mental model. It's clear that the raw materials are information (usually structured, sometimes unstructured).[4] It's also clear that the output is a product or service (potentially one that is improved by an insight implying new actions).

What's murkier is the mechanism that transforms the informational inputs into insightful, valuable outputs. It is some combination of a person's experience, abilities, critical thinking skills, learned trade processes and procedures, and maybe a little intuition, that enable the knowledge worker to turn information into insight and action. It is some even greater combination of those analyst-level mechanisms that compose an organization's ability to process information into something useful.

If we don't know what the precise mechanism or technology is that underlies transformation of our data inputs into business outputs, then how is it possible to operationally enable our enterprise using data, analytics, hypotheses, and insights?

Industry has made manufacturing plants, steel refineries, and the like more productive over time by using new technologies for operational enablement. One revolutionary technology was electricity, which enabled manufacturers to install custom machines to automate the manual work that was previously done by people. We can't exactly electrify an analyst[5] to enable them to produce more insights, but there is another means of increasing the efficiency of mechanisms that involve information work: *trade secrets*.

Trade Secrets: The Original Business Logic

To explain what a trade secret is in this context, consider a glassware manufacturer. Making common glassware used to require skilled artisans who, through hard work and experience making glass with other artisans, would gain inside information on techniques that would make them more productive, more efficient, or produce higher quality goods. Venetian glass manufacturers, for centuries, protected the secret glass recipes, heating techniques,

---

[4] Structured data are easily organized into a regularized format, like an Excel spreadsheet. Unstructured data come in the form of raw text, or raw images, that must be operated on, to put them into a regularized format.

[5] Or maybe we can electrify an analyst. We've never tried it.

and design templates that made their glassware the best in the world.[6] Nascent trade organizations for glassware artisans would vehemently protect their ability to make a profit and charge their own prices by preventing outsiders from learning how they made their glass.

These trade secrets represented special processes, learned over time through careful application, inference, and experimentation, that could reliably produce a higher quality—and more efficiently achieved—outcome. If we could learn these trade secrets, we could learn the process by which to produce a highly valuable good and make good money doing it.

The trade secrets of yesteryear are today known by another name: *business logic*. Knowledge workers and companies that use data as part of their everyday operations are familiar with business logic. It is the sequence of actions and transformation that are taken on a piece of information that prompt some output to be produced. These sequences of actions and transformations are so precious to today's companies that they require employees to sign nondisclosure agreements that prevent employees from ever revealing the trade secrets they learn there. The reason for these nondisclosure agreements is the same as the reason that the Venetian trade organizations were so aggressive in protecting their trade secrets: if we know the secret sauce, we, too, can produce highly valuable goods and make good money doing it.

How Hypothesis Validation Develops Trade Secrets and Business Logic

If you think about it, every insight we generate through the hypothesis generation and validation framework we've introduced in this book is a new "trade secret," or a new "rule" to be included in our business logic. For example, if we find that personalizing the customer's experience during the checkout process by adding their first name into the website header improves the probability that they convert on a purchase, then we have discovered a new step that we can take as part of our business logic to improve the quality of our products and services. If we find through a controlled experiment that higher ad frequency increases sales in the Midwestern region, then we have discovered a new step that we can take as part of our business logic to increase sales in that area.[7] If we find that using sand from the beaches of France creates better selling glass than sand from the beaches of Florida, we have discovered

---

[6] If not for the Venetian glassmakers, we would never have invented spectacles, telescopes, or microscopes. It was their perfected glass-making techniques that enabled the production of clear, durable glass that could magnify images by bending light.

[7] Recall from Chapter 9, however, that experimental results are often context specific, responding to the location of the subjects, the period in which the experiment was

a new step that we could take as part of our business logic in sourcing raw materials.[8]

Keep applying the hypothesis generation and validation framework, and before you know it, you will have a series of insights that together become the actual business logic that is needed to turn inputs into desired outputs. Whereas trade secrets in the past were more or less "stumbled upon" through coaching and targeted effort on the part of talented artisans, the framework we have outlined in this book is a structured way to ensure that we are constantly developing new ideas and insights that can feed back into our business logic to ultimately produce more efficient mechanisms and higher quality outputs. The hypothesis library we discussed in Chapter 6 is, seen through this factory lens, a trove of potential rules we may want to include as part of our business logic (when the validation renders a positive result).

Not all trade secrets must be developed through the process of hypothesis validation. Our human ability to simply articulate the steps that have worked for us in the past can generate mechanisms that work well. But there is value in taking a disciplined approach to testing the steps we use as part of that mechanism, or to introducing new steps into that mechanism that improve the quality and quantity of the output. We don't always know if all of the steps we are going through as part of a mechanism actually contribute to a better outcome; we may simply do them because "one time it worked really well and we didn't want to change anything."

Indeed, such is the same logic we use when carrying around lucky pennies and wearing our lucky baseball jerseys to games: we did it before and it usually works, so why change it? The reason: it probably costs more to do those extra steps, and those costs can add up over time. The hypothesis validation framework does not just have to introduce *new* rules into the process. It can also be used to verify whether *removing* certain rules improves the output.

Operational Enablement and Data in Defined Processes

Trade secrets—these business "rules"—are the basic building blocks of the defined processes that compose factory mechanisms. To get an idea for what those building blocks are, just ask an experienced professional to break down

---

run, and the nature of the treatment itself that would purport to create a new rule in the business logic.

[8] Look, we know it's not just any sand that gets used to make glass; it's purified silica sand—we're just talking about it this way to make the point.

their day-to-day task into discrete transformational steps that are required to achieve the business outcome their job supports. If we were to ask an artisanal glassmaker to break down the steps involved in their process to produce a basic piece of glassware, they would give us something like the following:

> *To create a basic piece of glassware, we need to melt a certain type of sand at a certain temperature, mold it to specification, and let it cool down in a controlled manner. Each individual step requires something I learned at some point, either by trial and error or training. The temperature at which we melt the sand is 3,090 degrees Fahrenheit, the shape of the mold that we use is a two-sided graphite slug with an inflatable cavity, and the precise manner in which we let the glass cool is in a kiln that reduces temperature gradually to 300 degrees over four days.*

The defined process has reliable, specific inputs, outputs, and mechanism steps. Similarly, we may ask an experienced operations consultant to break down the steps involved in helping their fulfillment team comply with state tax law:

> *If our fulfillment manager receives an order with an address in Texas, then they know the company will pay sales tax in Texas. The mechanism they use to ascertain the Texas tax rate is simple: they look up the sales tax rate in Texas in an Excel spreadsheet, reserve that amount for payment to the Texas revenue service, and add it to the reconciliations spreadsheet for the next check we cut for taxes. Our fulfillment manager may even develop shortcuts over time to accelerate the lookup speed, linking the cell in the spreadsheet to the state's tax rate automatically by using a lookup for the state.*

In both cases above, operational data may be used to replace tasks that we previously would need a person to manually look up or monitor. We may want to track the temperature at which the kiln is running; we may want to know what the latest tax rate is in Texas, which can change with each legislative session. But major transformations of that data—and actions that require nuanced interpretation of that data—are unnecessary.

Because the inputs and outputs are well defined, we can create defined, rules-based processes that deal with the tasks using only operational data: if the kiln is at temperature X, remove the glass; when we get the order's subtotal, multiply the tax rate by the subtotal to yield the tax payment contribution. These steps are possible to automate using a machine or computer.

In simple, defined cases like both of the examples we just described, the steps required to process the information are easy enough that we could build a computer program to do them. We could, in effect, "replace the human in the loop" with a computer program that ingests data and automatically acts upon it.

In fact, such simple business logic has been automated so greatly in industry that when simple processes are not automatic and use people instead, we jokingly refer to the mechanism as "human middleware:" humans performing tasks that computer software should perform instead. The second case involving tax rate data lookups, for instance, is an exceedingly simple mechanism that is today usually (but, not always!) automated using data and software at a very low cost (and the work-hours to execute it manually are much more expensive).

Output Complexity and Automation Costs

The processes required to change an input into an output are more difficult to explain when their complex outputs require accordingly complex mechanisms to be produced. Consider the glassware artisan's response, now tasked with decomposing their process for an expensive piece of artistic glassware, commissioned by a discerning client:

> *Customers are finicky about what they want and may have custom requirements about the glassware we produce, and the interpretation of what the customer wants can be subject to a good deal of nuance. To create an artistic piece of glassware, we need specific knowledge about how to mix different types of sand and special combustible materials together to achieve the right hue and texture, and how to use a specific and special glass blowing or molding instrument that we created for the design desired by the customer. For many pieces, such as those inspired by Chihuly, we must know how to structure the glass components so that the work does not collapse in on itself.*

The mechanism in this case is complex, and the outputs a customer might desire are numerous. We can see that it is hard to constrain a factory mechanism to a series of steps that can produce the customer's desired output.

Similarly, consider the following business case from an executive responsible for the operations of a payment processing company's call center:

> *If our call-center representative receives a call from a customer who is irate because their credit card was suspended due to fraudulent activity, then the representative knows that they need to solve the problem quickly so that the customer does not cancel their credit card. The mechanism is*

complicated. First, the representative has to ascertain what the problem is by searching through recent transactions to discover if any unusual charges were made to the card. Second, the representative has to verify with the customer that the unusual charges were, indeed, inauthentic. Third, the representative has to either (a) *coach the customer through proactively putting a hold on their card and ordering a replacement, in the case that the unusual charges were fraudulent, or* (b) *put the customer at ease, so that they do not cancel their card out of rage.*

This more complicated process requires the call center employee to do on-the-fly data transformations while using their soft skills to quell the customer's emotional state, which takes time. It requires operational data to make it work, but it also requires the synthesis of several other data sources, some of which are not machine-readable, to produce the desired outcome.

It would be difficult to build a computer program that can deal with the many vagaries entailed in this type of customer service call. The output is well-defined (customer complaint resolution), but some of the inputs are ambiguous, and the mechanism required to get to the output is not clearly explicated.

Operational enablement with data can help make complex processes more efficient by automating small parts of those complex processes. For instance, we could hire a development team to write database queries that make parts of the call center representative's process faster. The program they develop could automatically pull transactions associated with the customer's phone number from the company's database and flag the transactions that have fraudulent data signatures associated with them. With this program, by the time the customer is connected with a call center representative, the representative would already have a pretty good idea of what they need to do and wouldn't need to spend any time talking the customer through their recent transactions. This could reduce costs by reducing the amount of time any given representative has to spend with a customer. This could also improve quality, because customers will feel at ease sooner during a call.

We could extend this logic to every part of the process that has been delineated by the artisan and the executive responsible for the payment processing company's call center. We could break the very complex tasks down into their constituent parts, each of which was put in place in response to some expectation or insight by knowledgeable trade experts. We could then build small rulesets that help people who do not have experience execute each one of these tasks. And, if each ruleset was simple enough, we could potentially write a computer program that could do the tasks for the people. But then there is the trade-off we discussed earlier: at what point does breaking this ambiguous process into discrete defined processes become too expensive?

An ambiguous process with ambiguous inputs and outputs can require an undefined number of mechanisms to complete the task. The attempt to automate such undefined processes can get expensive in a few ways.

First, *defined processes are brittle* because they tend to break down when confronted with unexpected inputs. Every time the process breaks, a person has to intervene in order to backstop the inability of the process to deliver the outcome that was desired. In cases with material production automation, when the process breaks, the output being produced is often mangled, forcing the person who intervenes to discard the materials that were originally used to start the process. These "human backstops" must be paid, and that is often at a higher rate than first order resources, because they must be skilled in debugging the process. The materials that are lost become a sunk cost. If you've ever been on the phone with a call-center representative who asks you to repeat all of the information you already gave to the IVR system, you have experienced the redundancy that is required when the process breaks down. And the business pays for it!

Second, with an undefined number of mechanisms, we can get stuck trying to define a new process for every potential situation, effectively building a cumbersome architecture around what originally would have just been *easier and cheaper for a person to just execute themselves.*

For example, consider data entry specialists who must correct poorly OCRed documents (i.e., computers have been used to transcribe a scanned image's text into machine-readable characters using optical character recognition—OCR—like when we have to enter someone's email from a sign-up sheet into a computer database). The correction process is longer than the original entry process: reading the faulty outputs, reading the original source, and then re-inputting the data is a three-step process. Simply transcribing the data takes only one step.

Third, there are *technology costs* involved in enabling such a system that can grow to be considerable given the amount of engineering effort required to create (and maintain!) a custom process for each potential input. Operational enablement always entails costs associated with providing the tooling necessary for employees to be able to do their jobs.

The beauty of humans is that they can "learn on the fly" and apply transferable knowledge and skills to the task at hand, drawing on knowledge they've gained in the past or on a preternatural understanding of how physical movement works. This helps them deal with situations that they haven't seen before to achieve outcomes that are comparable to situations that they *have* seen before. The call center representative, for instance, can deal with new information by simply exercising human judgment, and paying that call center representative to do that may just be cheaper than having to engineer thousands of processes.

Operational enablement is effectively limited by the complexity of the mechanisms required to produce the desired output. We may wish to reduce the need for a call center representative's soft skills by using automated scripts, but, as we discussed in the introduction to this chapter, to implement a system that does that may cost just too much to justify the investment. That's where machine learning and AI come into the picture.

MACHINE LEARNING AND AI

The emergence of AI in recent years has been marked by computer processes that can execute complex responsibilities we once thought only humans could manage. This includes use cases such as recognizing cancer in a radiological scan, tutoring children on their homework, and even deciding whether to make million-dollar bets on Wall Street. The popularization of LLMs, which produce textual outputs nearly indistinguishable from the textual outputs we could have paid a person to produce—but in far less time and at far less expense—have triggered a revolution in our ability to operationally enable ideas that previously seemed too expensive, or impossible, to automate. So, what do these technologies mean for our ability to use data for operational enablement?

In short, machine learning and AI enable us to scale complex processes and business logic at lower cost. While the cost is not trivial, it is much lower in many cases than the costs we would incur if we had human beings execute those complex processes, or if we were to build brittle rule-based workflows to execute them. Harkening back to the trade-offs we introduced in this chapter, these lower costs can enable businesses to provide higher quality outputs and remain profitable.

Machine Learning: Discovering Mechanisms Without Manual Intervention

Machine learning is a field of computer science that uses algorithms that let computers learn rules from the world about how to transform inputs into outputs without having to be programmed explicitly with the rules it eventually discovers. These algorithms enable the computer to construct sets of rules that reflect the process we otherwise would need a trade expert to create for us. The fact that these algorithms can find a way to transform inputs into outputs—by creating their own complex set of rules—is important because it allows us to delegate tasks that previously we would not have been able to define processes for (and, therefore, have been unable to automate) to machines and computers that can automate them. And it is usually much cheaper to use a computer to do a task than asking a human to do that same task.

Humans are great at intuitively performing tasks. If we validated a hypothesis that reading each day's summarized news improved our ability to close important sales because we would be more relevant to our clients, then we might decide to implement a process by which we read the summarized news each day. To act on that hypothesis, we may ask one of our employees to summarize the news for the day: that employee would go and read the newspapers, sketch out common themes, and then come back to us with a summary of what was published. We would not have to delineate explicitly the process for how to summarize the news; they would just "get" how to do it (perhaps with a little training).

If we, instead, had to create from scratch an elaborate and explicitly defined process—a process that does *not* use machine learning, but, rather, relies on specifically defined rules and logic that we create—for a machine to summarize the news, it could easily get out of hand. We would have to teach the machine to recognize the words on the news websites. We would have to teach the machine how to extract meaning from the words they recognize. We would have to teach the machine how to form a thematic thought about those words. We would have to teach the machine how to transform those thoughts into written language that would then enable us to recover a summary of the news. And we would have to do this for every potential theme that could exist in the news, which is nearly impossible to do, because the events of the world will not consistently fit into buckets that we've already defined. The inputs are too ambiguous, and ultimately, the string of text being produced as an output is too ambiguous to define a pre-ordained, reliable, rule-based mechanism to turn those inputs into *durable, valuable* outputs.

Machine learning approaches invert the problem. They work backward, asking, "What is the output I wish to produce, and what are the inputs from which I must produce that output?" They then use different types of algorithms to discover the mathematical functions that can map the inputs they're given to the outputs desired. They can discover the set of rules that compose the mechanism without ever having to be told what those rules should be. As a matter of fact, if you were reading this example and thinking, "I've seen something that does something very similar to this," then you've almost certainly seen machine learning in action.

Simple Machine-learned Rulesets

Some of the rulesets machine learning models discover are simple. For instance, a random forest regression may be used to figure out what characteristics are associated with a customer who buys a BMW instead of another make of car.[9] This regression may output a ruleset as follows: if the customer makes more than $100,000 a year, has shown an interest in sports cars, and subscribes to a travel magazine, then they are more likely to buy a BMW, and we should advertise to them.

These rules are intuitive: if a customer makes more money, they have the disposable income to buy a more expensive vehicle; if a customer likes sports cars, they are more likely to buy a sports car; if a customer subscribes to a travel magazine, they are more likely to see luxury vehicle advertisements placed by BMW in that magazine because its readers are more likely to have disposable income (they have income to spend on "reading for pleasure" periodicals *and* they have an interest in travel, which means they are more likely to have the financial means to travel periodically for leisure).

We can use this "machine-learned" ruleset as part of our business logic that inputs customer data and outputs an advertisement rendering decision to improve the efficiency of our advertising spend. In fact, this simple ruleset is something that we likely could have come up with ourselves. If we had the long-held expectation that we should advertise BMWs to customers like those described in the preceding paragraph, then this mathematical discovery of those same rules can serve as an independent validation, which is something, even if it's not a surprising and impactful insight.

As we discussed in earlier chapters, to *definitively* say that the characteristics of income, interests, and advertising exposure affect a customer's likelihood to buy our products and services, we would need to embark on a journey of counterfactual reasoning. Nonetheless, the machine-learned ruleset can give us confidence that the rules we generated ourselves aren't too far off from the ones a mathematical approach would have generated. If the machine generates a different logical tree than we would have, it doesn't mean that ours is wrong. But it can be reassuring when a bootstrapped model[10] converges to the answer we would have expected at the outset. We stop short of considering this ruleset-to-ruleset comparison as an exercise in generating anything more than weak evidence.

---

[9] Random forest regression is another topic that has had entire books devoted to it. It is a popular machine learning technique that, to oversimplify to the point that some readers could be offended, recreates "trees of rules" that will accurately classify inputs into the desired outputs.

[10] A "bootstrapped model" is a model that has been run several thousand times to observe the distribution of potential rulesets it might generate. It's more jargon, we realize, but a useful takeaway is that "several thousand times" bit—computers don't balk at running through a somewhat tedious set of statistical calculations again and again and again to arrive at an end result.

Simple machine-learned rulesets can also help us tune rulesets that already exist as part of our business logic. For example, our advertising team may already have made the decision to advertise BMWs to customers with high incomes, but they have been using an income level that is different from the one that the algorithm identified as the ideal cutoff point. By using the machine-learned threshold, our team can more accurately target converting customers, thereby saving dollars from advertising impressions that don't move the needle.

Finally, a simple machine-learned ruleset can be applied wholesale as part of our business logic if we don't already have a process in place to transform the input in consideration into the output desired. We strongly recommend piloting the deployment of rulesets generated by machine learning approaches within the hypothesis validation framework:

> *"I **believe** that we will save money and increase our conversion rate by changing our advertising targeting criteria **because** my machine learning model generated a new set of rules for targeting customers more likely to convert. If I'm right, I'll update my business logic to employ the rules the machine learning model identified."*

We will explore the relationship between operational enablement and hypothesis validation in more detail in Chapter 11.

Complex Machine-learned Rulesets

Whereas defined processes require smaller, well-understood rulesets to make the process manageable and feasible to implement, the sets of rules machine learning approaches discover can be incredibly complex. We would venture so far as to say that the rules that today's best deep learning algorithms discover are so numerous that, in most cases, no human-readable "rulebook" could be realistically cut from the rules they discover. They deal with underlying data representations—intermediate transformations of the inputs that mark important steps along the way to the desired outputs—that may make sense to those who have taken a graduate level course in the vagaries of Hilbert spaces but are impractical for most people in business to understand. Many machine learning approaches are considered "black box," in that, once an input goes in, it is impossible to know what happens as part of the mechanism inside.

Up to this point, we have characterized machine learning as a tool to produce sets of rules (mechanisms) that can be implemented in business logic to operationally enable the insights we generate by transforming an input into an output. But it gets more complicated when thinking about complex rulesets. In cases with complex machine-learned rulesets, it is impossible to create new business logic, processes, or rules that mimic the discovered mechanism because the rules themselves are not practically intelligible. It is impossible to do ruleset-to-ruleset comparison—as discussed in the previous section on simple rulesets—to build confidence in existing business processes.

To employ machine learning models with complex mechanisms for operational enablement, we need to simplify the complex rulesets the algorithms create. The way we do that is to...well...*plug the algorithm's trained model into our process*. We plug it into our business logic as a new step! Essentially, we insert a miniature and computerized "trade expert" in the process who we trust to "figure it out." Our delegation of the complex mechanism and its outputs to a computer gets that computer a gold-star promotion: it becomes commonly known as *artificial intelligence*.

AI: Executing Mechanisms Autonomously

Linear regression, LLMs, advanced robotics—they all fall under the broadening umbrella of AI. The reason the AI umbrella has been broadened so wide is because of the role of data, analytics, and machine learning in operational enablement. Linear regression and similar techniques were used by payment processing companies in the early 2000s to determine whether charges might be fraudulent. LLMs power customer chat applications with interactions that appear practically human. Advanced robotic resources in distribution facilities can move boxes, jump up and down, and even fold laundry. These technologies are increasingly used to enable businesses to turn inputs into outputs through the automation of business logic.

As such, we define AI for operational enablement as the *delegation of complex responsibilities to a machine*, which acts as a substitute for a trade expert who otherwise would need to intervene in the business process.

Once a machine learning model is trained—creating a mechanism that converts inputs into outputs—we call the outputs it creates *predictions*. The reason we call them predictions, and not *outcomes*, is because machine learning models operating on data can envision outcomes that haven't happened yet: it takes an action, based on the algorithm's prediction, to produce an outcome. For example, consider the use of a trained machine learning model to predict whether a customer will convert on a purchase *if the customer is given a coupon*:

- The **inputs** are customer characteristics relevant to purchase conversion, along with an indicator for whether they were given the coupon.
- The **mechanism** is the complex ruleset the algorithm learned to classify customers as converters, depending on their characteristics and whether they had a coupon.
- The **output** is the predicted probability that the customer will convert with a coupon.

To get the customer to convert (and generate an outcome), we must still *give them the coupon.* Someone, or something, must make the *judgment* as to whether the business should offer the customer the coupon and, if so, then get that coupon into the customer's hands. The ability to execute autonomously on a judgment is what distinguishes AI from machine learning.

Judgment: Deciding to Act on a Prediction

Judging whether to take an action is nuanced. Judgment requires the business, through its process or its employees, to weigh the costs of implementing an action per a prediction generated by a machine learning model against the potential return the business could get from it.

In fact, the process of judgment, regardless of whether it is based on a prediction or an output from another business process, is the most critical part of the business logic. It is judgment and action that achieve business outcomes, balancing the value created by an automated business process against the broader picture of the costs involved in doing so.

Consider the previous case of the coupon. It is not free to offer the customer a coupon. The coupon must be issued to the customer somehow, either through the mail or through digital means. The coupon itself reflects some decreased amount of money that can be made from the purchase of the good, because it discounts the price of the good. And the company must have a way of verifying at the point of purchase that the coupon is authentic. We may decide to issue a fixed number of coupons given cost constraints, and therefore, the business must make a judgment as to whether the customer in question should get a coupon. And then, there's always a chance that even if we give the customer a coupon, they don't use it to convert. In Chapter 3, we discussed uncertainty in the importance of making good judgments at length.

The steps required to make a judgment can be executed by an expert, a computer, or some combination of both. We refer to these degrees of delegation by whether they use a human "in-the-loop," "on-the-loop," or "out-of-the-loop." Each degree of delegation reflects a gradation of how much we let the model "take the wheel."

Degrees of Delegation: In-the-loop, On-the-loop, and Out-of-the-loop

There are three ways to use the outputs of the machine learning algorithm, and all of them count as AI given the definition we've offered. But they differ in the degree of autonomy the machine has over the execution of the process.

Human-in-the-loop Processes

The first is *human-in-the-loop* processing. In human-in-the-loop processing, the machine learning algorithm produces outputs (predictions) that are given to a human who can decide whether to act on them. The machine does not take action alone. Instead, it acts like a "heads-up display," giving humans additional information they can use to make their own decisions.

In our running example about issuing a customer a coupon, the algorithm would yield its prediction about a customer's probability of conversion back to a person who can decide whether it would make sense to issue that person a coupon. The human in this case brings their own information about the customer, along with information about the overall business context, to combine with the information that comes from the algorithm. Then, the human renders a decision based on all of that information available to them.

If we take a step back, the human-in-the-loop process looks a lot like the process we would put in place after testing a hypothesis. If we ran a controlled experiment (see Chapter 9) and found that customers convert at a higher rate when they are given a coupon, we would now have an additional piece of information with respect to how a customer would convert. We would then take into account the business context and any additional information we have about the customer to render a decision as to whether we should issue a coupon.

When we work on human-in-the-loop processes, we recommend packaging the predictions the algorithms make as recommendations to the user rather than as raw probabilistic outputs. For example, an algorithm might predict that a customer is 10 points more likely to convert if we give them a coupon, rendering a raw output of "0.10." But what does that really mean? It would be better if the system would render information such as, "I recommend we give a coupon to this customer because it will increase their probability of converting after controlling for all the other factors that could influence their decision."

In-the-loop processing is useful for catching mistakes that may have been introduced into the process by either the code or the data used to produce the machine learning model. If we don't trust the output of the model, then we need a human to review it. In-the-loop processing can also be useful in highly regulated industries like finance, where anti-money laundering policies require a person to verify that a bank account application was submitted by a real person. The drawback, of course, is that it requires the time of the human to implement, and that increases the cost to the business.

Human-on-the-loop Processes

The second type of processing is *human-on-the-loop*. In this type of processing, the machine is prepared to render a decision based on the information it gets, but the decision must be approved by a human. This can be helpful in cases where what the machine needs to do is routine but there is a risk that the final decision needs a quality check.

The main difference between human-in-the-loop and human-on-the-loop processing is that the machine's mechanism is given additional information about the business context that enables it to render a decision. Revisiting our running example, the machine may predict a 55% chance of converting based on a coupon, but a 50% chance of converting without it, but then it will conduct an additional operation to mimic what the human would do.

For instance, the human might decide that even though it is more likely than not that the customer converts, the expected value to the business is not worth it to act. The specific math works out as follows: if we would make $100 on a conversion, but it costs $40 to issue the coupon, inclusive of the discount and transaction costs involved in getting the coupon into the customer's hand, then the expected value of the conversion is ($100 − 40) × 0.55 = $33. If we were to leave it to the original chance without sending the coupon, then the expected value is $100 × 0.50 = $50. The business would expect to make $17 less by sending the coupon.

This more complex process weighs the model's predictions against the actual business value that may result from it, emulating the approach the human would take. Then, the human reviews the decision that is proposed before finally approving it.

When we work with human-on-the-loop processes, we recommend packaging the machine's proposed decisions with explanations for why those decisions were made. If we consider the coupon example yet again, the annotated decision proposal should read as follows: "I propose to send this customer a coupon because the expected value of sending them the coupon is $20 greater than if we didn't. I've checked the coupon fund utilization, and we have enough money in the fund to cover the cost of the coupon." The human is then given an interface to approve, deny, or dig deeper into the specific data inputs used to make the prediction.[11]

On-the-loop processing can be beneficial in that it turns a human, who may have previously been required to execute a business process that is now delegated to a machine, into the manager, or editor, of the process. This can free that person up to work on other tasks, effectively increasing their productivity.

Human-out-of-the-loop Processes

Human-out-of-the-loop processes are fully automated. The algorithm is given the authority to make a prediction about the result of an action, synthesize contextual information needed to make a judgment, and ultimately render that judgment to pursue the action. The process does this entirely without human intervention, substituting its own judgment for human judgment. The benefit to the business is huge: with a fully automated process, it can now produce business outputs at minimal cost.

Out-of-the-loop processes are similar to the operational data processes already used widely in business today, but with the tweak that no judgment is rendered with respect to their outputs. Data transfers and transformations from point A to point B are automated processes that require no human engagement to review or approve their outputs. What makes the processes rise to the level of AI is this fact that a business decision is being rendered autonomously, with authority delegated to the machine.

The challenge with out-of-the-loop processes is that they can produce judgments that, in retrospect, seem irresponsible. These judgments can even verge on the level of being entirely ludicrous, or even open the company up to significant legal risk.

For instance, in 2019 the US Department of Housing and Urban Development sued Meta Systems (formerly Facebook), alleging that Meta's advertising algorithms allowed marketers to violate fair housing laws by limiting certain groups of people from seeing housing ads on Facebook. Meta's "look-alike" feature—

---

[11] Although this is not in the scope of this book, new approaches to explainable AI are helping to make human-on-the-loop processes more effective.

a machine learning process that finds new people to show our ads to based on the people we already know we want to target with our ads—was one of the subjects of debate. Look-alike algorithms can use characteristics like gender and race to decide who should be included in the expanded audience.

These characteristics are protected by the Fair Housing Act, and if we choose an audience based on those characteristics when showing housing-related ads, we are in violation of the law. While Meta argued they were not intentionally trying to break the law, their generalized, autonomous advertising process—which they created to show any advertisement, including those related to housing—inadvertently broke the law because of the way its customers used it to target audiences. There were no people to verify that the algorithms were using compliant judgment on the advertisements they would promote; authority was given to the machines to make decisions.

Another problem with out-of-the-loop processes is that things break. The data coming into the process can become malformed. The code used to execute the machine learning model can accidentally have an update pushed to it that breaks it. The power can go out at the data processing center, resetting the application programming interface (API) through which business processes interface with the machine learning process, thereby causing it to fail until manually reconfigured. The machine learning services that support out-of-the-loop processes can be brittle, and when they break (notice, we did not say *if* they break!) without a fallback plan, the impact to the business can be catastrophic. Moreover, if the process is not monitored, it may fail without anyone noticing because the authority has been silently delegated to the machine.

When we work with human-out-of-the-loop processes, we recommend the following:

- At the outset of the process lifecycle—before it is even developed—convene a diverse group of people from your company or organization who can serve as an AI Review Board. Describe your idea and gather feedback from them about how it could go wrong and what data sources should, or should not, be included in its development.
- During the development of the process, use a robust red-teaming, testing, and evaluation procedure. Let trade experts "attack" the model, revealing where it is weak so that its weaknesses can be remedied.
- After the deployment of the process, use a system to constantly monitor the process and ensure any problems, such as model drift (in cases when the models are automatically retraining without oversight), are noticed quickly. The system should integrate new operational data back into your overall operational workflows.
- Include a "ripcord" mechanism that can be used to take the model out of production immediately without baseline service interruption, in the case the process needs to be moderated.

Why Machine Learning Is Important for Operational Enablement

The costs entailed in employing machine learning models to discover and implement the mechanisms required to turn inputs into outputs is usually much lower in the long run than the cost entailed in employing people to do the same thing.

We've already demonstrated that creating complex rulesets from the knowledge of trade experts is infeasible when it comes to complex processes. Paying trade experts by the hour to execute undefined mechanisms can cost hundreds of dollars per hour. The cost of using a computer by the hour is a few cents, *if* we can get reliable and trustworthy outputs.

There are, of course, costs associated with the development of machine learning mechanisms. We must hire the right people who can build, train, and deploy the models. We must develop the appropriate data sets that the models need to be trained. We must establish a governance approach that will ensure that our machine learning models are not breaking the law, that the people within our organization are not irresponsibly consuming company resources, and that the downside risk of a catastrophic model failure is mitigated.

But with the advent of widely available algorithms that can be fit fast and efficiently, at low-cost—and with the broad availability of data that are already being used for operational purposes—the costs are comparable to what the business would pay to trade experts anyway.

With lower costs necessary to discover and execute mechanisms, there's a greater chance that you can implement actions suggested by your validated hypotheses at a profit!

MEASURE THIS CHAPTER

And now, it's the second-to-last time we will prompt you to contribute to the performance measurement of this book by visiting https://analyticstrw.com and answering the two-question survey for this chapter. And yes, we are using an automated process to render our results, but it's not human-out-of-the-loop. If you're not at least thinking about smirking at that quip, you might have skimmed this chapter too quickly!

11

Bringing It All Together

A h, the last chapter of a business book. This is where we will do the briefest of recaps of the material covered in this tome, reinforce the connective tissue between the different concepts covered up to this point, and then extract and explore some broader takeaways that have underpinned everything we have covered. Let's jump in!

THE INTERCONNECTED NATURE OF THE FRAMEWORK

We've spent the last six chapters diving into the three distinct ways that data can be used to deliver value to an organization:

Performance Measurement (Chapter 5) is about objectively and quantitatively answering the question: "Where are we today relative to where we expected to be today at some point in the past?"

Hypothesis Validation (Chapters 6 through 9) is about making decisions: given the magnitude of the decision being made and the available data that exists (or that could be gathered), selecting the most appropriate method to reduce the uncertainty regarding that decision (and then executing that method responsibly).

Operational Enablement (Chapter 10) is, among other things that build organizational capacity, about using data when it is embedded directly into a business process—some set of data is an input or an output to an operational process, or it is generated as part of the process itself to be employed as an input to another process.

These are *distinct* uses of data, and they each require a different mindset and approach to apply them effectively. However, these three uses of data are not entirely independent. In this chapter, we will explore how they are often interconnected, in that one type of data use may trigger another type of data use. The result when all three are operating in unison is like that of a well-conducted orchestra: each use of data knowing its place and purpose but working in harmony with the other uses to effectively deliver a symphony of productive information.

Operating in unison is the key phrase, so let's dive into the different connections among these three types of data uses.

Performance Measurement Triggering Hypothesis Validation

Performance measurement done well is all about removing ambiguity. With a quick glance at a well-designed performance measurement dashboard, a business manager can immediately identify which, if any, areas of the project or initiative are falling short. Critically, though:

> *The dashboard does* not *tell the manager* why *the effort is falling short or* what the manager should do about it.

The "why," ultimately, is a hypothesis validation activity, which means it can be triggered by performance measurement, as shown in Figure 11.1.

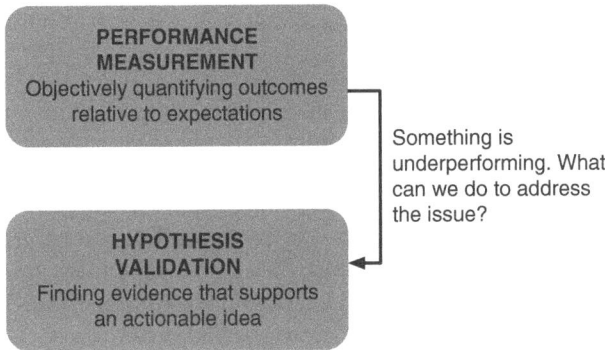

FIGURE 11.1   Performance measurement triggering hypothesis validation

Realistically, three levels of hypotheses can emerge from below-expectations performance.

Level 1: Manager Knowledge

The performance shortfall may be expected or readily explainable by the manager himself:

- "We missed our revenue target pretty badly, but I knew that was coming, since our largest customer was hit by supply chain issues and, as a result, pushed out a lot of the work we were slated to do for them."
- "We had a budget misconfiguration issue with Google Adwords in the middle of last week, which meant we had two full days where we were not doing any Google Search advertising. I expected website revenue to drop as a result, and the performance measurement dashboard reflects that. We've already addressed the issue, so no further action is needed."
- "Yep, I knew it would look like that once our CNC (a metal fabrication machine) broke."

- "Our employee turnover jumped last quarter, but our HR team had already given us a heads-up from their exit interviews that the trimming of the pool for raises this year, combined with our main competitor announcing a surge in hiring, appeared to be driving higher-than-expected attrition."

These are often rapidly formed and self-validated hypotheses—either "I was already expecting a miss because [some reason]" or "I wasn't expecting a miss, but once I saw it, I could quickly identify the root cause just based on my knowledge of the current operating environment for the organization."

Level 2: Peer Knowledge

In other performance measurement situations, a target gets missed, and it is *not* immediately obvious to the manager—or whomever is reviewing the results—as to why. But the manager is just one person. Often, *someone* has knowledge as to why the results missed expectations. This is why it is useful to share performance measurement results as quickly as they are available rather than holding them close until they have been fully analyzed and explained: it's not productive to spend cycles digging into the data only to find something that the fellow two cubicles over already knew!

As a matter of fact, the previous Google Adwords example was directly drawn from an experience one of the authors had years ago when he was working at a creative agency. He spent several hours digging into the marketing data before arriving at the "insight" that the company had apparently stopped their advertising in Google Search mid-week. He dashed off a note to the team responsible for managing that marketing channel, and he was excited to have found something so clear and actionable ("Turn that back on!"). Several hours later, he got a note back, "Oh, yes. We knew that happened, and we've already addressed it. We're sorry we neglected to let you know."

Consider an alternate approach (which the same author has employed every day since): develop an extreme bias toward sharing performance measurement results with as little latency as possible. It's okay to take a quick look to ensure there is not something obviously broken in the dashboard or report, but then sharing the results with all of the stakeholders with an invitation for them to share any information that explains why any key metrics missed their targets is wildly more efficient.

To be clear, these explanations, too, should be treated as *hypotheses* with varying levels of evidence that support them. If the evidence is overwhelming (like the earlier Google Search example), then no additional validation of the hypothesis may be warranted. If the hypothesis lacks strong evidence, though, it should be added to the hypothesis library and considered along with other hypotheses as to if and how it should be validated.

Level 3: Not Readily Apparent

Finally, there are performance misses that are genuine head-scratchers: *no one* on the team has a strong idea as to what the root cause of the miss was. In this scenario, the default—but unhealthy—reaction in many organizations is one of two responses:

- "The target we set was unrealistic. We need to reset the target."
- "We need to have an analyst dive into the data to figure out why this happened."

While a mis-set target is certainly a possible explanation, simply adjusting the target without a disciplined review of the target is dangerous. Remember: targets were set to capture the *expectations* as to what results could be expected. Those expectations represented the team's collective wisdom regarding what was realistic, and the decision to continue with the initiative—and the investments required to do that—were based on that expectation. If that expectation was missed, then a real evaluation of whether the investment is worth continuing is often warranted.

Before simply re-setting the targets, this result should trigger a round of hypothesis ideation: what ideas, *as a team*, do we have for *why* we missed our target and what might we do differently if that turns out to be the case? While no one may have an immediate idea as to what happened, forcing a pause and some collaboration will almost always generate some plausible theories. Expecting an analyst to simply find a root cause (that would point to corrective action) *may* bear fruit, but it's unnecessarily narrowing the scope of the investigation.

More rarely, but not impossibly, the target set was ludicrous to begin with, and the leadership need to do some soul searching about how their goal-setting process should run. If no hypotheses are forthcoming, then it's possible that the targets were, indeed, overly ambitious. *But this does not mean they should simply be adjusted.* Those targets represented the expectations that got the initiative funded in the first place. So, if they're going to be lowered, then the question has to be asked, "If these were our expectations back in the initial planning, would we still have funded this initiative?" If the answer is, "No," then serious consideration needs to be given to halting the effort.[1]

---

[1] The "sunk cost fallacy" comes into play with this. That's another popular concept from business school that we're simply not going to elaborate on here, even though it is a very real and dangerous phenomenon.

Hypothesis Validation Triggering Performance Measurement

Conversely, hypothesis validation can trigger performance measurement! This can happen in a couple of ways.

Did the Corrective Action Work?

If performance measurement *triggers* hypothesis validation, as discussed in the last section, then the successful validation of one or more hypotheses should lead *back* to performance measurement: "We had a problem, we identified what to do to address it, we did that, so now we're looking back to confirm that it had the desired result." Figure 11.2 illustrates this.

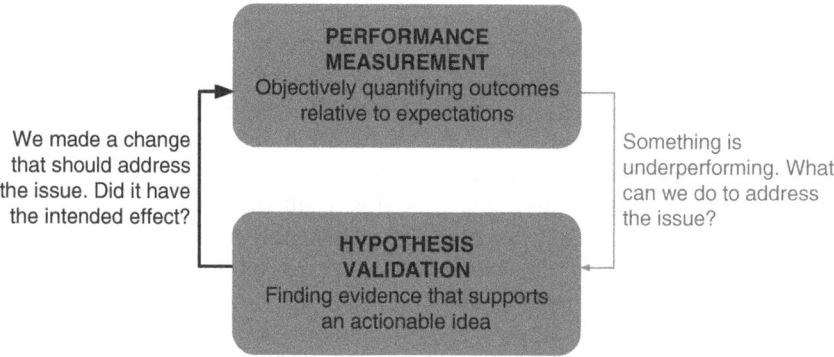

FIGURE 11.2   Hypothesis validation triggering performance measurement

This symbiosis is at the core of any organization that is meaningfully putting data and analytics to effective use. It's a signal that the entire team is putting data to productive use by using it to both efficiently identify where there are problems that need to be addressed (performance measurement) and also using it to address those problems (hypothesis validation). It provides a clear view—for everyone—as to the what and why of their roles and their activities.

"Performance Measurement" as a Validation Technique

Note the quotation marks around "Performance Measurement" in the heading for this section. They are used here as so-called "scare quotes" (which, honestly, seems a bit melodramatic), but we *are* nervous that the use of the phrase here may inject some confusion into a subject that we have gone to great lengths to keep clear up to this point. However, in the interest of pragmatism, we are going to go ahead and dip our toes into those waters.

There *will* be cases where a hypothesis is best "validated" (there are those scare quotes again!) simply by identifying one or more metrics and targets that, if achieved, we have decided will be sufficient evidence for the validation of the hypothesis.

We can illustrate this with a silly example. Consider the following hypothesis: "**We believe** that hanging a bundle of garlic around our dog's neck when she goes outside will prevent her from having any olfactorily unpleasant interactions with skunks **because** we read an article that said that 'garlic repels skunks with a sulfuric compound that is unpleasant to skunks, but not to dogs.' **If we are right**, we'll create a special collar attachment for our dog that holds a bundle of garlic, and we'll put it on her any time she goes out in our yard between dusk and dawn."

How could we validate this hypothesis? The most rigorous way would be to get several hundred volunteers who all had a dog who was allowed out into its yard to roam on a regular basis. *Randomly* assign some of those volunteers to *always* put a bundle of garlic around their dogs' necks when they let them outside. Instruct the other volunteers to *never* put garlic around their dogs' necks when they let them outside. Then, have each group report the number of run-ins their dogs had with skunks. This would be a *controlled experiment*—scientific evidence as described in Chapter 9—and would be the best way to determine if there is strong evidence that the garlic collar is effective.[2]

Is it practical to conduct such an experiment? Perhaps, but it would be expensive—recruiting and monitoring the volunteers to ensure the experiment is rigorously conducted would get complicated in a hurry!

Consider another validation option: we put a garlic collar around *our own* dog's neck every time she goes outside for 3 months during peak skunk-spotting season and see if she gets sprayed. If she doesn't, then consider the hypothesis validated.

---

[2] Despite this being a silly example, it would work as an experiment if it was properly designed and executed. We've said "several hundred" volunteers here, but the design could take into account various factors to determine if more or fewer study participants were needed. For instance, if the volunteer pool was limited to people who had *seen* a skunk in their yard within the past 12 months, as long as the treatment—the garlic necklace—was *randomly* assigned, fewer participants would be needed. Conversely, if the volunteer pool was much more open—including participants in places where skunks had never or very rarely been seen—the number of participants would need to be higher to get an equally valid result. Additionally, since it would be impossible—we think—to have a "placebo garlic necklace," the participants would need to be coached to take no greater and no lesser measures to avoid skunk interactions than they were already taking before the experiment.

This *is* a legitimate way to validate the hypothesis, but it comes with a whopper of a caveat: it is *really weak* evidence—it is *anecdotal evidence*, which we explored in Chapter 7. It's more than *no* evidence, but it's entirely possible that some contextual vagary determined why we didn't see any skunks rather than our garlic cloves:

- Perhaps there were simply no skunks in the area during that 3-month window when the dog was let out into the yard.
- It's also possible that multiple neighbors read the same "garlic repellant" article (which, for the sake of making the point, we'll say was an article grounded in strong scientific evidence) and had liberally treated their own yards throughout the same period that we were trying out the garlic collar, thus keeping skunks entirely away from the area. In that case, we could have hung a can of tuna, a peanut butter sandwich, or a miniature whiskey barrel from our dog's neck, and we would have seen the exact same result as the garlic!

There could be any number of reasons that our dog didn't get sprayed during our validation window that had nothing to do with the garlic collar. *Or* the garlic collar might have been the actual reason. We simply wouldn't know, as we chose a validation technique that was cheap and expedient at the cost of the strength of the evidence that it provided.

The reality: the garlic is relatively inexpensive, our dog didn't get sprayed by a skunk, and if we continue the practice indefinitely, there is neither harm nor foul to any nostrils other than our own. Hopefully (especially after reading this book), we know that, while we have *some* evidence of a causal relationship between a garlic neckpiece and skunk avoidance, we know that this evidence is weak, and we stop ourselves from declaring a Grand Finding on social media (which will happily take the finding at face value) or in scientific journals (which will, correctly, reject it faster than a skunk can spray a charging dog).

The point here is that, in this admittedly silly example, we made the choice to simply "choose a metric and a target" as a means of validating our hypothesis. Given the stakes (low) and the cost of more rigorous validation techniques (high), we simply *defined a result* that, if achieved, we would consider the hypothesis validated (*with weak evidence*).

In this case, we just picked a result that seemed reasonable: zero sprayings in a 3-month period. If this seems a lot like the "pick a number" technique for setting a target for a KPI that we described in Chapter 5, that's because it is!

We could have used *any* of the target-setting techniques from Chapter 5 in this situation. For instance, we could have gathered a set of friends with dogs who were all interested in skunk deterrence and asked them to each come up with how many non-sprayings in what time frame they would need to see for them to start bulk-buying garlic for their canine companions—a miniature "wisdom of the crowds" approach. Perhaps our group of neighbors (who raised an eyebrow when we referred to them as "stakeholders") settled instead on a 6-month window with no more than one spraying of *any* of the dogs in the entire group. If that was the case, then we would have used a different metric and target as our validation criteria. It still would be *evidence* of the garlic's effect, but it would still only be *anecdotal* evidence.

In the day-to-day of business, we often have ideas that we put into action, and every idea can be viewed as a hypothesis. Hopefully, we've made the case that hypothesis generation and validation is a healthy and productive way to view the world!

Many ideas—hypotheses—can require undue cost to scientifically validate them. It takes very little effort to pause and ask the question, though: "Given the stakes involved with this hypothesis, what is the best way to validate it?" In a world of infinite resources and no time constraints, the default answer to this question would be, "Design a controlled experiment!" (see Chapter 9). In the real world, this is often not practical, so the fallback is to use descriptive statistics. We covered some of the caveats and considerations for this approach in Chapter 8.

If even *a small analysis* is not feasible, then we can still make a lot of assumptions, pick a metric or two that we will use to assess the hypothesis, and set a threshold (target) for each metric such that, if the threshold is exceeded, we will declare the hypothesis validated...but *validated anecdotally*. This devil-may-care approach looks a lot like performance measurement, but as we opened with, it's really just "performance measurement" (scare quotes!) put to use in the service of weakly validating a hypothesis.

Operational Enablement Resulting from Hypothesis Validation

Operational Enablement (Chapter 10) is when data are embedded directly within a process. This use of data often has a direct line from hypothesis validation, in that the *idea* to incorporate data into an operational process was, itself, a hypothesis! And once again, it behooves us to treat every idea as a hypothesis, as this allows for deliberate thought and effort to determine whether the idea has merit—will the data embedded in the process *actually* provide value, or will we simply be adding complexity to the process that will need to be indefinitely maintained (at a cost) with no meaningful benefit? Figure 11.3 illustrates this relationship.

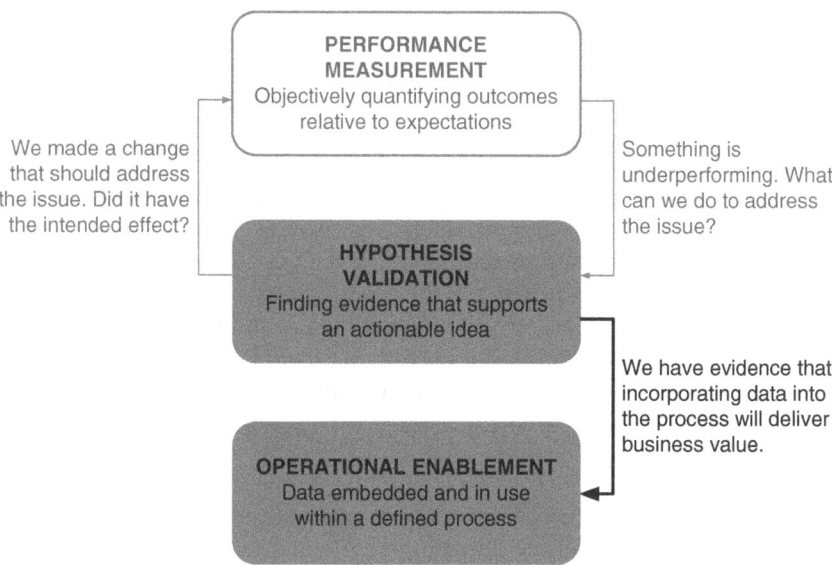

FIGURE 11.3 Hypothesis validation triggering operational enablement

Consider a scenario where the marketing team at a B2B organization has an idea to implement a "lead nurturing" program. These are reasonably common, and they have never had one. The basic idea is that, once they have the contact information for a prospect, they will communicate with them in a highly personalized way. The more they learn about the individual—based on what communication the prospect responds to, information they've gleaned about the individual from other data sources (Married or single? How many kids? What zip code do they live in?), and how often and how recently they have had an interaction with the brand, the more personalized these communications will be and, as a result, the more effective they will be at nudging the prospect to make their next purchase.

This all seems like a reasonable idea, right? It's not a particularly original one, as the idea was outlined in *The One to One Future: Building Relationships One Customer at a Time* by Don Peppers and Martha Rogers in...1993! The idea was compelling, and it's got a strong theoretical basis (as consumers, we're more likely to respond to messaging that we find relevant), but it's also *expensive* to fully go after *one-to-one* marketing. The supporting content that needs to be created and maintained, the technical integrations that need to be developed, the monitoring that needs to be in place to ensure the complex machine does not misfire, is...a *lot!*

In the case of our scenario—a marketing team diving into the development of an automated lead nurturing program—there are two broad options:

- Design a system that is as involved as they feel they can sustain (which won't come close to true "one-to-one") and roll it out.
- Treat the entire idea as a series of hypotheses that can be tested incrementally to ensure that the *only* complexities rolled out are ones that actually move the needle with their prospects.

Time and again, we've watched organizations take the first approach. And since nothing involving technology is as straightforward as it is supposed to be, these programs are always complex and costly. Partly, this is because they are so involved that, by the time they are up and running, they have too much organizational momentum to turn them off, *even if there is no strong evidence that they are effectively driving results.*

In fact, when we delegate authority to machines with complex rules, machine learning, and artificial intelligence, we can paradoxically become incompetent with respect to the business need that initially prompted the creation of the process. Just try to give a 2020s kid a road atlas and see if they know how to use it. Navigational skills aren't taught anymore because smartphones have GPS available to take care of for us. What would happen if they were placed in an area without satellite reception and needed to navigate without the GPS? And would they even know if the GPS was more effective than the road atlas to begin with, having never used it?

The latter approach—developing the marketing program as a series of testable hypotheses—is usually a much better way to start. It does require articulating and prioritizing hypotheses up front, but as we discussed in Chapter 6, this can be a relatively quick exercise. Many of the hypotheses may be around specific types of identifiable information about the prospect and how that could be used to tailor follow-up communications. Each of those hypotheses can be tested as a controlled experiment or as part of a minimum viable product (MVP)—manually or semi-manually tried to see if they bear fruit before going to the expense of building out a fully automated capability. And it helps the team to surgically figure out what they truly need to do before they try to crystallize the entire process at the outset.

This sort of incremental approach allows the team to *not* do things for which there is no evidence that they are worth rolling out permanently!

Operational Enablement Needs Performance Measurement

To complete the interconnectedness of the three ways we can use data, we need to look at the relationship between performance measurement and operational enablement. This one is straightforward: if there is a process in place, that process *should* be delivering business value, and that value should be measured to ensure it is delivering the amount of value that is expected!

In today's age of machine learning and artificial intelligence, there is a temptation to abdicate human intervention as part of the process in favor of an "almighty" computer program that can "see things we could never see." Similarly, leaders increasingly hear an imperative from their stakeholders to wedge AI technologies into their operational processes when in fact there may be little real need to do so.

The truth is that these complex and advanced processes are not better just because they are more complex and advanced. They still must pass the same sniff test that every other hypothesis must pass as part of the validation process. And they need to do so at a cost that generates an acceptable return on investment—performance measurement!

Figure 11.4 completes the view of the relationships between these three types of data usage by showing the relationship between performance measurement and operational enablement.

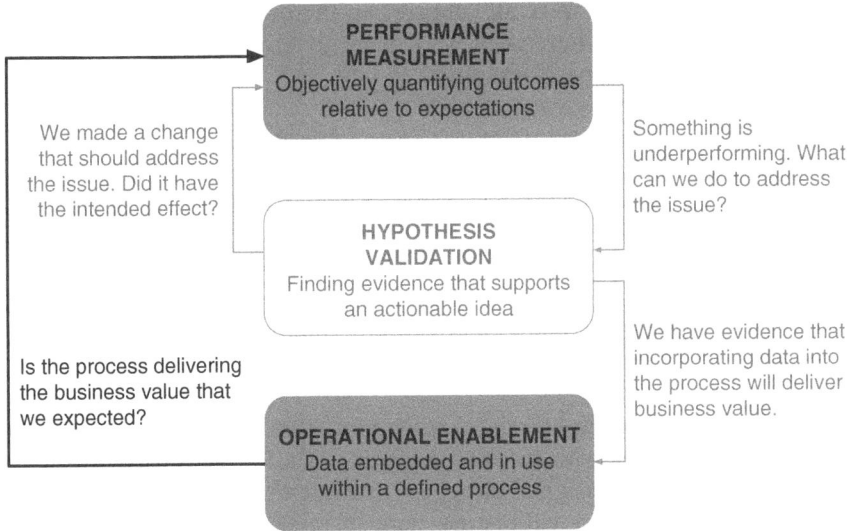

FIGURE 11.4 Performance measurement in support of operational enablement

A Call Center Example

To illustrate this interconnectedness, let's consider a call center for a large retailer and walk through how the three elements of performance measurement, hypothesis validation, and operational enablement work together.

First, there is the *performance measurement* for the call center overall. The head of the call center, along with her manager and peers, used the two magic questions (Chapter 5) to identify three KPIs with targets:

- More than 97% of calls handled in under 6 minutes
- More than 90% of calls (completed post-call surveys) receiving a "Satisfied" or "Very Satisfied" rating
- Less than 5% abandonment rate

Unfortunately, the customer satisfaction ratings are consistently under the target of 90%. The team sits down and brainstorms ideas as to what the root cause could be. This brainstorm includes several of the most experienced customer service representatives (CSRs), who act as trade experts. The group develops a series of *hypotheses* as to what is causing dissatisfaction.[3] These were all captured in the organization's hypothesis library (Chapter 6), where they were prioritized. The team decided the most promising hypothesis was this:

> **We believe** *that many of our customers get frustrated with how much they have to interact with our interactive voice response (IVR) system before they are able to speak to a human* **because** *almost one quarter of the unsatisfied customer calls that we listened to referenced their frustration with having to navigate the automated menu so extensively before getting to talk to the CSR.* **If we are right**, *we will add logic to the IVR system that routes the caller to a human automatically once they've had three automated interactions.*

To *validate this hypothesis*, the team runs a controlled experiment whereby each caller who reaches the point of a fourth interaction with the IVR is *randomly* assigned either to continue through the IVR or to get routed to a CSR. These callers are flagged in the system as (1) having reached the point in their engagement with the IVR that they were *eligible* for the experiment and (2) which experience ("treatment") they were randomly assigned to (continuing with the IVR or being routed to a human).

This experiment runs for several weeks, at which point the customer satisfaction scores for both groups are compared. The result is a detectable improvement in the customer satisfaction scores for callers who were more quickly routed to a CSR, so that change gets rolled out for all callers. The call center software is updated to include a new set of rules that will *operationally enable* the routing insight.

The performance measurement continues, and the customer satisfaction scores do improve, but they are still below the 90% target that the team had set. They go back to their hypothesis library and begin validating additional hypotheses as to how they can improve customer satisfaction for their callers. The process is continuous—performance measurement as an ongoing (and automated) process that triggers hypothesis validation as needed—with some additional data (the number of IVR interactions occurring in real-time on a caller-by-caller basis) being used to drive one decision point (when to route to a human) in the process!

---

[3] Several members of the team pulled a sample of low-scoring calls and listened to them to spark some of the ideas they brought to the brainstorming session.

ENABLING GOOD IDEAS TO THRIVE: EFFECTIVE COMMUNICATION

We've talked a lot about new mental models and methodologies for how to create, test, and deploy new ideas. But even the smallest ideas and actions can be hard to implement if the person attempting to do so is ill-equipped for the task. We now turn to a "softer" skillset that is hard to represent mechanically, but which still is critical to the effective use of the framework we've explored in this book.

At the individual level, analysts need to be confident in the insights they generate, or else others will recognize their lack of confidence and abandon the idea. To ensure they are confident in their ideas, analysts need access to the following:

- **Subject matter expertise appropriate for the task at hand**. Analysts may be skilled in the application of methodologies, but they don't always know enough about the subject matter at hand to know which methodology to choose, or what hypotheses to posit.[4]
- **Practical experience using analytics methods**. Analysts must know that they have the skills required to have done the analysis appropriately. If analysts aren't confident in their own abilities, others won't be confident in them either.
- **Data they can trust**. Even the best analytic methodology is useless without quality data capture (sometimes we call this measurement).[5]
- **The resources to fully conduct their analysis**. An analyst may know what to do and how to do it, but without the appropriate budget or cloud computing resources to do it, it's simply impossible to do.
- **The ability to communicate the results of their analysis effectively**. Analysts' own confidence in their analysis is not enough. They must also gather the confidence of others to encourage adoption of the actions their hypotheses suggest.

---

[4] The idea that you can simply run a regression and get the answer is ludicrous, but this is the view that permeates the industry. Analytics is not an engineering task; it's a thinking task.

[5] Data governance approaches are not the subject of this book, but it is important to point out that without an effective approach to governance, it's nearly impossible to have an effective approach to analytics.

Because we've discussed many of these components at length in the earlier chapters of this book, let's assume that the analyst already has practical experience, used data they trust, possesses subject matter expertise, and had the resources to successfully conduct their analysis (altogether these can feel like a tall order!). Let's further suppose that the action implied by the analysis will truly help the company.

That leaves one last thing for the analyst to do: effectively communicate their results. Communication is king in analytics. The success of any project hinges on purposeful, transparent communication. In business, the "readout" is the primary way the results of projects are communicated with stakeholders. The purpose of a readout is to convey actionable insights to the team and then arm them with compelling next steps relevant to their strategy.

Readouts can be quite effective when they inspire confidence and action. To inspire confidence and action, the analyst must frame the results of a hypothesis testing exercise in terms that the business values and understands. This is something through which the framework we have outlined throughout this book directly aims to aid the analyst: establishing *business-oriented* clarity for performance measurement with the two magic questions (Chapter 5), and clearly articulating hypotheses *including outlining actions to be taken if they are validated* (Chapter 6) are critical inputs to the analysis processes. This information—available to analysts before, during, and after they start laying their hands on the data itself—provides them with important context that they can (and should!) incorporate in how they deliver the results of their efforts back to their business partners.

Analysts can develop the best model in the world or build the most fantastic application that they demo to their customers or demonstrate the power of their methodology to prove their theory right with complex statistics. But, ultimately, in those rare few minutes of focus from their business partners, they have to clearly demonstrate the value, reasoning, and next steps implied by the analysis or experimentation work they have conducted.

ALRIGHT, ALRIGHT: YOU DO NEED TECHNOLOGY

We have admittedly, at times, taken some shots at the overhyped expectations and over-investment by many organizations in analytics technologies, data lakes, machine learning platforms, and the like as part of this book. Our comments with respect to technology are not meant to devalue its role; rather, they are meant to challenge the prevailing received wisdom that simply by buying a technology platform, we can gain transformative insights about our organization.

Technology is not the whole story. But it is a part of enabling transformative insights, and it is worth discussing briefly (a detailed discussion is outside the scope of this book).

What Technology Does Well

Technology is powerful for the exact reasons we discussed in Chapter 10 on operational enablement: it enables the organization to do expensive things more cheaply. Chapter 10 focused on the processes and mechanisms we use in business to **provide and capture end-user value at low costs**, but there are other ways technology is indispensable to the modern enterprise:

- Technology can **decrease coordination costs** by providing a single source of truth to all parts of the business. What we don't mean here is providing automation to the team that is responsible for business intelligence. What we're talking about instead is using technology to avoid the situation in which various units and subunits run off in different directions, make competing decisions based on competing information sources for competing priorities (a death wish for the company's P&L). Gaining the ability to coordinate effectively based on an instantaneous set of shared facts is a necessity in today's world of diverse, diffuse, and sprawling business interests. In fact, this proposition is the genesis of most operational data and governance protocols.

- Technology can accelerate the development and deployment of **new business interests** by providing company executives and technicians with lower bars for innovation and testing. It's easy to ignore the value of sandboxing and testing environments, but with the right tools, a junior employee 2 years out of college can take data from a shared environment, test a hypothesis, and deploy an actionable insight worth several multiples of their salary and the basic cost of having the tools available.
- Technology can **increase employee satisfaction and retention** by creating a more flexible work environment. With the right security protocols and cloud resources in place, analysts can access the raw materials they need to do their job from the family farm out in southeast Georgia (for instance). Having flexibility is critical in the post-pandemic era.

This is by no means a comprehensive or exhaustive list, but these few items alone represent tremendous business value enabled by technology.

What Technology Doesn't Do Well

What technology does poorly is—you guessed it—replace human thinking. We would like to make a few points here.

First, technology platforms do not give you governance. Governance is an organizational solution to the collective action problems we see so often in business and life:

- *The tragedy of the commons* is where there is an abandonment of stewardship for publicly used resources (because it's "everyone else's" responsibility to take care of them). Too many organizational databases and data lakes are in disarray, and a primary driver is that once someone has created a new table (often duplicating an older table), or a new data field, they will just let it sit there and consume resources without it ever being used again—without it being documented well enough to enable someone else to use it. We could say the same about sprawling farms of never-used dashboards and proofs-of-concept dumped into the void.
- *Free riding* is where people use things without paying their fair share. When a group produces a data product and publishes it out to the rest of the organization, there's usually this idea that "we will one day be able to generate a chargeback, or revenue, based on this product." But in reality, the cost for any one user of the data product is too high for them to be able

to pay for it, and lots of users want to use it but can't pay the individual price. And so the group that published the data product ends up servicing it as a cost center, usually at the behest of some politically charged agreement by the higher-ups. The same could be said about granting sandboxing privileges to the entire organization for training models; inevitably, there's a data scientist who runs up a $300,000 bill for letting a model train for too long that accidentally wasn't configured correctly. Things like that happen when there's no incentive for the data scientist to carefully manage their spending.

- The *prisoner's dilemma* is where people choose options that are collectively worse for the organization than they would if they could have coordinated. For example, when it comes to auditing products and services powered by artificial intelligence and machine learning models, the organization would be better off if both the team that produced the model and the rest of the group's stakeholders collectively agree that when they find problems with the approach (e.g. it's biased, it makes too many errors) they will fix those problems through a shared process before making the model generally available—thereby reducing costs and creating value. Instead, it's easier for the team producing the model to obfuscate issues so as not to raise any eyebrows; it's easier for the stakeholders to either ignore the impetus to check the model (reducing the amount of work necessary) or publicly blow up the model once a problem is discovered (gaining credibility while axing the idea). This devolution can result in catastrophic press when the model fails.

The list of specifics could go on, as we are sure you're thinking of several instances in your own organization that could use better collective action solutions. But we hope you notice that none of these problems can be solved by another technology platform *per se*; we cannot "buy" governance from a technology vendor. Technology can be the apparatus through which we attempt to enforce protocols, but protocols are not the full picture. Instead, we must embark on an organizational change management exercise to build cultural norms, institutions, incentives, and penalties that promote outcomes that are better for everyone.

Second, technology doesn't help you "think" about how to reduce costs. The storage of data; the compute cycles required to analyze the data and train models; the platforms required to inventory, manage, and deploy microservice APIs associated with machine learning models; monitoring and logging; auditing—these things aren't cheap. The smartest thing an analyst can do before running up a technology bill is thinking carefully about what really needs to happen to create, validate, or deploy an idea. Too often, a "big data" problem turns out to be something that "small data" could have remedied faster and cheaper; analysts in search of "firepower" embark on an expensive boondoggle while the rest of the business taps their foot waiting for what seemed like an easy and quick answer.

Third, technology does not generate insights. We hope that in this book we've made it clear that you still need a structured thought process to generate insights.

We could further introduce numerous topics and discuss both sides of the argument about benefits and drawbacks, but we don't have the time. Technology can both help and hurt in the process of developing analytics and insights. To the point we make in this book: when you invest, make sure that you know what you're going to get back before doing so.

FINAL THOUGHTS ON DECISION-MAKING

Hopefully, over the course of reading this book, you've started to think about data and analytics differently. Did we provide you with a simple formula or tool that, if you pushed enough of your data into it, you would realize a steady stream of actionable insights and deep wisdom? No. That's because no such thing exists. While data in the twenty-first century is abundant, readily accessible, and often quite precise, it is not a vessel for deterministic omniscience.

As human beings, we accept uncertainty constantly in our daily lives, but we have let a range of industry forces and understandable misconceptions set an expectation of data that it will *eliminate* uncertainty when, even at its very best, it can only *reduce* uncertainty. We have let ourselves confuse the ability for data to provide facts about the past with its ability to provide certainty about the future, and as such, we have let ourselves start believing that, given sufficient data and sufficiently advanced analytical techniques (and AI!), the importance of human thought and creativity is steadily diminishing.

This simply is not the case. The steadily increasing volume and complexity of the data, along with the increasingly broad range of analytical tools and techniques available, means that focus and clarity powered by human thought have *never been more important.*

Focus and clarity powered by human thought have *never been more important.*

In this book, we've done our best to provide you with techniques and frameworks and ways of thinking that you can use to productively and efficiently put the data in your organization to use. These techniques are equally applicable if you are working with data directly in Excel or Google Sheets or a BI platform, or if you are working with an analyst or data scientist whose full-time job is to access, analyze, visualize, and summarize data on your behalf. So go forward with confidence remembering that data is a powerful resource, but it's your brain and your ideas that will determine the extent to which the data powers your business.

MEASURE THIS CHAPTER AND THE BOOK

For the final time, it's time to contribute to the performance measurement of this book by visiting https://analyticstrw.com and answering the two-question survey for this chapter and for the book as a whole. If you've been diligently completing the survey as you've finished each chapter, thank you for doing that. It's the core of how we're measuring the performance of this book—two outcome-oriented metrics identified and with targets established before we even completed the book's outline!

Index